W. Gaebel and A. G. Awad (eds.)

# Prediction of Neuroleptic Treatment Outcome in Schizophrenia

## Concepts and Methods

Springer-Verlag Wien New York

**Prof. Dr. W. Gaebel**
Department of Psychiatry, Heinrich-Heine-University, Rheinische Landes- und Hochschulklinik, Düsseldorf, Federal Republic of Germany

**Prof. Dr. A. G. Awad**
Department of Psychiatry, The Wellesley/St. Michael's Hospitals, University of Toronto, Toronto, Ontario, Canada



Printed in Austria



Typesetting: Tau-Type, A-7202 Bad Sauerbrunn
Printing: Eugen Ketterl GesmbH, A-1180 Wien
Printed on acid-free and chlorine-free bleached paper

With 23 Figures

ISBN 3-211-82602-5 Springer-Verlag Wien New York
ISBN 0-387-82602-5 Springer-Verlag New York Wien

# Preface

Since the introduction of neuroleptics in the early 1950s interest in prediction of outcome as well as understanding the factors contributing to variability of response to therapy has preoccupied researchers and clinicians although with variable degree of success so far. A number of conceptual and methodological factors have contributed to the lack of major progress in this important area. An additional factor has been the uncritical acceptance of the notion that regardless of any identified predictor of response to neuroleptics, patients will be treated regardless with neuroleptics since medications have proven to be the most effective available approach for the management of most patients with schizophrenia. In spite of having neuroleptics and extensively using them over the past 40 years, unfortunately a good number of basic research issues relevant to clinical practice are not clear or poorly understood. We are still largely unclear about dosages, differential effects of various neuroleptics, when to switch from one medication to another, how long to wait before declaring a neuroleptic as ineffective, etc. The recent re-introduction of Clozapine and its demonstrated efficacy in chronic schizophrenics resistant to treatment has generated major interest in issues related to response and/or nonresponse to neuroleptics. With the recent accelerated development of new neuroleptics that possess different pharmacological profiles, a re-examination of our approaches to prediction of response and outcome to neuroleptics has become a pressing issue. In addition, the introduction of new and frequently expensive methodologies as positron emission tomographic studies has opened a new vista for exploration of brain functioning. Such new technology has also forced the need for reviewing methodological approaches in clinical trials of new neuroleptics as well as outcome studies.

In this context it proved timely that a group of experts in the field ought to examine the state of the art and make recommendations for future directions. We are thankful to all the contributors as well as participants who took part in a two-day meeting in Düsseldorf at the *Rheinische Landes- und Hochschulklinik,* Department of Psychiatry, Heinrich-Heine-University. We are fortunate that we were able to publish the contributions made in the conference. As many important concepts, comments and ideas have evolved during the extensive panel discussions, we felt strongly that we should include an abridged version of such discussions, realizing some of the inherent difficulties in attempting to put panel discussions in a reasonable printable form.

It is our hope by trying to reach a consensus on future directions by holding the conference and publishing the proceedings, that prediction research of response to neuroleptic therapy moves forward with renewed vigour and rigor. It is also our hope that the contributors to the conference and this book can become an international resource network for future collaborative projects. The editors would like to acknowledge with particular thanks all those companies (listed in the acknowledgement section) that have made it possible to hold the conference. However, particular thanks has to go to Promonta Lundbeck Arzneimittel GmbH & Co, Hamburg, whose generous sponsorship has made it possible to publish this book.

Düsseldorf, Toronto, August 1994 **W. Gaebel, A. G. Awad**

# Acknowledgements

The editiors gratefully acknowledge the conference support by the following pharmaceutical companies (in alphabetical order):

Astra Chemicals, Wedel
Bristol-Myers Squibb, München
Ciba-Geigy, Wehr/Baden
Hoffmann La Roche, Grenzach
Janssen GmbH, Neuss
Lilly Deutschland GmbH, Bad Homburg
Organon GmbH, Oberschleißheim
Sandoz-Wander, Nürnberg
SmithKline Beecham, München
Tropon Bayer, Köln

The publication of the conference proceedings was sponsored by Promonta Lundbeck Arzneimittel GmbH & Co, Hamburg.

Not the least we want to thank all those who helped in realizing the conference with their personal assistance.

# Contributors
(first authors only)

A. G. Awad, Professor of Psychiatry, University of Toronto, Psychiatrist-in-Chief, Department of Psychiatry, The Wellesley/St. Michael's Hospitals, 160 Wellesley Street East, Toronto, Ontario/Canada M4Y 1J3

R. M. Bilder, Assistant Professor of Psychiatry, Chief of Clinical Neuropsychology, Albert Einstein College of Medicine, Hillside Hospital, Long Island Jewish Medical Center, Glen Oaks, NY, 11004/USA

M. S. Buchsbaum, Professor of Psychiatry, Director Neuroscience, Department of Psychiatry, Mt. Sinai School of Medicine, 1 Gustave L. Levy Place, New York, NY, 10029/USA

P. Falkai, Dr. med., Psychiatrische Klinik der Heinrich-Heine-Universität, Rheinische Landes- und Hochschulklinik, Bergische Landstrasse 2, D-40629 Düsseldorf/FRG

W. W. Fleischhacker, Prof. Dr. med., Psychiatrische Klinik der Universität, Allgemeines Krankenhaus, Anichstrasse 35, A-6020 Innsbruck/Austria

W. Gaebel, Prof. Dr. med., Psychiatrische Klinik der Heinrich-Heine-Universität, Rheinische Landes- und Hochschulklinik, Bergische Landstrasse 2, D-40629 Düsseldorf/FRG

I. D. Glick, Professor of Psychiatry and Behavioral Sciences, Department of Psychiatry, Stanford University School of Medicine TD 114, Stanford, CA, 94305/USA

J. M. Kane, Professor of Psychiatry, Department of Psychiatry, Albert Einstein College of Medicine, Hillside Hospital, Long Island Jewish Medical Center, Glen Oaks, New York, NY, 11004/USA

J. L. Kennedy, Assistant Professor, Head Neurogenetics Section, University of Toronto, Clarke Institute of Psychiatry, 250 College Street, Toronto, Ontario/Canada M5T 1R8

W. Köpcke, Prof. Dr. phil., Institut für Informatik und Biomathematik der Universität, Domagkstrasse 9, D-48419 Münster/FRG

J. A. Lieberman, Professor of Psychiatry, Albert Einstein College of Medicine, Hillside Hospital, Long Island Jewish Medical Center, Glen Oaks, NY, 11004/USA

S. R. Marder, Professor of Psychiatry, Department of Veterans Affairs, Medical Center, Wadsworth and Brentwood Divisions, 13201 Wilshire and Sawtelle Boulevards, Los Angeles, CA, 90073/USA

H.-J. Möller, Prof. Dr. med., Psychiatrische Klinik der Universität, Sigmund-Freud-Strasse 25, D-53105 Bonn/FRG

F. Müller-Spahn, Prof. Dr. med., Psychiatrische Klinik der Universität, Nußbaumstrasse 7, D-80336 München/FRG

D. Naber, Prof. Dr. med., Psychiatrische Klinik der Universität, Nußbaumstrasse 7, D-80336 München/FRG

M. V. Seeman, Professor of Psychiatry, Head of the Schizophrenia Program, University of Toronto, Clarke Institute of Psychiatry, 250 College Street, Toronto, Ontario/Canada M5T 1R8

# Contents

# Prediction research of neuroleptic treatment outcome in schizophrenia – state of the art: 1978–1993

**A. G. Awad**

Department of Psychiatry, The Wellesley Hospital, Toronto, Ontario, Canada

## Introduction

In spite of the proven benefits of neuroleptics in reducing acute psychotic symptoms and in preventing relapse in many schizophrenic patients, not all patients benefit equally from neuroleptic therapy. The marked variability of the course in schizophrenia and its response to drug therapy are widely recognized (Awad 1989). Not surprisingly then, a good deal of interst has been devoted to predictive research and prognostic issues in general. Bellak (1948), surveying almost three decades of extensive literature on schizophrenia research concluded;

> *"...the criteria for improvement, recovery*
> *and all other factors pertaining to prognosis*
> *are vague and disorderly."*

Such statement reflected the various methodological shortcomings that limited the usefulness of outcome research at that time. Thirty years later, May and Goldberg (1978) published their extensive review; "Predictions of Schizophrenic Patients' Response to Pharmacotherapy." The authors lamenting about the state of the art at that time, could only conclude based on their review that chronic illness is likely to remain chronic, people are most unlikely to do any better after treatment than they did at their best before, and in general, those who responded in the past are likely to respond in the future. In spite of these rather pessimistic conclusions, the review was significant in shaping thinking and steering research in the subsequent 15 years into events that occur early in the course of treatment as potential predictors. In the last fifteen years there have been numerous major reviews for predictors of illness outcome, but only very few major reviews that dealt specifically with prediction of outcome to neuroleptic therapy (Lydiard and Laird 1988, Awad 1989,

Stern et al. 1993). The interesting observation from these last three reviews is the consistency and similarity of the conclusions though the reviews were several years apart. This likely points to the somewhat slow progress in the field in spite of the extensive research efforts.

## Potential predictors of neuroleptic response

Generally, factors that have been identified as potential predictors can be grouped into three major categories.

- Clinical predictors
- Biological/pharmacological predictors
- Neurophysiological/neuropsychological predictors

In my review of the extensive predictive research over the last 15 years, I have selectively taken into consideration only those reports where there is good evidence from reasonably designed studies and adequately replicated by other groups.

### *Clinical predictors*

Demographic characteristics in general including such factors as socioeconomic status, educational level, marital status, have generally yielded inconsistent results. Sex difference is likely the only exception; female sex has been correlated with more favourable outcome (Young and Meltzer 1980, Seeman 1983, Kolakowska et al. 1985). Studies of psychiatric history characteristics as age of onset, acute onset and short duration of illness have similarly reported conflicting results (Kolakowska et al. 1985, Awad and Hogan 1988a, Bartko et al. 1990). Though one of the important aspects of any diagnostic system is its ability to predict outcome in a consistent way, several studies comparing the predictive value of several diagnostic criteria in common use in schizophrenia have failed to confirm the utility of such approach (Carpenter et al. 1978, Helzer et al. 1981, Awad and Hogan 1988b, Kulhara and Chandiramani 1988, Carpenter and Strauss 1991). The presence of specific clinical symptoms as Schneiderian first rank symptoms, affective symptoms or paranoid symptoms have been inconsistently correlated with outcome (Gift et al. 1980, Ritzler 1981, Carpenter and Strauss 1991). Though positive symptoms as thought disorder, delusions, hallucinations, hostility and agitation have been consistently reported to be sensitive to neuroleptics, there is no agreement on the responsiveness of negative symptoms to such treatment (Angrist et al. 1980, Crow 1981, Goldberg 1985, Meltzer et al. 1986, Breier et al. 1987). Similarly, the presence of neurologic soft signs though confirmed in a number of studies, an equal number has failed to substantiate its predictive significance (Manschreck et al. 1982, Kolakowska 1985, Schulz et al. 1983, Bartko 1990).

In spite of such extensive research one can identify only three clinical factors that have evolved as potential predictors with a good degree of consistency and replication:

## Baseline symptomatology

Several studies have consistently reported that a high degree of baseline symptomatology has correlated with favourable outcome following treatment with neuroleptics for various periods ranging from 3–6 weeks (Möller et al. 1985, Breier et al. 1987, Awad and Hogan 1988a, Bartko et al. 1990, Harvey et al. 1991). In most of the studies, improvement was significant generally with more positive symptoms. In our prospective studies, the good outcome group on neuroleptic therapy compared to the poor outcome group had significantly more conceptual disorganization, hallucinations, higher scores in thinking disturbance, hostile suspiciousness as well as the total BPRS pathology (Table 1) (Awad and Hogan 1988a). Obviously, such favourable outcome may reflect at least in part some "floor effect."

**Table 1.** Baseline symptomatology and outcome to neuroleptic therapy

| | Poor outcome | Good outcome |
|---|---|---|
| *BPRS scales* | | |
| Emotional withdrawal | 3.22 | 3.75 |
| Blunted affect | 2.93 | 3.25 |
| Conceptual disorganization | 3.76 | 5.18[1] |
| Hallucinations | 2.96 | 4.44[1] |
| Grandiosity | 1.72 | 2.07 |
| Depressive mood | 1.64 | 1.41 |
| *BPRS factors* | | |
| Withdrawal-retardation | 7.74 | 8.75 |
| Thinking disturbance | 12.16 | 14.77[1] |
| Hostile suspiciousness | 5.80 | 8.04[1] |
| Anxiety-depression | 5.20 | 5.52 |
| *BPRS total pathology* | 41.68 | 50.63[1] |
| *Global Assessment Scale* | 32.93 | 35.64 |

[1] $p<0.01$

## Early symptom change

Initial improvement in symptomatology within a few days of initiation of neuroleptic therapy has been correlated with favourable outcome (May et al. 1980, Nedopil and Ruther 1981, Nedopil et al. 1983, Neborsky 1982, Awad and Hogan 1985a, Moeller et al. 1985, Bartko et al. 1987, Gaebel et al. 1988, Rifkin et al. 1988). In our studies (Table 2), the more the patients' condition is improved at 24 hours in thinking disturbance, hostile suspiciousness and total BPRS score, the better was the eventual outcome to neuroleptics at three weeks.

**Table 2.** Twenty-four hours symptom change and treatment response to neuroleptic therapy at three weeks

| | Correlations | |
|---|---|---|
| | Pearson | Partial |
| Withdrawal-retardation | 0.20 | 0.16 |
| Thinking disturbance | 0.41[2] | 0.29[1] |
| Hostile suspiciousness | 0.40[2] | 0.15 |
| Anxiety-depression | 0.10 | 0.12 |
| BPRS total score | 0.48[3] | 0.32[1] |

[1] $p<0.05$; [2] $p<0.01$; [3] $p<0.001$

## Early subjective response

An increasing number of reports habe confirmed the predictive value of early subjective responses to neuroleptics 24–72 hours following initiation of therapy. The evidence from the majority of reports is markedly consistent in that early negative subjective response to neuroleptics (dysphoric response) positively correlated with less favourable outcome to neuroleptic therapy (Van Putten et al. 1978, 1980a, b, 1981, Awad and Hogan 1985a, b, 1988a, 1994, Bartko et al. 1987, Hogan and Awad 1992). Though little is known about factors that contribute to the genesis of such dysphoric responses, it does not seem to be related to the type of neuroleptic since it has been reported with different classes of neuroleptics including phenothiazines, butyrophenons and thiothexines (Awad 1993a).

On balance then, early symptomatic improvement appears to be a strong predictor of outcome on neuroleptic therapy. In our prospective studies we examined the contributions of five predictor sets to the process of outcome to neuroleptic therapy (Awad and Hogan 1988a): 1) drug predictors, 2) pretreatment symptomatology and early symptom change, 3) psychiatric history variables, 4) demographics, 5) diagnostic criteria. Multiple regression analysis of significant factors identified in these five predictor sets has confirmed that only 24 hours subjective response and more so the 48 hour symptom change have significantly contributed to the variance in outcome ($R^2$0.29 and 0.52 respectively).

## *Biological predictors*

### Structural brain changes

Several studies have already demonstrated structural abnormalities in the brain of schizophrenic patients, mainly an enlargement of cerebral ventricles. Though the area has suffered from numerous methodological shortcomings, the weight of the evidence links structural brain changes to outcome of neuroleptic therapy. Morphologic brain abnormalities as demonstrated by higher VBRs and/or enlarged lateral brain ventricles on CT scans were associated with less fabourable response to neuroleptics (Weinberger et al. 1980, Schulz et al. 1983, De Lisi et al. 1983, Smith et al. 1983, Luchins et al. 1983, Williams et al. 1985, Gattaz 1988, Kaplan et al. 1990, Lieberman et al. 1993).

### Indices of dopamine receptor blockade – plasma HVA

Three indices of dopamine receptor blockade have been extensively investigated; CSF and plasma homovanillic acid (HVA), increased plasma prolactin and extrapyramidal symptoms. The correlation of prolactin and extrapyramidal symptoms to outcome of neuroleptic therapy has been mostly contradictory with no reasonable agreement among studies. On the other hand a good number of studies have demonstrated that higher baseline plasma HVA levels can predict a favourable treatment response (Bowers et al. 1984, 1986, 1987, 1991, Pickar et al. 1986, Van Putten et al. 1989, Chang et al. 1990, Mazure et al. 1991). Similarly, several studies have positively correlated changes in plasma HVA concentrations with changes in severity of symptoms (Pickar et al. 1984, Davilla et al. 1988, Sharma et al. 1989, Van Putten et al. 1989, Chang et al. 1990, Javaid et al. 1990, Davidson et al. 1991, Mazure et al. 1991). Though there are a number of other studies that failed to confirm such correlations, the balance of the evidence indicate with increasing consistency, a good correlation exists between baseline HVA levels, early changes in HVA and outcome of neuroleptic therapy.

### Functional brain changes – PET studies

Results from studies of brains of schizophrenic patients are slowly coming in view of the high cost and complex methodological aspects of the procedure. One recent study has already negatively correlated dopamine receptor occupancy with response to neuroleptics (Coppens et al. 1991). In their study of striatal metabolism after 18-F-fluorodeoxyglucose, Buchsbaum et al. (1992) reported a low metabolic rate in the caudate nucleus and putamen predicted a favourable clinical response to haloperidol in a sample of 25 patients with schizophrenia. Obviously, the area is in its beginning and more studies are needed to prove or disprove the predictive value of such approach.

## *Pharmacological predictors*

### Differential response to neuroleptics

Till recently, the type of neuroleptic did not figure in the process of outcome to therapy. Though there were a number of studies that attempted to correlate drug response of certain classes of neuroleptics to certain subtypes of schizophrenia, yet the results were largely negative. However, the recent reintroduction of clozapine in the last few years has challenged such conclusion and refocused attention once more on possible differential response to various neuroleptics of different pharmacological properties (Kane et al. 1988, Deutch et al. 1991).

### Pharmacological challenges and neuroendocrine responses

Several studies have investigated such approach using growth hormone response to the dopamine pre-synaptic agonist apomorphine as well as behavioral responses to challenges with amphetamine, methylphenidate, or fenfluramine (Rotrosen et al. 1979, Ferrier et al. 1984, Cowen et al. 1985, Lieberman et al. 1993). Unfortunately results from various studies are not consistent though the approach appears to be promising as it may provide a tool for dealing with the recognized heterogeneity in schizophrenia.

### Pharmacokinetics – neuroleptic blood levels

It is recognized that considerable inter-individual variability exists among schizophrenic patients in the process of absorption and metabolism of neuroleptics. Since therapeutic response is dependent on serum and ultimately brain levels of drugs, measurement of plasma blood levels has become an important tool in assessing drug response. Though this area appears to be promising, in reviewing the extensive literature, many studies have suffered from methodological shortcomings that have to do with design and patients' selection. Though a number of studies reported a kind of relationship between neuroleptic blood levels and therapeutic response for chlorpromazine, thioridazine, fluphenazine, butaperazine, perazine and haloperidol, equally many other studies failed to confirm such relationship (Cohen and Baldessarini 1981, Dysken et al. 1981, May et al. 1981, Magliozzi et al. 1981, Dixon et al. 1982, Extein et al. 1982, Bleeker et al. 1984, Bigelow et al. 1985, Davis et al. 1985,

Van Putten et al. 1985, 1991, Van Putten and Marder 1986, Volavka and Cooper 1987, Baldessarini et al. 1988, Volavka et al. 1990). In view of these variable results, the only conclusion at present is that therapeutic relationship for many neuroleptics may exist but the evidence for it is not yet strong nor consistent.

### *Neurophysiological/neuropsychological predictors*

#### Computerized EEG

Though only relatively few studies habe been reported, the results from computerized EEG studies suggest that schizophrenic patients who have more high frequency fast activity and a lesser degree of alpha and slow waves before treatment are likely to have a more favourable therapeutic response to neuroleptics. Similarly, a larger increase in alpha activity shortly after the administration of a neuroleptic has been reported to be correlated with more favourable response (Davies and Neil 1979, Itil 1981, May et al. 1982, Ulrich et al. 1988, Czabor and Volavka 1991). On balance this approach appears to be promising, but in view of the few studies so far reported, further studies are needed before any definitive conclusions can be made.

#### Autonomic nervous system reactivity

Resting heart rates, abnormal skin conduction and non habituation of skin conduction have all been explored in various studies as predictors of outcome to neuroleptic therapy (Frith et al. 1979, Zahn et al. 1981, Schneider 1982, Straube et al. 1987, 1989, Lindstrom et al. 1992). The conclusion at present is that many of these studies have produced conflicting results which are likely related to design and methodological problems.

#### Neuropsychological deficits

A number of neuropsychological deficits have been reported in schizophrenia and involve attention, perception, memory, problem solving, sensation and spatial orientation. The literature is extensive but suffers from critical methodological problems. Not withstanding such limitations few recent studies correlated the interaction of specific neurocognitive performance with neuroleptic dose in predicting symptomatic relapse (Golden et al. 1983, Marder et al. 1984, Asarnow et al. 1988). A number of studies reported enhanced predictive value of neurocognitive deficits when associated with demonstrated morphological brain changes (Weinberger et al. 1979, Donnaly et al. 1980, Kemali et al. 1985, Smith et al. 1983, 1992).

## Discussion

In reviewing the extensive literature over the past 15 years, the only conclusions that can be made is that only a few predictors have been consistently correlated with outcome of neuroleptic therapy:

- Early symptom change
- Early subjective response
- Severity of baseline symptomatology
- Plasma HVA
- Structural brain changes – CT scan

A good number of the studies have suffered from many methodological problems that may have confounded the results and contributed to a lack of consistency among studies (Awad 1989, 1993b):

### *Approach to the diagnosis of schizophrenia*

Some studies have used different criteria for the diagnosis of schizophrenia which makes comparisons between studies not possible.

### *Specificity of drug response*

Many studies have not controlled for non specific responses which makes it difficult to separate specific drug predictors from general illness related factors.

### *Selection of patients and length of follow-up*

Many studies in an effort to facilitate the conduct of study tend to include patients whose illness is generally mild to moderately severe or those chronic patients who frequently are less sensitive to neuroleptic effects. This introduces bias in that the study population is chosen from one tail of the distribution. The length of follow-up varies considerably among studies with the majority of studies tend to be of short duration. It is well known that some patients tend to respond slowly, an observation that raises the question of what would be an optimum length of follow-up. Similarly, several studies did not account for patients lost to follow-up.

### *Choice of outcome measures and the appropriateness of scales used for measurement*

Certain schizophrenic symptoms such as delusions, hallucinations or agitation are generally sensitive to the effects of neuroleptics. Other features such as lack of insight or community adjustment may be altered by different interventions. Generally outcome has been assessed in the majority of the studies using the criterion of symptomatic improvement. Very few studies included measures of functional status or quality of life as a component of outcome (Awad 1992).

### *Definition of response*

Different studies have employed different definitions for response and mostly unidimensional. Such a definition has to be multidimensional and established in the context of the population studied. A small change in a chronic drug treatment resistant population may prove significant, but it may not be enough in an acutely psychotic population.

### *Ensuring compliance*

There is an agreement among clinicians and researchers that the level of noncompliance of schizophrenic patients concerning prescribed medications can be as high as 30 %–50 %. With more reliance on outpatient outcome studies, compliance becomes a critical concern. Obviously, efficacy or lack of efficacy cannot be demonstrated unless medications are taken.

### *Recognition of the role of "extrapharmacological" factors*

Issues like the quality of therapeutic relationship, role of concomitant psychotherapy or occupational therapy, dysphoric negative subjective responses to neuroleptics are a few among the issues that frequently do not receive adequate attention in outcome studies.

## Conclusions

Over the past 15 years only a few predictors have proven their utility in predicting outcome and explaining some of the variability in response to neuroleptic therapy. These predictors include: early symptom change, early subjective response, severity of baseline symptomatology, plasma HVA and structural brain changes. However, it is clear that none of these factors can stand by itself as a strong predictor. Though combining predictors certainly improve their predictive power, this approach still does not explain but a limited proportion of variance in response to neuroleptic therapy.

In 1978, May and Goldberg rhetorically raised the following questions:

- Would it be that psychiatric outcome is inherently unpredictable?
- Are the statistical models used appropriate?
- Is it possible that the wrong variables are being examined?

In 1993, 15 years later, these questions are still valid and relevant to future directions of prediction research of response to neuroleptic therapy.

## References


Asarnow RF, Marder Sr, Mintz J et al. (1988) Differential effects of low and conventional doses of fluphenazine on schizophrenic outpatients with good or poor information processing abilities. Arch Gen Psychiatry 45:822–826

Awad AG, Hogan TP (1985a) Early treatment events and prediction of response to neuroleptics in schizophrenia. Prog Neuropsychopharmacol Biol Psychiatry 9:885–888

Awad AG, Hogan TP (1985b) Towards the development of strategy for individualized drug therapy in schizophrenia. The predictive value of early subjective response and symptom change. J Clin Pharmacol 6:461

Awad AG, Hogan TP (1988a) Drug therapy in schizophrenia – prediction of outcome. Schizophr Res 1:222

Awad AG, Hogan TP (1988b) Diagnostic criteria as a predictor of drug response in schizophrenia. Med Sci Res 16:199–200

Awad AG (1989) Drug therapy in schizophrenia – variability of outcome and prediction of response. Can J Psychiatry 34:711–720

Awad AG (1992) Quality of life of schizophrenic patients on medications and implications for new drug trials. Hosp Comm Psychiatry 43:262–265.

Awad AG (1993a) Subjective response to neuroleptics in schizophrenia. Schizophr Bull 19:609–618

Awad AG (1993a) Methodological and design issues in clinical trials of new neuroleptics: an overview. Br J Psychiatry 163 [Suppl] 22:51–57

Awad AG, Hogan TP (1994) Subjecitve response to neuroleptics and quality of life: implications for treatment outcome. Acta Psychiatr Scand 89 [Suppl] 380:27–32

Baldessarini RJ, Cohen BM, Teicher MH (1988) Significance of neuroleptic dose and plasma level in the pharmacological treatment of psychoses. Arch Gen Psychiatry 45:79–91

Bartko G, Herezeg I, Bekesi M (1987) Predicting outcome of neuroleptic therapy on the basis of subjective response and early clinical improvement. J Clin Psychiatry 48:363–365

Bartko G, Frecska E, Horvath S et al. (1990) Predicting neuroleptic response from a combination of multilevel variables in acute schizophrenic patients. Acta Psychiatr Scand 82:408–412

Bellak L (1948) Dementia precox. Grune & Stratton,New York

Bigelow LB, Kirch DG, Braun T et al. (1985) Absence of relationship of serum haloperidol concentrate and clinical. Psychopharmacol Bull 21:66–68

Bleeker JAC, Dingemans PM, Frohn-De Wunder ML (1984) Plasma level and effect of low dose haloperidol in acute psychosis. Psychopharmacol Bull 20:317–319

Bowers MB, Swigar ME, Jatlow PI et al. (1984) Plasma catecholamine metabolites and early response to haloperidol. J Clin Psychiatry 45:248–251

Bowers MB, Swigar ME, Jatlow PI et al. (1986) Early neuroleptic response in psychotic women and men: correlation with plasma HVA and MHPG. Compr Psychiatry 27:181–185

Bowers MB, Swigar ME, Jatlow PI et al. (1987) Early neuroleptic response in clinical profiles and catecholamine metabolites. J Clin Psychopharmacol 7:83–86

Bowers MB (1991) Characteristics of psychotic inpatients with high or low HVA levels at admission. Am J Psychiatry 148:240–243

Breier A, Wolkowitz OM, Doran AR et al. (1987) Neuroleptic responsivity of negative and positive symptoms in schizophrenia. Am J Psychiatry 144:1549–1555

Buchsbaum M, Potkin SG, Siegel BV et al. (1992) Striatal metabolic rate and clinical response to neuroleptics in schizophrenia. Arch Gen Psychiatry 49:966–974

Carpenter WT, Bartko JJ, Strauss JS et al. (1978) Signs and symptoms as predictors of outcome. A report from the International Pilot Study of Schizophrenia. Am J Psychiatry 135:940–945

Carpenter ET, Strauss JS (1991) The prediction of outcome in schizophrenia. IV. Eleven-year follow-up of the Washington IPSS Cohort. J Nerv Ment Dis 179:517–525

Chang WH, Chen TY, Lin SK et al. (1990) Plasma catecholamine metabolites in schizophrenics: evidence for the two-subtype concept. Biol Psychiatry 27:510–518

Cohen BM, Baldessarini RJ (1981) Haloperidol and clinical response. Am J Psychiatry 138:1513–1514

Coppens HJ, Sloff CJ, Paans AMJ et al. (1991) High central $D_2$ dopamine receptor occupancy as assessed with positron emission tomography in medicated but therapy-resistant schizophrenic patients. Biol Psychiatry 29:629–634

Cowen PJ, Gadhiri B et al. (1985) Response of prolactin and growth hormone to L-tryptophan in fusion: effects in normal subjects and schizophrenic patients receiving neuroleptics. Psychopharmacology 86:164–169

Czabor P, Volavka J (1991) Pretreatment EEG predicts short-term response to haloperidol treatment. Biol Psychiatry 137:383–386

Davidson M, Kahn RS, Knott P et al. (1991) The effect of neuroleptic treatment on plasma homovanillic acid concentrations and schizophrenic symptoms. Arch Gen Psychiatry 48:910–913

Davies RK, Neil JF (1979) Cerebral dysrythmia in schizophrenics; clinical correlates. In: Bellak L (ed) Psychiatric aspects of minimal brain dysfunction in adults. Grune & Stratton, New York, pp 139–150

Davilla R, Manero E, Zumarraga M et al. (1988) Plasma homovanillic acid as a predictor of response to neuroleptics. Arch Gen Psychiatry 45:564–567

Davis JM, Ericksen SE, Hurt S et al. (1985) Haloperidol plasma levels and clinical response: basic concepts and clinical data. Psychopharmacol Bull 21: 48–51

DeLisi LE, Schwartz CC, Targum SD et al. (1983) Ventricular brain enlargement and outcome of acute schizophreniform disorder. Psychiatry Res 9:169–171

Deutch AY, Moghaddam B, Innis RB et al. (1991) Mechanism of action of atypical antipsychotic drugs, implications for novel therapeutic strategies for schizophrenia. Schizophr Res 4:129–156

Dixon PA, Oforah E, Makanjuala R (1982) Predicitve indices for chlorpromazine therapy in schizophrenia. Br J Clin Pharmacol 14:273–277

Donnely EF, Weinberger DR et al. (1980) Cognitve impairment associated with morphologic brain abnormalities on computerized axil tomography in chronic schizophrenic patients. J Nerv Ment Dis 168:35–39

Dysken MW, Javaid JI, Chang SS et al. (1981) Fluphenazine pharmacokinetics and therapeutic response. Psychopharmacology 73:205–210

Extein I, Augusthy KA, Gold MA et al. (1982) Plasma haloperidol levels and clinical response in acute schizophrenia. Psychopharmacol Bull 18:156–158

Ferrier IN, Johnston EC, Crow TJ (1984) Hormonal effects of apomorphine in schizophrenia. Br J Psychiatry 144:349–357

Frith CD, Stevens M, Johnstone EC et al. (1979) Skin conductance responsivity during acute episodes of schizophrenia as a predictor of symptomatic improvement. Psychol Med 9:101–106

Gaebel W, Pietzcker A, Ulrich G et al. (1988) Predictors of neuroleptic treatment response in acute schizophrenia: results of a treatment study with Perazine. Pharmacopsychiatry 21:384–386

Gattaz WF, Rost W, Kohlmyer K et al. (1988) CT Scans and neuroleptic response in schizophrenia: a multidimensional approach. Psychiatry Res 26:293–303

Gift TE, Strauss JS, Kokes RF (1980) Schizophrenia, affect and outcome. Am J Psychiatry 137:580–585

Golden CJ, Carpenter B, Wilkening B et al. (1983) The relationship of the Brief Psychiatric Rating Scale to neuropsychological deficits in phenothiazine treated schizophrenics. Psychopharmacol Bull 19:513–517

Harvey PD, Davidson M, Powchik P et al. (1991) The course and clinical predictors of treatment response in schizophrenia. Schizophr Res 5:161–166

Helzer JE, Brockington IF, Kendall RE (1981) Predictive validity of DSM-III and Feigner definitions of schizophrenia. Arch Gen Psychiatry 38:791–797

Hogan TP, Awad AG (1992) Subjective response to neuroleptics and outcome in schizophrenia: a re-examination comparing two measures. Psychol Med 22:347–352

Itil TM, Shapiro D, Schneider SJ et al. (1981) Computerized EEG as a predictor of drug response in treatment resistant schizophrenia. J Nerv Ment Dis 169:629–637

Javaid JI, Sharma R, Janicak P et al. (1990) Plasma HVA in psychotic patients: longitudinal studies. Psychopharmacol Bull 26:361–365

Kane J, Hornigfeld G, Singer J et al. (1989) Clozapine for the treatment-resistant schizophrenic – a double blind comparison with chlorpromazine. Arch Gen Psychiatry 45:789–796

Kaplan MJ, Lazoff M, Lukin R et al. (1990) Enlargement of cerebral third ventricle in psychotic patients with delayed response to neuroleptics. Biol Psychiatry 27:205–214

Kemali D, Maj M (1985) Clinical and neuropsychological correlates of cerebral ventricular enlargement in schizophrenia. J Psychiatr Res 4:587–596

Kolakowska T, Williams AO, Ardren M, Reverley MA, Jambor K, Gelder MG, Mandelbrote BM (1985) Schizophrenia with good and poor outcome. 1. Early clinical features, response to neuroleptics and signs of organic dysfunction. Br J Psychiatry 146:229–239

Kulhara P, Chandiramani K (1988) Outcome of schizophrenia in India using various diagnostic systems. Schizophr Res 1:339–349

Lieberman JA, Jody D, Geislar S et al. (1993) Time course and biologic correlates of treatment response in first episode schizophrenia. Arch Gen Psychiatry 50:369–376

Lindstrom EM, Ohlund LS, Lindstrom LH et al. (1992) Symptomatology and electrodernal activity as predictor of neuroleptic response in young male schizophrenic inpatients. Psychiatr Res 42:145–148

Luchins DJ, Lewine RJR, Meltzer HY (1983) Lateral ventricular size in the psychosis in relation to psychopathology and therapeutic and adverse response to medications. Psychopharmacol Bull 19:518–523

Lydiard BR, Laird LK (1988) Prediction of response to antipsychotics. J Clin Psychopharmacol 8:3–13

Maglozzi JR, Jollister LE, Arnold KV et al. (1981) Relationship of serum haloperidol level to clinical response in schizophrenic patients. Am J Psychiatry 138:365–367

Manschreck TC, Ames D (1984) Neurologic features and psychopathology in schizophrenic disorders. Biol Psychiatry 19:703–719

Marder SR, Asarmow RF, Van Putten T (1984) Information processing and neuroleptic response in acute schizophrenic patients. Psychiatry Res 13:41–49

May PRA, Goldberg SC (1978) Prediction of schizophrenic patients' response to pharmacotherapy. In: Lipton MA, DiMascio A, Killam KF (eds) Psychopharmacology: a generation of progress. Raven Press, New York, pp 1135–1139

May PRA, Itil TM, Van Putten T (1982) Preliminary attempt to relate individual differences in EEG, test dose response to clinical effect. Biol Psychiatry 17:599–603

May PRA, Van Putten T, Jenden D et al. (1981) Chlorpromazine levels and the outcome of treatment in schizophrenic patients. Arch Gen Psychiatry 38:202–207

May PRA, Van Putten T, Yale C (1980) Predicting outcome of antipsychotic drug treatment from early response. Am J Psychiatry 37:1088–1090

Mazure CM, Nelson CJ, Jatlow PI (1991) Plasma free homovanillic acid as a predictor of clinical response in acute psychosis. Biol Psychiatry 3:475–482

Meltzer HY, Sommers AA, Luchins DJ (1986) The effect of neuroleptics and other psychotropic drugs on negative symptoms in schizophrenia. J Clin Psychopharmacol 6:329–338

Möller HJ, Scharl W, von Zerssen D (1985) Can the result of neuroleptic treatment be predicted? An empirical investigation of schizophrenic patients. Pharmacopsychiatry 18:52–53

Neborsky R, Janowsky D, Munson E et al. (1982) Behavioral prediction of response to haloperidol in a test dose strategy. J Clin Psychiatry 43:157–158

Nedopil N, Ruther E (1981) Initial improvement as a predictor of outcome of neuroleptic treatment. Pharmacopsychiatrica 14:205–214

Nedopil N, Pflieger R, Ruther E (1983) The prediction of acute response, remission and general outcome of neuroleptic treatment in acute schizophrenic patients. Pharmacopsychiatry 16:201–205

Pickar D, Labarca R, Linnoila M et al. (1984) Neuroleptic induced decrease in plasma homovanillic acid and antipsychotic activity in schizophrenic patients. Science 225:954–957

Pickar D, Labarca R, Doran AR et al. (1986) Longitudinal measurements of plasma homovanillic acid levels in schizophrenic patients. Arch Gen Psychiatry 43:669–676

Rifkin A, Seshagiri D, Karajgi B et al. (1988) Neuroleptic treatment and prediction of response. Psychopharmacol Bull 24:169–171

Ritzler B (1981) Paranoia – prognosis and treatment. A review. Schizophr Bull 7:710–728

Rotrosen J, Angrist O, Gershon S et al. (1979) Neuroendocrine effects of apomorphine, characteristics of response patterns and applications to schizophrenia research. Br J Psychiatry 135:444–456

Schneider SJ (1982) Electrodernal activity and therapeutic response to neuroleptic treatment in chronic schizophrenic in-patients. Psycho Med 12:607–613

Schulz SC, Sinicrope P, Kishore P et al. (1983) Treatment response and ventricular brain enlargement in young schizophrenic patients. Psychopharmacol Bull 19:510–512

Seeman MV (1983) Interaction of sex, age and neuroleptic dose. Compr Psychiatry 24:125–128

Sharma R, Javaid JI, Janicak P et al. (1989) Plasma and CSF HVA before and after pharmacological treatment. Psychiatry Res 28:79–104

Smith RC, Largen J, Calderon M et al. (1983) Morphological and neuropsychological abnormalities as predictor of clinical response of psychotropic drugs. Psychopharmacol Bull 19:505–509

Smith RC, Largen J, Vroulis G et al. (1992) Neuropsychological test scores and clinical response to neuroleptic drugs in schizophrenic patients. Compr Psychiatry 33:139–145

Stern RG, Kahn RS, Davidson M (1993) Predictors of response to neuroleptic treatment in schizophrenia. Psychiatr Clin North Am 16,2:313–338

Straube ER, Schiad HW, Rein W et al. (1987) Autonomic nervous system differences as predictors of short-term outcome in schizophrenia. Pharmacopsychiatry 20:105–110

Straube ER, Wagner W, Foerster K et al. (1989) Findings significant with respective to short and medium-term outcome in schizophrenia – preliminary report. Prog Neuropsychopharmacol Biol Psychiatry 13:185–197

Ulrich G, Gaebel W, Pietzker A et al. (1988) Prediction of neuroleptic on drug response in schizophrenic in-patients by EEG. Eur Arch Psychiatr Neurol Sci 237:144–155

Van Putten T, May PRA (1978) Subjective response as predictor of outcome in pharmacotherapy. Arch Gen Psychiatry 35:477–480

Van Putten T, May PRA, Jenden DJ et al. (1980a) Plasma and saliva levels of chlorpromazine and subjective response. Am J Psychiatry 137:1241–1242

Van Putten T, May PRA, Marder SR (1980b) Subjective responses to thiothixene and chlorpromazine. Psychopharmacol Bull 16:36–38

Van Putten T, May PRA, Marder SR et al. (1981) Subjective response to antipsychotic drugs. Arch Gen Psychiatry 38:189–190

Van Putten T, Marder SR, May PRA et al. (1985) Is a plasma level of haloperidol clinically useful? Psychopharmacol Bull 21:61–64

Van Putten T, Marder SR (1986) Low-dose treatment strategies. J Clin Psychiatry [Suppl] 47:12–16

Van Putten T, Marder S, Aravagiri M et al. (1989) Plasma homovanillic acid as a predictor of response to fluphenazine treatment. Psychopharmacol Bull 1:89–91

Van Putten T, Aravagiri M, Marder SR et al. (1991) Plasma fluphenazine level and clinical response in newly admitted schizophrenic patients. Psychopharmacol Bull 27:91–96

Volavka J, Cooper TB (1987) Review of haloperidol blood level and clinical response: looking through the window. J Clin Psychopharmacol 7:25–30

Volavka J, Cooper TB, Meisner M et al. (1990) Haloperidol blood levels and effects in schizophrenia and schizo-affective disorder: a progress report. Psychopharmacol Bull 26:13–17

Weinberger DR, Torrey EF, Neophytides AN (1979) Lateral cerebral ventricular enlargement in chronic schizophrenia. Arch Gen Psychiatry 36:735–739

Weinberger DR, Bigelow LB, Kleinman JE et al. (1980) Cerebral ventricular enlargement in chronic schizophrenia: an association with poor response to treatment. Arch Gen Psychiatry 37:11–13

Williams AO, Reveley MA, Kolakowska T et al. (1985) Schizophrenia with good and poor outcome. II. Cerebral ventricular size and its clinical significance. Br J Psychiatry 146:239–246

Young MA, Meltzer HY (1980) The relationship of demographic, clinical and outcome variables to neuroleptic treatment requirements. Schizophr Bull 6:88–101

Zahn TP, Carpenter WT, McGlashan TH (1981) Autonomic nervous system activity in acute schizophrenia. II. Relationship to short-term prognosis and clinical state. Arch Gen Psychiatry 38:260–266

**Author's address:** Prof. Dr. A. G. Awad, The Wellesley Hospital, Department of Psychiatry, 160 Wellesley Street East, Toronto, Ontario M4Y 1J3, Canada

# Prediction research of outcome in neuroleptic treatment – definitions and concepts

**W. Gaebel**

Psychiatrische Klinik, Heinrich-Heine-Universität,
Rheinische Landes- und Hochschulklinik, Düsseldorf, Federal Republic of Germany

## Introduction

Prognosis is a core concept in medicine. It is a prerequisite for the clinical evaluation of spontaneous course and effective treatment. Since the introduction of effective treatment methods in psychiatry, interest in prediction of outcome as well as understanding the factors contributing to variability of response to therapy has preoccupied researchers and clinicians. One reason for the limitation of results thus far is the inconsistent conceptual and methodological foundation of research.

Successful research on response prediction requires explicit concepts, definitions and operationalizations of illness course (spontaneous "prognosis"), response, dimensions of outcome, and predictors. In addition appropriate statistical methods are also required for analysing their relationship. A superordinate concept of prediction has to make explicit how these elements relate to each other in bio-psycho-social terms. Finally, valid predictions can only be made if there are recognizable rules operative in illness course and treatment outcome. Hence, the more we learn about the pathophysiology of the illness, its course and potential determinants the better we will be able to develop a valid predictive algorithm.

In this contribution the following conceptual and methodological aspects of prediction research will be discussed:

- Treatment outcome and response
- Predictors
- Predictor-outcome relationship

## Treatment outcome

The outcome of schizophrenia is the result of an as yet poorly under-

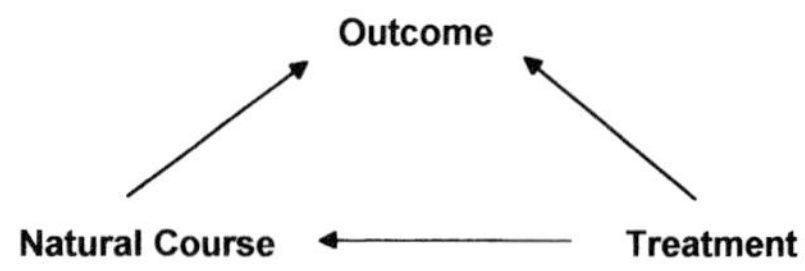


**Fig. 1.** Interaction of natural course and treatment in the development of illness outcome

stood interaction of biological and non-biological processes building up the "natural course", which is further "complicated" by treatment influences (Fig. 1).

Methodological factors contribute heavily to the characteristics of "outcome" and related measures such as treatment response. Measurement of outcome therefore requires a multidimensional conceptual framework, appropriate instruments, and adequate timing of assessment.

### *Illness course*

To model the true continuum of the illness course with respect to time coordinates ($t_1$, $t_2 \ldots t_n$) a sufficiently close time frame of assessment ($\delta t \rightarrow 0$) is required (see Fig. 3). Depending on the illness stage (acute/postacute/chronic) and the corresponding gradient of change to be expected a relatively narrow time frame should be chosen. However, since assessment instruments usually cover a certain time period in retrospect, a too narrow time frame is neither necessary nor feasible to model the illness course longitudinally with respect to certain treatment conditions.

### *Outcome*

"Outcome" refers to a cross-sectional aspect of the illness course either under spontaneous conditions or after a certain treatment intervention. According to a multidimensional concept of outcome, measures are required for different target areas sensitive to the applied treatment. Again, depending on the stage of illness/treatment (e. g. acute vs long-term) varying target areas have to be assessed. Main areas to be covered are symptomatology, work function, social contacts, need for and duration of hospitalization. Quality of life – although inconsistently defined – is another outcome concept related to social adaptation, subjective well-being and treatment side effects and which has recently been given more attention in drug studies (Awad 1992). Both self-ratings as well as observer-ratings can be employed. In schizophrenia various outcomes are cross-sectionally moderately intercorrelated but are best predicted longitudinally by themselves (Gaebel et al. 1986). Therefore, having been conceptualized as "open linked systems", according to Strauss and

Carpenter (1974) "each system is open in the sense of influencing and being influenced by outside variables; the systems are linked in the sense of having definite but incomplete interdependence; conceived in this framework each outcome process, work, social relationships, symptoms, and need for hospitalization might be considered as a system". Accordingly, at a given point in time there are many outcomes instead of a single outcome.

The characterization of a biological variable as a state- or trait-marker depends not the least on a clear definition of the pre-, intra- and post-episodic illness state by means of a target symptom measure. Schizophrenic patients remitted on a positive symptom scale often still demonstrate substantial negative symptoms. It therefore depends on our definition, whether we call these patients remitted or not and hence declare a variable as a state- or trait-marker.

Hence there is no outcome besides what is arbitrarily defined as such and is applied at a certain time point of the illness course.

### *Response*

Response is clearly a treatment-related concept of illness course. It refers to an either pre- or post-treatment defined change of illness course in a certain outcome system due to the influence of treatment. However, a causal treatment influence may only be inferred, if an appropriate study design (e. g. a randomly assigned placebo group) allows to control for spontaneous change in the illness course. Depending on the kind and

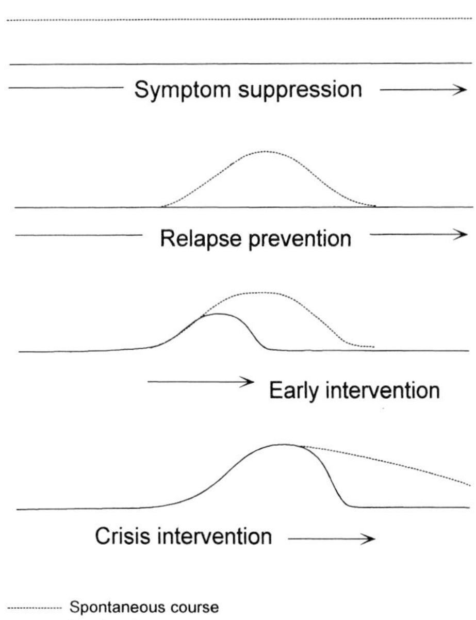


**Fig. 2.** Treatment interventions and illness course

time course (e. g. latency) of treatment effects, target symptoms, treatment duration, and time frame of measurement have to be adapted. Different therapeutic interventions depend on the illness stage. Acute treatment (early intervention, crisis intervention) and long-term treatment (symptom suppression, relapse prevention) can then be distinguished (Fig. 2).

### *Acute treatment*

Symptom change measured as a function of time [$f(t_1–t_2)$] may be the result of spontaneous remission, placebo response or treatment response. Therefore, in evaluating drug treatment effects response "on drug" has to be distinguished from response "to drug" (May and Goldberg 1978). This, however, is impossible in the individual case, if not an experimental A-B-A treatment design is applied.

In acute drug treatment, signs and symptoms of a given disorder are the target areas for measuring response. Usually, they are combined in a syndrome score or total score of a rating scale – reflecting global illness intensity (i) – which is applied repeatedly, at least once at the beginning and once at the end of a trial (Fig. 3).

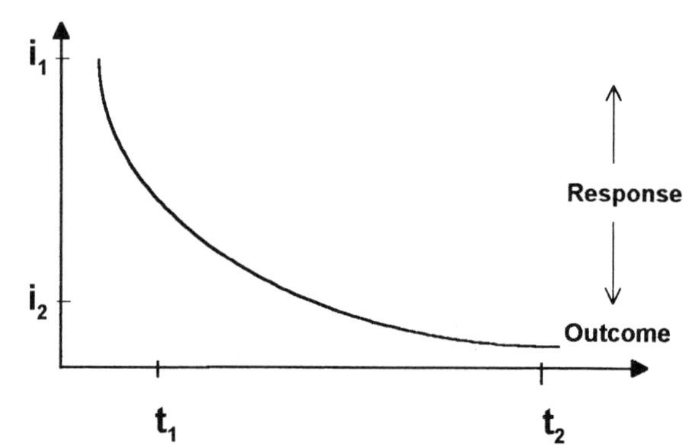


**Change (f ($t_1$ - $t_2$)) by:**
- **Spontaneous remission**
- **Placebo response**
- **Drug response (on vs to drug)**

**Measures of :**

| | | |
|---|---|---|
| ◆**Course:** | Δi/Δt, t 0 (i = signs/symptoms) | |
| ◆**Outcome:** | Residual score (RS) $i_2$ | |
| ◆**Response:** | Difference score (DS) | $(i_1 - i_2)$ |
| | Percent change (%C) | $(i_1 - i_2) \times 100 / i_1$ |

**Operationalization of:**
- **Response:** >= X %C
- **Non-Response:** < X %C

**Fig. 3.** Schematic illness course under acute neuroleptic treatment

Whereas outcome is indicated by the residual scale score $i_2$ at $t_2$, response is measured by means of a difference score ($i_1$–$i_2$) or by percent change [($i_1$–$i_2$)x100/$i_1$] to correct for interindividual differences in the initial scale score $i_1$. Response may then be operationally defined by a certain amount of percent change which has to be met, otherwise non-response would be inferred. However, it has to be kept in mind, that these definitions are arbitrarily applied to a continuum of response.

Comparable to global response statements such as "better" or "worse", there are at least two potential disadvantages of composite scale scores. First, the mixture of signs and symptoms blurs any differential effects of a drug, informing just about change in illness severity. Second, signs and symptoms are sampled from different data sources: The former are directly observable by the rater and can be measured or coded, the latter rely on the patient's introspection and verbal abilities (Alpert 1985). Not only from the viewpoint of reliability, but also validity, signs (i. e. objectively monitored illness behaviors) might be sometimes more preferable than patients' selfreports. With respect to a more "functionally" oriented psychopathology (Van Praag et al. 1987) aiming at underlying neurobiological dysfunctions and their responsivity to drug, target areas of drug response should be conceptually refined and subjected to objective measurement under more experimental assessment conditions (Gaebel and Renfordt 1989).

Response to psychoactive drugs, such as typical neuroleptics, develops with a time delay depending on certain neurobiological changes (Freed 1988, Pickar 1988). However, if one looks at the exponential time-curves of change, the group of responders (*on* or *to* drug) appears to improve more rapidly than that of non-responders. It is not known, whether the longer time course of change in "non"-responders reflects the slow but natural self-limitation of an illness episode (accelerated by drug only in the case of responders), or whether it reflects a kind of partial (e. g. placebo) responding. Whatsoever, this observation could help to reconceptualize response/non-response in terms of differences in the underlying time-dependent biological processes relevant for spontaneous illness course and treatment reactivity as well.

### *Long-term treatment*

Under long-term treatment conditions prevention of relapse is the most important response criterion. The concept of relapse means reappearance of an acute illness episode of a predefined magnitude after remission, irrespective whether it requires rehospitalization or not. To index an illness episode, related concepts such as full or partial remission, prodromal symptoms and recovery have also to be defined. Moreover, clinical deterioration has to be distinguished from relapse. In depression research the term relapse has been applied to early deterioration after an acute episode, whereas symptom re-exacerbation after a defined time period of remission has been termed recurrence (Frank et al. 1991).

Neuroleptic long-term treatment – usually of the kind of low-dose maintenance treatment, since intermittent early intervention treatment has not turned out equally effective (Pietzcker et al. 1993) – serves either for relapse prevention or symptom suppression. Accordingly, prediction of response (relapse prevention) under long-term treatment aims at the virtual drug mechanism of suppressing/preventing/delaying a relapse. Obviously relapse is not prevented by symptom suppression but instead by a delay of symptom reappearance (Hogarty et al. 1973). However, the neurobiological mechanisms of neuroleptic maintenance treatment are far from clear.

## Predictors

Besides treatment the spontaneous illness course is shaped and modified by various factors, which are referred to as potential outcome/response "predictors" sampled from a wide area of patient and environmental characteristics. Although mainly described in psycho-social terms, these predictors are not necessarily non-biological in nature. Since the kind and mechanism of their illness/treatment relationship is far from clear, the more preferable neutral term for them would be "non-drug" factors. However, there are other types of classification of predictors, e. g. state/trait, static/dynamic or subjective/objective. With respect to the illness course and its treatment pre-treatment and treatment-dependent predictors of response may be distinguished (Fig. 4).

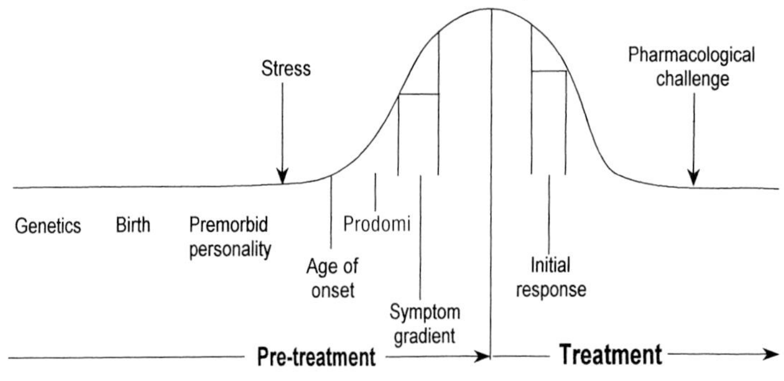


**Fig. 4.** Illness course and potential predictors of treatment response

If one conceptualizes the patient as a multilevel system in bio-psycho-social terms (Engel 1980), the following intervening levels may contribute to the complexities of drug treatment outcome (Fig. 5).

According to this model – besides environmental characteristics such

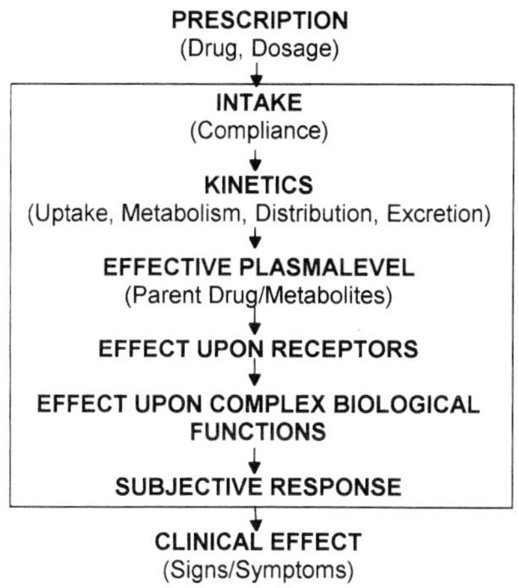


**Fig. 5.** Intervening system levels contributing to the complexities of outcome in drug treatment (from Helmchen and Gaebel 1987)

as treatment milieu, planned psychosocial interventions, and patient family environment (Gaebel 1993) – variables from all levels may be evaluated as potential outcome predictors (Table 1).

**Table 1.** Potential predictor variables (modified from Awad 1989)

| | |
|---|---|
| Patient | Demographics<br>(sex, SES, marital status)<br>Psychiatric history<br>(age of onset, family history, premorbid adjustment, prev. response)<br>Clinical characteristics<br>(Positive/negative symptoms, other symptoms)<br>Diagnostic criteria<br>Attitudes<br>(compliance) |
| Neuroleptic drug | Drug type |
| Effective plasma level | Drug blood levels<br>(test dose, steady state) |
| Effect at receptor | Indices of DA receptorblockade<br>(HVA, PRL, EPS)<br>Challenge tests<br>(GH, amphetamine) |
| Complex biolog. functions | Brain morphology<br>(CT, NMR)<br>Soft signs<br>Perinatal complications<br>Neurocognitive functions<br>Psychophysiology<br>(EDR, EEG) |
| Subjective interpretation | Early subjective response |
| Behavioral reactivity | Early symptom change |

Various chapters of this book deal with different kinds of predictors. Variables that measure atypical clinical features, chronicity, or past social performance have been identified as general prognostic indicators. Unfortunately, some of these predictors such as premorbid adjustment are often not easily distinguished from outcome itself, rendering their "predictive" value at least minimal. Moreover, most predictors have not been validated by replication studies (May and Goldberg 1978). Even with multivariate combinations of single predictors, usually no more than 30-40 % of the outcome variance has been explained. The beneficial effect of neuroleptic treatment seems to override the power of most predictors, i. e. most patients improve at least partially despite unfavorable characteristics. In the individual case, however, prediction of treatment success is particularly difficult. This may be explained by the extensive interindividual variability of treatment-related intervening processes (Fig. 5). Accordingly, in addition to static background variables without direct bearing on the treatment process itself treatment-related dynamic variables have been introduced into predictive models (May et al. 1976). They refer to cybernetic principles of the underlying illness process and its treatment-responsiveness (e. g. Selbach 1961) or the "elasticity" of biological systems as measured by PET (Dewey et al. 1993).

The so-called test dose model combines several predictors from different assessment levels, e. g. early psychopathological response, subjective response, pharmacokinetic, psychophysiological, biochemical, and other functional predictors after test dose application (Gaebel et al. 1988). Findings on the relationship between (early) pharmacokinetic data and treatment outcome are inconsistent (Gaebel et al. 1992) and may ultimately be replaced by more direct measures of drug effects at the receptor. Early subjective response has turned out as a response predictor in some studies (e. g. Van Putten and May 1978, Awad and Hogan 1985), but not in others (Gaebel et al. 1988). One of the more easily accessible and also replicated parameters is the early clinical response (May et al. 1980, Nedopil and Rüther 1981, Möller et al. 1983, Woggon and Baumann 1983, Awad and Hogan 1985, Bartko et al. 1987, Gaebel et al. 1988). From these findings it must be concluded, that – contrary to the imputed "latency" of neuroleptic response – specific clinical improvement takes place already in the first few days of treatment.

## Predictor-outcome relationships

The scientific meaning of statistical associations between predictors and outcome is far from clear. Generally, most of the "predictors" are "indicators" of unknown processes, relating in unknown ways to various outcome dimensions. Many of these relationships depend on the particular definition and operationalization of outcome or response – they change by altering such definitions. The scientific status of a predictor is almost never that of an outcome/response "determinant" – it is at best a statisti-

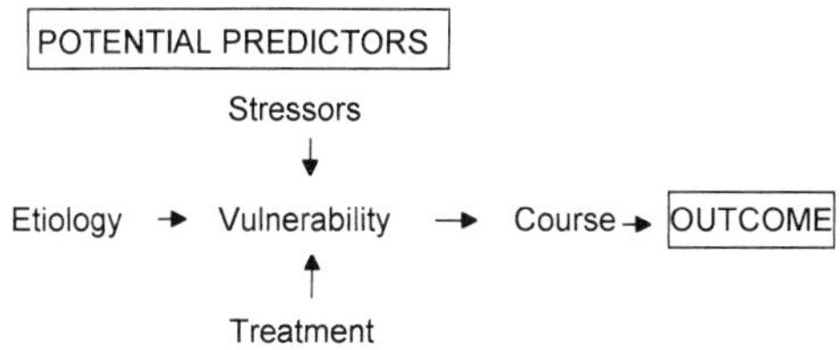


**Fig. 6.** Modified vulnerability-stress-model for use in prediction research

cally associated "risk factor" for treatment success/failure and/or side-effects, or an unspecific "indicator" of treatment response itself.

A heuristic integrative concept for prediction research is the vulnerability-stress model (Nuechterlein 1987, Clements and Turpin 1992). According to this model, pathogenetic as well as pathoplastic (Birnbaum 1923) determinants of illness course and treatment response (predictors) can be conceptualized on a biological, psychological and environmental level (Fig. 6).

To assess the relationship between treatment and response the concept of vulnerability – referring to a predisposition for psychic destabilization – has to be translated into the concept of instability. Potential clinical instability and hence relapse-proneness – thought to be mediated by a dysfunctional status of the dopaminergic system – can be assessed by the reactivity of the psychobiological system to pharmacological probes, e. g. methylphenidate (Lieberman et al. 1987). In a functional context the steepness of the symptom gradient of spontaneous destabilization as well as of drug-induced (early) restabilization are also predictors of treatment response. This kind of objective predictors are even more important since subjective antecedents of destabilization such as prodromal symptoms have not turned out as valid relapse predictors (Gaebel et al. 1993).

It is a task for future research to redefine in neurobiological terms the various predictor variables which have been proven effective. The final common pathway of drug and non-drug related influences on illness course may ultimately be reflected by postsynaptic regulatory processes of signal transduction and gene expression, which constitute plasticity in a given neural network (Hyman and Nestler 1993). It is possibly these processes which build the more enduring "structural" basis for different types of treatment outcome – and its prediction.

## Future research recommendations

To further scientific development in the field of prediction research, potential predictors of treatment response should be routinely included in clinical trials (Carpenter et al. 1981). According to the bio-psycho-social model of etiopathogenesis and treatment (Engel 1980, Goodman 1991), which is now generally accepted in psychiatry, the various components of the vulnerability-stress-outcome model should be conceptualized and defined in biological and non-biological terms as well. Generally, a hypothesis-driven functional approach should be given more attention in prediction research: testing the function of a treatment relevant psychobiological system could reveal more about the capacity of responding to treatment than any epidemiological variable, which is at best an indicator of as yet not understood course modifying processes.

Finally, to make study results better comparable, the calculation of sensitivity (true positive rate) and specificity (true negative rate) of a predictive measure with respect to different cut-off points of predictor and outcome variables should be encouraged. The so-called ROC method (Receiver Operating Characteristics) allows to quantitatively assess and compare the significance of different outcome predictors (Hsiao et al. 1989). Generally, appropriate statistical methods should be applied to prediction research (see chapter by Köpcke).

## Conclusions

The clinical picture and (treatment) outcome of schizophrenia are heterogeneous and variable. Neuroleptic treatment response is a complex, in its pathophysiology still poorly understood and inconsistently operationalized phenomenon. Reliability and validity of many predictors are rather low, particularly in the individual case. Most patients (60–70 %) respond to typical neuroleptics; therefore, developing predictors of non-response or severe side-effects is of special importance. At present, predictions can best be made from psychobiological changes after test dose, pharmacological challenge or from previous treatment response. Future prediction research should prospectively assess potential predictors derived from the vulnerability-stress-model – defined in biological, psychological and social terms, using adequate methods for statistical analysis.

## References

Alpert M (1985) The signs and symptoms of schizophrenia. Compr Psychiatry 26:103–112

Awad AG, Hogan TP (1985) Early treatment events and prediction of response to neuroleptics in schizophrenia. Prog Neuropsychopharmacol Biol Psychiatry 9:585–588

Awad AG (1989) Drug therapy in schizophrenia: variability of outcome and prediction of response. Can J Psychiatry 34:711–720

Awad A (1992) Quality of life of schizophrenic patients on medications and implications for new drug trials. Hosp Commun Psychiatry 43:262–265

Bartko G, Herczeg I, Bekesy M (1987) Predicting outcome of neuroleptic treatment on the basis of subjective response and early clinical improvement. J Clin Psychiatry 48:363–365

Birnbaum K (1923) Der Aufbau der Psychose. Grundzüge der psychiatrischen Strukturanalyse. Springer, Berlin

Carpenter WT, Heinrichs DW, Hanlon TE (1981) Methodologic standards for treatment outcome research in schizophrenia. Am J Psychiatry 138:465–471

Clements K, Turpin G (1992) Vulnerability models and schizophrenia: the assessment and prediction of relapse. In: Birchwood M, Tarrier N (eds) Innovations in the psychological management of schizophrenia. Wiley, Chichester New York Brisbane Toronto Singapore, pp 21–47

Dewey SL, Smith GS, Logan J, Brodie JD, Fowler JS, Wolf AP (1993) Striatal binding of the PET ligand $^{11}$C-Raclopride is altered by drugs that modify synaptic dopamine levels. Synapse 13:350–356

Engel GL (1980) The clinical application of the bio-psycho-social model. Am J Psychiatry 137:535–544

Frank E, Prien RF, Jarrett RB, Keller MB, Kupfer DJ, Lavori PW, Rush J, Weissman MM (1991) Conceptualization and rationale for consensus definitions of terms in major depressive disorder. Remission, recovery, relapse, and recurrence. Arch Gen Psychiatry 48:851–855

Freed WJ (1988) The therapeutic latency of neuroleptic drugs and nonspecific postjunctional supersensitivity. Schizophr Bull 14:269–277

Gaebel W, Pietzcker A, Baumgartner A (1986) 3-Year follow-up of schizophrenic patients – outcome dimensions and neuroleptic treatment. Pharmacopsychiatry 19:208–209

Gaebel W, Pietzcker A, Ulrich G, Schley J, Müller-Oerlinghausen B (1988) Predictors of neuroleptic treatment response in acute schizophrenia. Pharmacopsychiatry 21:384–386

Gaebel W, Renfordt E (eds) (1989) Objective methods for behavioral analysis in psychiatry and psychopharmacology – examples and concepts. Pharmacopsychiatry 22 [Suppl]:1–50

Gaebel W, Müller-Oerlinghausen B, Schley J (1992) Early serum levels of neuroleptics do not predict therapeutic response in schizophrenia. Prog Neuropsychopharmacol Biol Psychiatry 16:891–900

Gaebel W (1993) The importance of non-biological factors in influencing the outcome of clinical trials. Br J Psychiatry 163 [Suppl 22]:44–50

Gaebel W, Frick U, Köpcke W, Linden M, Müller P, Müller-Spahn F, Pietzcker A, Tegeler J (1993) Early neuroleptic intervention in schizophrenia: are prodromal symptoms valid predictors of relapse? Br J Psychiatry 163 [Suppl 21]:8–12

Goodman A (1991) Organic unity theory: the mind-body problem revisited. Am J Psychiatry 148:553–563

Helmchen H, Gaebel W (1987) Strategies of clinical research on neurobiological determinants of psychosis. Psychiatr Dev 5:51–62

Hogarty GE, Goldberg SC, Collaborative Study Group (1973) Drug and sociotherapy in the aftercare of schizophrenic patients. Arch Gen Psychiatry 28:54–64

Hsiao JK, Bartko JJ, Potter WZ (1989) Diagnosing diagnoses. Receiver operating characteristic methods and psychiatry. Arch Gen Psychiatry 46:664–667

Hyman SE, Nestler EJ (1993) The molecular foundations of psychiatry. American Psychiatric Press, Washington London

Lieberman JA, Kane JM, Sarantakos S, Gadeleta D, Woerner M, Alvir M, Ramos-Lorenzi J (1987) Prediction of relapse in schizophrenia. Arch Gen Psychiatry 44:597–603

May PRA, Van Putten T, Yale C, Potepan P, Jenden DJ, Fairchild MD, Goldstein MJ, Dixon WJ (1976) Predicting individual responses to drug treatment in schizophrenia: a test dose model. J Nerv Ment Dis 162:177–183

May PRA, Goldberg SC (1978) Prediction of schizophrenic patients' response to pharmacotherapy. In: Lipton MA, Dimascio A, Killam KF (eds) Psychopharmacology: a generation of progress. Raven Press, New York, pp 1139–1153

May PRA, Van Putten T, Yale C (1980) Predicting outcome of antipsychotic drug treatment from early response. Am J Psychiatry 137:1088–1089

Möller HJ, Kissling W, Zerssen von D (1983) Die prognostische Bedeutung des frühen Ansprechens schizophrener Patienten auf Neuroleptika für den weiteren stationären Behandlungsverlauf. Pharmacopsychiatry 16:46–49

Nedopil N, Rüther E (1981) Initial improvement as predictor of outcome of neuroleptic treatment. Pharmacopsychiatry 14:205–207

Nuechterlein KH (1987) Vulnerability models for schizophrenia: state of the art. In: Häfner H, Gattaz WF, Janzarik W (eds) Search for the causes of schizophrenia. Springer, Berlin Heidelberg New York, pp 297–316

Pickar D (1988) Perspectives on a time-dependent model of neuroleptic action. Schizophr Bull 14:255–268

Pietzcker A, Gaebel W, Köpcke W, Linden M, Müller P, Müller-Spahn F, Tegeler J (1993) Continuous vs intermittent neuroleptic longterm treatment in schizophrenia - results of a German multicenter study. J Psychiatr Res 27:321–339

Selbach H (1961) Über die vegetative Dynamik in der psychiatrischen Pharmakotherapie. Dtsch Med J 16:511–517

Strauss JS, Carpenter WT (1974) The prediction of outcome in schizophrenia. II. Relationships between predictor and outcome variables. Arch Gen Psychiatry 31:37–42

Van Praag HM, Kahn RS, Asnis GM et al. (1987) Denosologization of biological psychiatry or the specificity of 5-HT disturbances in psychiatric disorders. J Affect Disord 13:1–8

Van Putten T, May PRA (1978) Subjective response as a predictor of outcome in pharmacotherapy. Arch Gen Psychiatry 35:477–480

Woggon B, Baumann U (1983) Multimethodological approach in psychiatric predictor research. Pharmacopsychiatry 16:175–178

**Author's address:** Prof. Dr. med. W. Gaebel, Psychiatrische Klinik der Heinrich-Heine-Universität, Rheinische Landes- und Hochschulklinik, Bergische Landstrasse 2, D-40629 Düsseldorf, Federal Republic of Germany

# General aspects of predictor research in schizophrenia and depression

**H.-J. Möller**

Department of Psychiatry, University of Bonn, Federal Republic of Germany

Prediction has always been an important issue in psychiatry both from the aspects of clinical practice and scientific research.

Practical aspects of predictor research aims at the following issues:

1. Prognosis of subgroups related to outcome under natural conditions.
2. Prognosis of individual outcome under natural conditions.
3. Treatment-related prognosis as basis of therapeutic modality indication, e. g. drugs versus psychotherapy.
4. Treatment-related prognosis as basis of specific indication, e. g. drug A versus drug B.

The Munich follow-up study in which we analyzed more than 100 social, anamnestic and psychopathological variables is a good example of this type of prediction research. A number of these variables has proven their prognostic relevance (Table 1). Most of these predictors explain only a small degree of variance with only few exceeding the proportion of 10 % (Möller et al. 1981 a,b, 1982 a,b). Each of the predictors contribute a certain risk in the calculation of poor global outcome for the subgroup of those patients characterized by an unfavorable prognosis. Principally, the same is applicable also for the individual prognosis. However, most of these predictors are not strong enough to guarantee a meaningful individual prediction. Combining prognostically relevant characteristics, as for example in the Strauss-Carpenter scale, can lead to better predictive ability (Möller et al. 1984). However, even with this approach, sensitivity and specificity are not very high, as demonstrated in our original sample of the Munich follow-up study on schizophrenics (Fig. 1) (sample I), as well as in the subsequent replication sample (sample II).

**Table 1.** Predictors of global outcome. Munich follow-up study on schizophrenia, sample I (n=81) (Möller et al. 1986)

| | | Predictors of Global Outcome (GAS) | Explained variance | |
|---|---|---|---|---|
| | | | ≤ 10 % | 11–20 % |
| (–) | ● | Higher socioeconomic status of the parents | x | |
| (–) | ● | Premorbid working dysfunction | x | |
| (+) | ● | More advanced age at first manifestation | x | |
| (+) | ● | More advanced age at first hospitalization | x | |
| (+) | ● | Precipitating factors before first manifestation | x | |
| (–) | ● | Duration of psychiatric hospitalization (5 years before index admission) | x | |
| (–) | ● | Duration of occupational disintegration (5 years before index admission) | | x |
| (+) | ● | Lasting heterosexual relationship | x | |
| (–) | ● | Impairment of working ability (1 year before index admission, | | x |
| (–) | ● | Personality change (1 year before index admission) | | x |
| (–) | ● | Diagnosis of schizophrenia | x | |
| (–) | ● | Poor psychopathological state at discharge | | x |
| (–) | ● | IMPS superfactor of organic syndrome at discharge | x | |
| (–) | ● | IMPS superfactor of depressive-apathetic syndrome at discharge | x | |
| (+) | ● | Ratio of amelioration of the IMPS superfactor of psychotic excitement | x | |
| (–) | ● | Self-rating factor of paranoid tendencies at discharge | | x |
| (+) | ● | Ratio of amelioration of the self-rating factor of paranoid tendencies | | x |

(+) = good prognosis, (–) = poor prognosis. *IMPS* Inpatient Multidimensional Psychiatric Scale

Theoretical aspects of predictor research aim at the following issues:

1. Differences in global prognosis as one element of nosological differentiation, e. g. schizophrenic versus affective psychosis.
2. Similarities in the predictor profile as one possible indicator of nosological similarities.
3. Biological (psychosocial) predictors for response to treatment as indicator of different biological (psychosocial) mechanisms.

To illustrate these abstract descriptions by concrete examples from our Munich follow-up study, we looked for the predictive power of three different diagnoses – schizophrenia, schizoaffective disorder and affec-

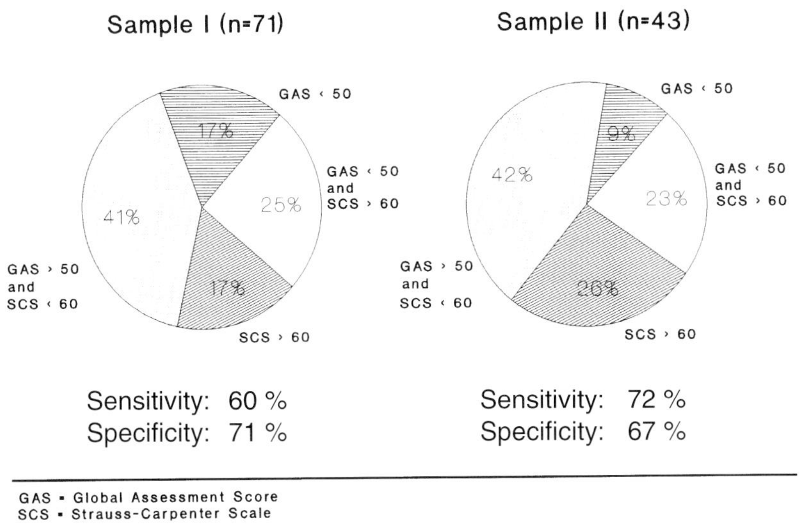


**Fig. 1.** Sensitivity and specificity of prognosis on the basis of the Strauss-Carpenter Scale. Munich follow-up study on schizophrenia (Möller et al. 1988)

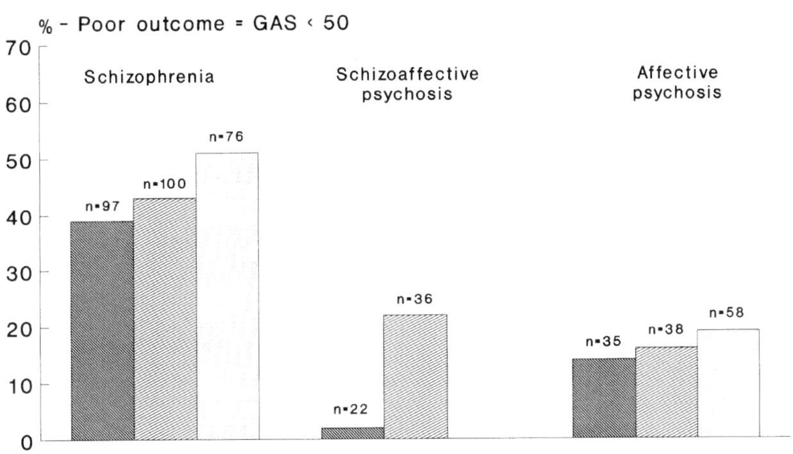


**Fig. 2.** Prognosis for different diagnoses with respect to global outcome. Munich follow-up study on schizophrenia (Möller et al. 1989)

tive disorder – with respect to global outcome according to three different diagnostic systems – ICD-8, RDC and DSM-III (Möller et al. 1989). As expected, the diagnosis "schizophrenia" was in all diagnostic systems associated with the poorest outcome compared to the affective and schizoaffective disorders. The DSM-III diagnosis "schizophrenia" was linked with the worst outcome. This can be explained by the fact that the strong exclusion of affective symptoms and the time-criterion in DSM-

**Table 2.** Predictors of response to antidepressive treatment. Confirmation by cross-validation (Möller et al. 1987, 1993)

| ICD Endogenous Depressives (n=159) | ICD Neurotic Depressives (n=134) |
|---|---|
| (–) ● Disturbed premorbid social adjustment (Premorbid Scale) | (–) ● Poor professional adjustment |
| (–) ● Orality | (–) ● Orality |
| (–) ● Neurotic structure (AHOS) | (–) ● Neurotic structure (AHOS) |
| (+) ● Apathetic syndrome (IMPS) at admission | (+) ● Apathetic syndrome (IMPS) at admission |
| (+) ● Superfactor depressive-apathetic syndrome (IMPS) at admission | (+) ● Depressive syndrome (IMPS) at admission |
| (–) ● Mood disturbances (Bf-S) after 3 weeks | (–) ● Mood disturbances (Bf-S) after 3 weeks |
| (–) ● Improvement of mood disturbances (Bf-S) after 3 weeks | |

(+)=good prognosis, (–)= poor prognosis

III apparently defines a core-group of schizophrenics (Fig. 2).

In our studies of the short-term response to antidepressant treatment, our results demonstrated that the predictor profile was similar in endogenous depressives and neurotic depressives. This may indicate that the traditional nosological subclassification seems not quite meaningful (Möller et al. 1987, 1993) (Table 2).

In the field of depression, several biological variables as the dexamethasone suppression test (DST) have been tested as predictor of different specific biological mechanisms (noradrenergic, serotonergic or anticholinergic). However, neither these specific hypotheses nor the predictive utility of DST in general response to antidepressant therapy could be confirmed (Arana et al. 1985).

Prediction research in psychiatry is generally faced with a number of deficiences and methodological problems:

1. Many studies included relatively small patient samples.
2. The specifity of predictors for certain outcome variables is frequently not considered.
3. In most studies no attempt was made to differentiate between predictors of the natural course of illness and predictors of response to treatment.
4. Multivariate procedures were only seldom used to increase the proportion of explained variance.
5. Cross-validation for testing the stability of predictors or sets of predictors was seldom carried out.

In our Munich follow-up study (Table 1), taking into account other outcome criteria other than the global outcome, as for example the Global Assessment Scale (GAS), it becomes evident that predictor variables for the

**Table 3.** Instability of predictors in relation to different outcome criteria. Munich follow-up study on schizophrenia, sample I (n = 81) (Möller et al. 1986)

| | Impairment of "level of functioning" (GAS) | Global psychopathology | Personality change | Impairment of work. ability | Impairment of social adaptation | Psychotic excitement | Paranoid-halluc. syndrome | Depr.-apathetic syndrome | Duration of occupational disintegration | Duration of psychiatric hospitalization | Duration of paranoid-halluc. symptoms |
|---|---|---|---|---|---|---|---|---|---|---|---|
| **Anamnestic data** | | | | | | | | | | | |
| Age at first manifestation | ● | ● | ● | ● | ● | | | | ●● | ● | |
| Age at first hospitalization | ● | ● | ● | ● | ● | | | ● | ●● | ●● | |
| Age at index admission | | | | ● | | | | | ●● | ● | |
| Number of phases/episodes | | | | | | | | ● | | | |
| Duration of illness | | | | | | | | | | | |
| Duration of psychiatric hospitalizations | ● | | | | | | ● | ●● | | ●● | |
| Duration of occupational disintegration | ●● | ● | ●●● | ●●● | ●● | | | ● | ●●● | ●●● | ● |
| Personality change | ●● | ●● | ●●●● | ●● | ●● | | ● | | ● | | ● |
| Impairment of work. ability | ●● | ●● | ●●● | ● | ●● | ● | ● | | | | |
| **Index manifestation** | | | | | | | | | | | |
| Duration of hospitalization | | | | ● | | | | | | | |
| State of discharge | ●● | ●●● | | | | | ● | | | | ● |
| Psychotic excitement | | | | | | ● | | | | | |
| Paranoid-hallucinat. | | | | | | | ●● | | | | ● |
| Depr.-apathetic | ● | | ● | ● | ● | | | ● | | | ● |
| Phobic-anancastic | | | | | | | | | | | |
| Organ. psych. | ● | | ●● | ●● | ●● | | | ●● | ● | | ● |

Explained variance: ● = ≤ 10 %, ●● = 11–20 %, ●●● = 21–30 %, ●●●● = 31–40 %

**Table 4.** Best combination of 5 predictors of "level of functioning" (GAS). Munich follow-up study on schizophrenia (n=81) (Möller et al. 1986)

| | | |
|---|---|---|
| 5 Best predictors: | ● Impairment of work ability (1 year before index admission) | (–) |
| | ● More advanced age at first hospitalization | (+) |
| | ● Poor psychopathological state at discharge | (–) |
| | ● Duration of occupational disintegration (5 years before index admission) | (–) |
| | ● Precipitating factors before first manifestation | (+) |
| Variance explained by 5 best: | 36 % | |
| Variance explained by all: | 62 % | |

(+) = good prognosis, (–) = poor prognosis

GAS score are not always predictors for other outcomes and vice versa (Table 3). Using multivariate statistical procedures the proportion of explained variance is increased as well as the stability of predictor results. A stepwise multiple regression analysis can select an optimal set of predictors out of a larger group of predictors (Möller et al. 1986) (Table 4). There are also other, more simple strategies to combine predictors, for example, to construct a total score of the most important individual predictors. Several prognostic scales in the literature are based on the latter procedure. Some of these scales do not cover the whole spectrum of data but only certain areas as for example psychopathology or social adaptation. Other scales cover a wide range of possible predictors like the Strauss-Carpenter scale. Six of these scales were tested in our first sample of the Munich follow-up study on schizophrenia. Using such approach allowed for an increase of the explained variance and provided higher stability concerning different outcome criteria (Table 5). Similar findings were obtained in the replication sample, which underlines the prognostic stability of these scales (Möller et al. 1986). Based on different statistical procedures and taking into account different aspects, we constructed four prognostic scales based on the data of the first sample of the Munich follow-up study (Table 6). Apart from the scale which was based only on psychopathological data, the validity of the three other prognostic scales was demonstrated, not only in the first sample but also in the replication sample (Table 7). Such prognostic scales were able to predict different aspects of outcome. Though theoretically it is preferable to have a more specific predictor, still this general approach can prove helpful clinically.

In general it has to be understood that predictor variables are not causal factors, although some of them can have a causal meaning. It is

**Table 5.** Predictive power of prognostic scales. Munich follow-up study on schizophrenia, sample I (Möller et al. 1986)

| Prognostic Scales | Impairment of "level of functioning" (GAS) | Global psycho-pathology | Person-ality change | Impairment of work ability | Paranoid-halluc. syndrome (IMPS) | Depr.-apathetic syndrome (IMPS) | Duration of occupational disintegration | Duration of psychiatric hospitalization |
|---|---|---|---|---|---|---|---|---|
| Gittelman-Klein Scale (n=55–70) | ● | | ●●● | ● | | ●● | | ●● |
| Goldstein Scale (n=55–61) | | | ●● | | | ●● | | ● |
| Phillips Scale (n=75–78) | ● | | ●● | ●● | | ●● | ● | ●●● |
| Vaillant Scale (n=72–76) | ●● | | ●● | ●●● | | ● | ●● | ●● |
| Stephens Scale (n=72–76) | ●●● | ●● | ●●● | ●●● | ● | ● | ●● | ●●● |
| Strauss-Carpenter Scale (n=67–77) | ●● | ●● | ●●● | ●● | ●● | ●● | ● | ●●● |

Explained variance: ● = ≤ 10 %, ●● = 11–20 %, ●●● = 21–30 %

**Table 6**. Items of the self-constructed prognostic scales. Munich follow-up study on schizophrenia (Möller et al. 1986)

| Score items | Score 1 | Score 2 | Score 3 | Score 4 |
|---|---|---|---|---|
| ● Premorbid working dysfunction | | | | x |
| ● No precipitating factors before first manifestation | x | x | | x |
| ● Younger age at first hospitalization | | x | | |
| ● No signs of manic-depressive disorder at first manifestation | | | | x |
| ● Duration of occupational disintegration (5 years before index admission) | x | x | | x |
| ● Duration of psychiatric hospitalization (5 years before index admission) | x | | | |
| ● No lasting partnership at index admission | x | | | |
| ● Impairment of working performance (during the year before index admission) | x | x | | x |
| ● Residual syndrome (personality change) before index admission | x | | | |
| ● Poor psychopathological state at discharge | x | x | | x |
| ● IMPS superfactors | | | | |
| • Organic syndrome at discharge[1] | | | | x |
| • Depressive, phobic-compulsive syndrome[2] at discharge[3] | | | | x |
| ● IMPS factors | | | | |
| • Disorientation at admission[3] | | | x | |
| • Obsessional-phobic at admission[3] | | | x | |
| • Retardation and apathy at discharge | | | x | |
| • Paranoid projection at discharge | | | x | |
| • Motor disturbances at discharge | | | x | |

[1] IMPS factors disorientation + retardation and apathy
[2] IMPS factors anxious depression + obsessional phobic
[3] The value (10 % of the theoretical score = 1, 20 % = 2, etc.) must be substracted from the total score

also equally important to state that predictors characterizing poor responders to a treatment should not be overinterpreted in the sense that these patients do not respond to the treatment in question at all.

In reviewing the literature on prediction research, it is clear that most of the results are so far controversial. To improve the consistency of the results, some basic preconditions for prediction research should be considered:

1. Reliable diagnosis according to operationalized classification systems.
2. Standardized assessment of predictors and outcome variables.
3. Large sample size, especially in situations when the predicted outcome is infrequent (e. g. suicide).

**Table 7.** Predictive power of prognostic scales. Munich follow-up study on schizophrenia. Replication sample (n=39–46) (Möller et al. 1986)

| Prognostic Scores | Impairment of "level of functioning" (GAS) | Global psycho-pathology | Person-ality change | Impairment of work ability | Paranoid-halluc. syndrome (IMPS) | Depr.-apathetic syndrome (IMPS) | Duration of occupational disintegration | Duration of psychiatric hospitalization |
|---|---|---|---|---|---|---|---|---|
| Score 1 | ●● | ●●● | ●●●● | ●●● | | ●● | ●●● | ●●● |
| Score 2 | ●● | ●●● | ●●●● | ●● | | ●● | ●● | ●● |
| Score 3 | | ● | | | | | | ●● |
| Score 4 | ●● | ●●●● | ●●●● | ●●● | | ●●● | ●●● | ●●● |

Explained variance: ● = ≤ 10 %, ●● = 11–20 %, ●●● = 21–30 %, ●●●● = 31–40 %

4. Analyses of potential predictor variables in relation to different/multidimensional outcome criteria.
5. Differentiation if possible between course- and treatment-related predictors.
6. Adequate statistical procedures, including modern multivariate analyses.
7. Replication as "via regia" of predictor validation.

## References

Arana GW, Baldessarini RJ, Ornsteen M (1985) The dexamethasone suppression test for diagnosis and prognosis in psychiatry. Arch Gen Psychiatry 42: 1193–1204

Möller HJ, von Zerssen D, Werner-Eilert K, Wüschner-Stockheim M (1981a) Psychopathometrische Verlaufsuntersuchungen an Patienten mit Schizophrenien und verwandten Psychosen. Arch Psychiatr Nervenkr 230: 275–292

Möller HJ, von Zerssen D, Wüschner-Stockheim M, Werner-Eilert K (1981b) Die prognostische Bedeutung psychopathometrischer Aufnahme- und Entlassungsbefunddaten schizophrener Patienten. Arch Psychiatr Nervenkr 231: 13–34

Möller HJ, Werner-Eilert K, Wüschner-Stockheim M, von Zerssen D (1982a) Relevante Merkmale für die 5-Jahres-Prognose von Patienten mit schizophrenen und verwandten paranoiden Psychosen. Arch Psychiatr Nervenkr 231: 305–322

Möller HJ, von Zerssen D, Werner-Eilert K, Wüschner-Stockheim D (1982b) Outcome in schizophrenic and similar paranoid psychoses. Schizophr Bull 8: 99–108

Möller HJ, Scharl W, von Zerssen D (1984) Strauss-Carpenter-Skala: Überprüfung ihres prognostischen Wertes für das 5-Jahres-"Outcome" schizophrener Patienten. Eur Arch Psychiatry Neurol Sci 234: 112–117

Möller HJ, Schmid-Bode W, von Zerssen D (1986) Prediction of long-term outcome in schizophrenia by prognostic scales. Schizophr Bull 12: 225–234

Möller HJ, Fischer G, von Zerssen D (1987) Prediction of therapeutic response in acute treatment with antidepressants. Results of an empirical study involving 159 endogenous depressive patients. Eur Arch Psychiatry Neurol Sci 236: 349–357

Möller HJ, Schmid-Bode W, Cording-Tömmel C, Zaudig M, von Zerssen D (1988) Verlauf schizophrener Psychosen im Vergleich zu anderen endogenen Psychosen sowie Prädiktionsmöglichkeiten auf der Basis von Schizophrenie-Prognose-Skalen und operationalisierter Schizophreniekonzepte. In: Böcker F, Weig W (Hrsg) Aktuelle Kernfragen in der Psychiatrie. Springer, Berlin Heidelberg New York Tokyo, pp 146–156

Möller HJ, Hohe-Schramm M, Cording-Tömmel C, Schmid-Bode W, Wittchen HU, Zaudig M, von Zerssen D (1989) The classification of functional psychosis and its implications for prognosis. Br J Psychiatry 154: 467–472

Möller HJ, Krokenberger M, von Zerssen D (1993) Prediction of short-term outcome of neurotic-depressive inpatients. Results of an empirical study of 134 inpatients. Eur Arch Psychiatry Clin Neurosci 242: 301–309

**Author's address:** Prof. Dr. H.-J. Möller, Psychiatrische Klinik der Universität, Sigmund-Freud-Straße 25, D-53105 Bonn, Federal Republic of Germany

# Target dimensions in prediction of neuroleptic response: concepts and instruments

**J. M. Kane**

Department of Psychiatry, Hillside Hospital, Division of Long Island Jewish Medical Center, Glen Oaks, NY, and Albert Einstein College of Medicine, Bronx, NY, U.S.A.

A variety of conceptual and practical issues need to be addressed in the study of neuroleptic response predictors. This paper will attempt to review some major aspects of this topic.

## How should response be defined?

Traditionally response to neuroleptic drugs has been measured with rating scales focusing primarily on positive symptoms (e. g delusions, hallucinations) and to a lesser extent on negative symptoms (e. g. alogia, anhedonia). More recently research has highlighted the existence of three factors or syndromes and predictive efforts should now include attempts to make this discrimination as well.

Current research in predicting response should include adequate attention to these different domains of psychopathology, particularly since response in these areas may or may not be correlated or simultaneous. In general, instruments such as the BPRS have been utilized to document overall changes in psychopathology. Other instruments have been developed which may provide a richer array of items to assess negative symptoms (e. g. SANS, PANSS). Scales used in this context should be well-anchored, with demonstrated interrater reliability and appropriate to the context or setting in which the patient is assessed (i. e. inpatient ward or outpatient clinic).

Even within the core symptomatology of schizophrenia there may be a different time course of response for one aspect of psychopathology compared to another. For example, agitation may improve before delusional thinking which may improve before thought disorder.

When looking at the course of schizophrenia with treatment, it is also difficult to tease apart medication-treatment effects from the influence of other factors such as natural disease course or the influence of environmental factors, substance abuse, etc. There are a paucity of modern-day data on the natural course of schizophrenia given the ubiquitous use of neuroleptics and their dramatic effects on the illness.

Increasing recognition of the importance of other dimensions of outcome is leading to the inclusion of a variety of assessment measures for quality of life, social and vocational adjustment, family burden, subjective distress and adverse effects.

Defining response also requires a decision as to whether ultimate response or initial response (or both) are of interest. Ultimate response would refer to where the patient ends up after the greatest degree of eventual response is achieved. The problem with this measure is that the time course of response is very variable and the ultimate maximum degree of response may not occur for weeks or months. Most clinical trials involve a fixed-interval with an arbitrary cutoff, however, this may capture only one aspect of treatment response.

Several studies in recent years have focused on response after 24–48 hours, predicting response after several weeks or response at one week predicting response after several weeks. It may be that some of the variability in response relates to time frame, that is some patients respond more quickly than others, but the ultimate degree of response might be the same.

It is also important to consider differentiating absolute response from relative response. Absolute response would refer to the actual amount of change on a particular measure whereas relative response would refer to the proportion of the possible response or percent improvement. Percent improvement can be misleading when comparing outcome among patients. A patient whose Brief Psychiatric Rating Scale score goes from 60 to 30 is experiencing a 50 % improvement as is a patient whose score goes from 36 to 18, but the latter patient may be essentially asymptomatic whereas the former has considerable psychopathology.

It would be desirable to take both types of response into account in predictor studies. A related issue is the documentation of persistent response. In some placebo studies, for example, an initial improvement on placebo may be followed by a subsequent deterioration. What is of interest is that response which is enduring and stable rather than transient.

## Acute, prophylactic and discontinuation response

Response can be studied in different treatment stages. Most often acute response in an exacerbation or relapse is studied where the degree of improvement on measures of psychopathology over a relatively short time frame are the focus of interest. Maintenance or prophylactic response would involve the effectiveness of treatment in preventing subsequent exacerbation or relapse. A different pattern of predictive variables may be relevant in this context and very little research has been done attempting to relate these different types of treatment response. For example, do those patients who respond best acutely also tend to do better in terms of maintenance response?

Another type of response which is related to maintenance response but not necessarily identical is the response to treatment discontinuation. Some patients are able to maintain remission for lengthy intervals following treatment discontinuation while others are prone to relapse very quickly. This distinction has important clinical and heuristic implications, though it may be overlooked when pure "treatment" response is being discussed. (To some extent this is equivalent to the placebo response component of acute treatment.)

## Should relatively responsive patients be selected for specific predictor studies?

In some studies response is dichotomized by some a priori or post-facto criterion. In other studies, an attempt is made to correlate degree of response with proposed predictor variables. The goals of these strategies may be quite different. It is useful to conceptualize patients as being capable of different degrees of response. In some studies it might be useful to identify a subgroup of patients who appear to be capable of response and then assess the predictive power of various factors in correlating with the degree of response within that group. This eliminates those patients who may be for whatever reason incapable of response and therefore adding "noise" to the assessment of response predictors. In other situations the prediction of no response or poor response as opposed to partial or good response would be the focus and all patients should be included.

We cannot necessarily assume that the ability to respond at all and the degree of response to a particular treatment are necessarily influenced by the same variables or to the same degree.

## Treatment considerations

In predicting response among patient groups it is critical to attempt to provide treatment in as uniform and controlled a fashion as possible. Patients should undergo sufficient washouts to allow the determination of an appropriate baseline evaluation. Neuroleptic treatment if possible should be provided in a consistent fashion. Ideally fixed drug, fixed dose (or blood level controlled) trials should be conducted so that differences in outcome are less likely to be attributable to differences in treatment. Adjunctive medications (e. g. benzodiazepines or antiparkinsonian agents) should be carefully controlled and specific durations of treatment should be specified. Efforts to ensure compliance are obviously critical as are efforts to prevent concomitant substance or alcohol abuse.

In discussing treatment conditions, clearly there is a tradeoff in degree of control over treatment variables versus sample size. It may be difficult in many settings to control treatment to the extent suggested and investigators may choose to do large-scale naturalistic studies where variations in treatment conditions and their influence on treatment outcome may be hoped to average out, therefore, permitting the potential effect of predictor variables to emerge.

Since there remains considerable debate about optimum treatment conditions such as most effective and least behaviorally toxic neuroleptic dosage, the potential importance of treatment parameters in systematically influencing response should not be overlooked.

## Predicting poor response

An example of a fixed drug, fixed dose design is a study recently completed by our research group (Kinon et al. 1993). One hundred fifty six acutely ill schizophrenic, schizoaffective and schizophreniform patients who had been recently hospitalized on an acute care inpatient facility were treated openly with fluphenazine 20 mg/day (with prophylactic benztropine mesylate) for four weeks. Those subjects who failed to meet a priori criteria for substantial therapeutic response at the end of four weeks were randomized to receive double-blind treatment for an additional four weeks. The alternative treatments were: (1) to continue on fluphenazine 20 mg/day; (2) to receive fluphenazine 80 mg/day; (3) to receive haloperidol 20 mg/day. Of the 115 subjects who completed the four week initial open trial, 32 % were characterized as good responders. Higher negative symptoms scores at baseline and a greater degree of extrapyramidal side effects across weeks one through four distinguished the poor responder from the good responder group.

Of the non-responders who went into randomized treatment, only 4 of 47 subjects (9 %) subsequently met response criteria and no superior efficacy was associated with any of the specific alternative treatments.

In examining demographic and diagnostic variables, those patients with schizoaffective schizophrenia were more likely to respond well as were those patients who had a later age of onset.

This trial is cited as an example of an attempt to identify predictors of poor response. These findings are also relevant to the question of identifying the most effective treatment alternatives for poor responders and suggest that at least during the course of an eight week trial, substantial increases in dose or switching to a different drug do not bring about substantial further improvement.

It might be for example that a trial of clozapine (or other promising treatments for refractory patients which might be developed) should be considered after an initial failure on a single drug rather than waiting for three trials on three different drugs as has been the pattern in the U.S. (Kane et al. 1988). This hypothesis requires testing in double-blind trials before any recommendations should be made, but the clinical implications are important.

This is an example where predictor research could have clear clinical implications.

## Conclusion

Predictor research holds the promise of allowing treatment decisions to be made in a more individual fashion. The enormous heterogeneity of illness characteristics, course, treatment response and long-term outcome hold the need and the promise for careful study of predictive factors which might help to identify clinically meaningful subgroups.

## References

Kane J, Honigfeld G, Singer J, Meltzer H, and the Clozaril Collaborative Study Group (1988) Clozapine for the treatment-resistant schizophrenic: a double-blind comparison versus chlorpromazine/benztropine. Arch Gen Psychiatry 45:789–796

Kinon BJ, Kane JM, Johns C, Perovich R, Ismi M, Koreen A, Weiden P (1993) Treatment of neuroleptic resistant schizophrenic relapse. Psychopharmacol Bull 29(2):309–314

**Author's address:** Prof. Dr. J. M. Kane, Department of Psychiatry, Hillside Hospital, 75–59 263rd Street, Glen Oaks, NY 11004, U.S.A.

# Predictors of outcome in schizophrenia: the concept of time

**J. A. Lieberman**

Department of Psychiatry, Hillside Hospital, Long Island Jewish Medical Center, Glen Oaks, NY, U.S.A.

## Concept and definition

The ability to predict the treatment response of patients with schizophrenia has been the goal of an extensive number of studies (reviewed in Lieberman and Kane 1986, Lieberman and Sobel 1993, Lieberman and Koreen 1993, Lieberman et al. 1994). Measures that have been examined as potential predictors of treatment outcome can be classified into several categories. These include *historical, constitutional, environmental, phenomenologic* and *biologic variables*. The ability of these measures to be predictive of treatment outcome is dependent on in what phase of the illness they are being assessed and when in the course of illness outcome is being assessed. In addition, there are a number of factors that can influence the expression and ability to identify measures that might be predictive of treatment outcome (Table 1).

**Table 1.** Factors that affect expression and identification of outcome predictors

- State vs trait dependency
- Maturational development and stage of the life cycle
- Medication status and duration of exposure

Let me illustrate these concepts with a few examples. Some measures, specifically biologic markers, can be state or trait dependent. A state dependent measure will be present only during specific phases of the illness. An example of a state dependent measure would be a putative biologic measure that may be predictive of outcome during the acute stage of illness such as growth hormone (GH) secretory levels in response to apomorphine or plasma homovanillic acid (pHVA), but is not present during periods of remission or after sustained drug treatment. A trait dependent measure on the other hand, is present at all times presumably even prior to the onset of the illness. An example of a trait dependent measure would be smooth pursuit eye movement dysfunction or human leukocyte antigens (HLAs).

At the same time other variables will differ in when in the course of the illness they may be manifest. Female gender which has long been associated with better treatment outcome is obviously present and detectable from the time of birth if not before. Impairment in a patient's level of premorbid functioning may not be detectable until later childhood or adolescence. While a patient's development of negative symptoms of the deficit state may occur at anytime in the patient's pre- or post-morbid course, i. e. prior to the onset, early or late in the course of their schizophrenia. Any assessment of the presence of abnormal brain morphology will be dependent on when in the patient's life cycle the assessment is being performed. This is because there are age dependent changes that occur in the structures of interest for schizophrenia, specifically the ventricular system, cortical gyri and sulci and the subarachnoid space.

Finally, medication status and duration of exposure to medication can influence the expression and ability to identify potential predictors of treatment outcome. Plasma homovanillic acid (pHVA) levels which have been shown to be correlated with treatment outcome are altered by antipsychotic medication. Moreover, the duration of medication treatment will influence the level of pHVA at any given time. Similarly, plasma prolactin (PRL) levels are greatly influenced by the medication status of the patient and for how long the patient has been on or off antipsychotic medication at the time when PRL is being assessed.

## Time frame for prediction of treatment outcomes

Treatment outcomes can be defined in various contexts. For acutely symptomatic patients it would be extremely valuable to be able to predict reliably their response to antipsychotic treatment, i. e. predict acute antipsychotic treatment response. For patients who are stable outpatients, it would also be valuable if we could predict which patients will relapse and when, and what dose of medication would be necessary to prevent relapse. At the same time we know that some patients will not have the same level of treatment response and outcome in the early phases of their illness as they will in the later phases. A significant proportion of patients will experience some progression of their illness and deterioration in their ability to respond to treatment over the course of their illness. Therefore, the short-term and long-term outcomes of patients will not necessarily be the same.

In determining the ability of specific measures to predict outcome we must understand that the strength of the predictive power of any variable will vary depending on the time-frame of the outcome to which it is being applied. Clearly, the most powerful and useful predictor is one that can be identified prior to or at the onset of a patient's illness and can forecast a patient's short- and long-term outcome. Clinical psychiatry has very few such validated predictors. Consequently, measures that are relatively predictive of outcome within certain limits can be of significant heuristic as well as practical value.

Let us now examine some of the most commonly studied and potentially informative predictors of treatment outcome in light of these considerations (Tables 1–6).

## **Historical predictors** (Table 2)

Poor premorbid level of function and social adjustment has long been known to be a poor prognostic factor. Behavioral precursors to schizophrenia have been extensively described. However, relatively few patients have histories of lifelong poor functioning. In patients who appear to be normal in childhood but begin to show declines in functional capacity in adolescence or early adulthood, it is unclear if this represents a prodromal phase of the illness.

An earlier age of onset has also been associated with poorer outcome of schizophrenia. This measure is of course highly dependent on how we define the onset of illness. Does it begin with the earliest manifestations of general personality and behavioral changes that may not be specifically related to schizophrenia, the so-called prodromal phase, or does it begin with the first signs of psychosis. The mode of onset of illness has also been found to predict outcome. Specifically, a gradual or insidious onset has been associated with poor outcome in contrast to an abrupt and florid illness onset.

The variables of age, mode and definition of illness onset are closely correlated with another measure that has been strongly associated with the treatment outcome of schizophrenia, duration and number of psychotic episodes (May et al. 1981, Crow et al. 1986, Loebel et al. 1992, Wyatt 1991). The import of these studies is that the acute psychotic episodes reflect an active morbid phase of the illness which can impair patients' ability to respond to treatment and recover. Given this although it has long been known that past history of illness and treatment response

**Table 2.** Historical predictors of treatment outcome

- Premorbid level of function
- Age of onset
- Mode of onset
- Duration of illness
- Number of prior episodes
- Response to prior treatment and level of recovery in prior episodes

was the best predictor of future course, we cannot be confident that a past history of treatment response will invariably predict consistent responses in future episodes.

## Constitutional predictors of treatment outcome (Table 3)

These are factors that are from the genetic endowment of the patient and may or may not be related to the disease pathophysiology. Females have consistently been found to have a more benign form of schizophrenia and a better treatment outcome than males. Genetic loci for schizophrenia or any of its phenotypic features have not been successfully identified. None of these measures would appear to have any temporal dependence in their predictive value.

**Table 3.** Constitutional predictors of treatment outcome

| | |
|---|---|
| – | Gender |
| – | Genetic loci |

## Environmental predictors of treatment outcome (Table 4)

Stressful life events can have destabilizing effects on remitted patients. Included in these are family interactions of high "emotional expression". In addition, substance abuse can produce symptom exacerbation. These events when they act as precipitants, usually precede by short periods of time, i. e. days or weeks, symptom exacerbations, and have the greatest effect on patients when they are not receiving antipsychotic medication.

**Table 4.** Environmental predictors of treatment outcome

| | |
|---|---|
| – | Stressful life events |
| – | Family's emotional expression |
| – | Substance abuse |

## Phenomenologic predictors of treatment outcome (Table 5)

The paranoid subtype of schizophrenia has been associated with better treatment outcome compared to the other undifferentiated, hebephrenic and catatonic subtypes. However, this measure may vary over the course of the illness as subtypes may evolve over time with some patients progressing from paranoid to nonparanoid illness subtypes in the later stages of the illness. Primary negative signs and symptoms of the deficit

**Table 5.** Phenomenologic predictors of treatment outcome

- Paranoid subtype
- Primary negative symptoms
- Acute EPS
- Tardive dyskinesia
- Neurologic soft signs

state are associated with poor treatment outcome. However, identification of these signs and symptoms is complicated by a number of confounding factors including acute psychotic symptoms and drug side effects. Consequently, patients can only be reliably characterized as having primary negative symptoms after they have stabilized from an acute episode.

Various types of neurologic signs have been reported as predictive of treatment outcome. Acute EPS with typical neuroleptics has been found to be a predictor of good treatment outcome in first episode patients, poor response in chronic multiepisode patients and good response to clozapine in treatment refractory patients. Vulnerability to tardive dyskinesia (TD) has been reported to be associated with poor treatment outcome. Since this feature is vulnerablility and not solely the expression of TD, we are limited in its detection if we must wait until signs of TD develop many months or years after the institution of treatment. Neurologic soft signs may also be predictive of treatment outcome. These would appear to be stable signs that are present throughout the course of the illness. However, there have been no longitudinal assessments of soft signs that demonstrate this. In addition, antipsychotic medication could potentially interfere with the expression of soft signs through the production of EPS.

### **Biologic predictors of treatment outcome** (Table 6)

Abnormal brain morphology, specifically enlargement of the lateral and third ventricles, has been associated with poor outcome in schizophrenia. Although it is generally thought that pathomorphological brain changes develop prior to or at the onset of the illness, this has not been fully established. Moreover, even if pathological changes are present at the onset it could still be possible for further changes to occur.

Higher baseline levels of pHVA and their decline with antipsychotic treatment have been found to be associated with better outcome. With the initiation of treatment, pHVA increases and then declines to below drug free baseline levels over the subsequent weeks/months of treatment. When maintenance medication is withdrawn, pHVA eventually increases after a 1 to 4 week washout period. Since medication clearly af-

**Table 6.** Biologic predictors of treatment outcome

| | |
|---|---|
| – | Brain morphology |
| – | Plasma homovanillic acid |
| – | Plasma prolactin |
| – | Plasma norepinephrine |
| – | CSF HVA/5-HIAA ratio |
| – | Antipsychotic drug blood levels |
| – | Behavioral response to dopamine agonist stimulation |

fects pHVA levels the duration of prior treatment and drug washout are important factors that can influence pHVA levels and their potential predictive validity. Similarly, plasma PRL levels are directly influenced by the antipsychotic drug dose and duration of treatment. Thus, the predictive validity of PRL is dependent on the patient's pharmacologic status.

Measures of norepinephrine (NE) have been reported to predict outcome to various treatment manipulations. Elevated CSF NE is associated with increased risk of relapse following medication withdrawal. Plasma NE levels increase in response to clozapine treatment. Greater increases in pNE are associated with therapeutic response to clozapine. Low CSF HVA to 5-HIAA ratios in a drug free condition have been found to predict a therapeutic response to clozapine in treatment refractory patients.

Pharmacologic factors have also been found to be predictors of treatment outcome. Studies relating antipsychotic drug blood levels to clinical response have produced inconsistent results. Nevertheless, with several compounds, including fluphenazine, haloperidol and clozapine, threshold levels above which the probability of a therapeutic response is enhanced have been demonstrated. In another paradigm, behavioral response to acute administration of psychostimulants have been examined. With a surprisingly high degree of consistency the results across studies indicate that patients who experience transient symptom activation have a higher relapse rate if maintenance medication is withdrawn. This predictive test appears to be dependent on patients being in an unremitted state of the illness (Lieberman et al. 1987).

## Conclusion

A number of measures are predictive of treatment outcome in schizophrenia. The strength of their association and their predictive validity are limited in varying degrees by temporal factors that must be considered in interpreting their significance.

## Acknowledgements

This work was supported by a Research Scientist Development Award (MH00537) to Dr. Lieberman and the Mental Health Clinical Research Center of Hillside Hospital (MH41960) from the National Institute of Mental Health.

## References

Crow TJ, MacMillan JF, Johnson AL, Johnstone EC (1986) A randomised controlled trial of prophylactic neuroleptic treatment. Br J Psychiatry 148: 120–127

Lieberman JA, Brown AS, Gorman (1994) Biological markers in schizophrenia. American Psychiatric Press Review of Psychiatry 13: 133–170

Lieberman JA, Kane JM (eds) (1986) Predictors of relapse in schizophrenia. American Psychiatric Press, Washington DC

Lieberman JA, Kane JM, Sarantakos S, Gadaleta D, Woerner M, Alvir J, Ramos-Lorenzi J (1987) Prediction of relapse in schizophrenia. Arch Gen Psychiatry 44: 597–603

Lieberman JA, Koreen A (1993) Neurochemistry and neuroendocrinology of schizophrenia. A selective review. Schizophr Bull 19 (2): 371–429

Lieberman JA, Soebel SN (1993) Predictors of treatment response and course of schizophrenia. Curr Opin Psychiatry 6: 63–69

Loebel AD, Lieberman JA, Alvir JMJ, Mayerhoff DI, Geisler SH, Szymanski SR (1992) Duration of psychosis and outcome in first episode schizophrenia. Am J Psychiatry 149: 1183–1188

May PR, Tuma AH, Dixon WJ (1981) Schizophrenia: a follow-up study of the results of five forms of treatment. Arch Gen Psychiatry 38: 776–784

Wyatt RJ (1991) Neuroleptics and the natural course of schizophrenia. Schizophr Bull 17: 325–351

**Author's address**: Prof. Dr. J. A. Lieberman, Department of Psychiatry, Hillside Hospital, Long Island Jewish Medical Center, 75–59 263rd Street, Glen Oaks, NY 11004, U.S.A.

# Sex differences in the prediction of neuroleptic response

**M. V. Seeman**

Department of Psychiatry, University of Toronto, Toronto, Ontario, Canada

It is currently not possible to accurately predict neuroleptic response. It is not known which acutely psychotic patients will respond to drugs with relative speed and comprehensiveness, or at low, as compared to standard doses. It is not known which patients will remain relapse-free over a given time period on maintenance neuroleptic therapy. It is not known which patients will sustain full, as distinct from partial, remission in response to maintenance drug therapy. It is not known which patients, after a stable period, will be able to undergo dose reductions without a return of symptoms or of dysfunction (Gaebel et al. 1987).

Those variables which best predict good outcome while on neuroleptics (premorbid adjustment, acute onset, absence of defect symptoms, preservation of affect) are the same ones which predict good outcome without drugs. To quote Fenton and McGlashan (1987), "we reach the apparent contradiction that good prognosis schizophrenic patients are not only most likely to respond to neuroleptic medications but are also most likely to do well without them". While perhaps not surprising, such a conclusion confounds the quest for accurate prediction of neuroleptic response.

In addition, it seems to be impossible to predict which of the many neuroleptics in common use will produce the best response in a given individual. Although receptor profiles of individual drugs are beginning to be delineated quite sharply and specifically, there is no good correlation between the receptor-binding properties of a drug on which the patient preferentially improves and either the patient's symptom profile, the stage or subtype of his illness, the individual's response to neurochemical challenge, his brain structure, or his neurocognitive profile.

Prediction of the *percentage* of neuroleptic-responding subjects in a representative schizophrenia sample is generally accurate and reliable but it is not known in advance who will be among the responders and who will not. Those who appear to respond dramatically to a particular drug at one time may not do so at another. The converse is less often true, but does occur. It has become increasingly apparent that new strategies to promote accurate prediction are critically important.

## Purposes of accurate prediction

Successful prediction may clarify the basic mechanisms that trigger and moderate psychotic processes. Psychosis can be viewed as a disturbance of neural networks resulting from alteration in one or more genes and the subsequent interaction of these gene products with neuromodulators. For example, an aberrant D2 receptor-complex may be responsible for symptoms in some individuals. Putatively, inhibition by D2 blockade will prevent the cascade of events that culminates in psychotic symptoms in these patients. Other individuals may inherit an abnormality of the D4 receptor complex. For relief of symptoms they will require D4 blockers. Still other persons may be vulnerable to psychosis because of a 5HT receptor variant, and these individuals' psychotic symptoms may respond best to serotonin blockade.

Research strategies to identify individuals whose psychosis responds to one well-characterized drug but not to another will be able to subtype schizophrenic illness into meaningful, etiologically-distinct categories (Niznik and Van Tol 1992).

Neurotransmitter receptors are, of course, only some of many proteins with which central nervous system drugs interact and whose structure is genetically determined and potentially polymorphic. Insofar as gonadal hormones modulate such structures – nerve growth factors, for instance (Toran-Allerand 1990, 1991) –, a focus on sex differences can help to uncover basic mechanisms leading to differences in neuroleptic response.

## Prediction and new drug development

If populations which respond or do not respond to specific features of antipsychotic drugs can be recognized, new drug development can capitalize on these distinctive features. In this way, pharmaceutical products can be made maximally effective for the largest possible number of individual suffering from psychosis. This purpose of prediction overlaps with the first but the focus is changed from the identification of psychopathological mechanisms to the development of drugs which have high tolerability, low toxicity, and which benefit as large as possible a segment of afflicted individuals.

Industry research and academic research into predictive strategies have somewhat different purposes and research initiatives may be shaped by these different purposes. As an example, a drug which is toxic to many individuals and, thus, not of interest to pharmaceutical research may, nevertheless, prove invaluable in the discovery of specific causative pathways which contribute to psychosis. Insofar as potential drug toxicity in women affects not only the patient but also her fetus and neonate, and, inasmuch as women and men react differently to drugs, the perspective of sex differences is increasingly recognized as important in industry-directed research (Seeman 1989, Yonkers et al. 1992).

## Prediction and health service delivery

Administrators of mental health delivery systems are interested in neuroleptic response prediction so that they can treat those who are likely to respond and not divert resources to those who will not. The aim here is efficiency and effectiveness of a system of care for the majority. The concern is not only that some patients may be receiving ineffective treatment. It is also that this treatment may have adverse effects which render some patients more disabled than they might otherwise be.

Again, research strategies for purposes of optimal delivery of health services need to be somewhat different than those oriented to uncovering basic mechanisms or those aimed at the development of new and better drugs. They need to be able to screen out likely non-responders early, perhaps via test dose procedure, and to delineate populations where the cost/benefit ratio warrants neuroleptic treatment.

Behavioral toxicity for mothers and for children born to them is an especially important area of focus. In general, women treated for schizophrenia perform more caretaking tasks than do schizophrenic men. The women, even when relatively disabled, take care of infants and children, spouses, ill or elderly relatives. They may be employed in caretaking occupations, all of which makes the prediction of the behavioral toxicity of neuroleptic drugs particularly critical in women (Seeman in press).

## Prediction in order to optimize individual care

The concern of clinicians is to determine which drug to use at which dose in the treatment of their individual patients. For the patient, what is important in prediction is subjective benefit relative to subjective cost. Both immediate and long-term perspectives are important.

Patients are concerned about financial cost and about durability of effect. They want drugs which act quickly so that the acute psychotic state and the attendant hospitalization and interruption of meaningful life tasks is kept as short as possible.

Many patients want drugs which are specific to specific symptoms – i. e. they would like a drug that will reliably reduce terror, for instance, without also interfering with flights of fancy, subjective feelings of self-confidence, or creativity. In general, patients will tolerate (sometimes even welcome) certain specific side-effects, loss of libido, for instance, while being totally intolerant of other effects, weigth-gain being an example. Men and women differ markedly with respect to the varieties of adverse effects that they are able to tolerate. The ability to anticipate these is an important ingredient of neuroleptic-response prediction.

The rest of this paper is situated within this last perspective of individual prediction. It will deal with the literature on speed of neuroleptic action in men and women, time to relapse, maintenance dose levels, dose reduction hazard in men und women, and fullness of remission. I will review drug tolerability and toxicity in women and men. These data need to be appreciated against the background of the known patterns of symptom fluctuation in schizophrenia in women and men, differential phase of illness effects, and age effects. Specific issues of particular importance to women will be highlighted and research initiatives that take these issues into account will be recommended.

## Speed of effect

At onset of an acute psychotic episode, speed of action is an important component of neuroleptic response, both for the immediate well-being of the patient and because there is some evidence that long-term prognosis is improved if psychosis is treated early (Loebel et al. 1992). While the reason for this association is not known, it seems reasonable to assume that time-in-psychosis is responsible for laying down memory traces in neural circuits which become irreversible if prolonged.

The ability to reach the target site of action quickly and to exert beneficial effect promptly is an important property of all medication. There is much about the time-course of action of neuroleptics that we do not know. There is evidence that, for standard neuroleptic action to become initiated, 75 % – 80 % of brain D2 receptors have to be occupied (Farde et al. 1989).

The timing will depend on absorption, distribution, clearance, and initial numbers of target receptors (which may vary with age, sex and diagnosis). High loading doses do not appear to shorten the lag time (Kane and Marder 1993).

While plasma drug levels may not be critical, it is important to note that gastrointestinal absorption for all drugs is relatively slow in women (Datz et al. 1987). It is under hormonal influence in that it is affected by phases of the menstrual cycle. Gastrointestinal transit time is slowest during the luteal phase.

With respect to distribution, lipid-soluble neuroleptics are distributed comparatively widely in women because of women's relative excess of adipose tissue.

Portal blood flow and efficiency of liver enzymes determines the rate of metabolism. These are also affected by hormonal fluctuations. There is a significant impact of age, smoking, alcohol, and drugs. Concomitant drug use may be sex-specific, as for example, the use of contraceptives.

Liver enzymatic activity is generally thought to be more efficient in men (Ereshefsky et al. 1991). Age, as might be predicted, correlates with poorer enzyme efficiency and slower breakdown and elimination of active drug. Anticholinergics (more often prescribed to men) appear to enhance the clearance of neuroleptics. Antidepressants (more often prescribed to women) inhibit liver enzymes and increase neuroleptic serum levels (McCreadie et al. 1992).

Once adipose tissue storage is saturated, neuroleptics are released back into the blood stream so that down-the-road plasma concentrations will differ from immediate ones, even when the dose is kept constant. Haring et al. (1989), controlling for dose and weight, found men's plasma concentrations of clozapine to be, on average, only 69 % those of women's. Ereshefsky et al. in 1991 reported higher blood levels of thiothixene in women. Whether these higher blood concentrations or, possibly, women's reportedly increased cerebral blood flow [15 % higher in women than men (Gur et al. 1982)] is responsible, the clinical consensus is that women respond to neuroleptics more quickly than men.

This is particularly interesting since acutely psychotic men have been reported to exhibit a superior placebo response relative to women (Goldberg et al. 1966). If this were possible to confirm it would untangle the early course of illness effect from neuroleptic response. In other words, are women's shorter acute psychotic episodes (see below) due to drug response or, alternatively, to other, non-specific factors? In 1978, Wode-Helgodt et al. studied acutely psychotic men and women treated for two weeks at three levels of daily chlorpromazine (200 mg, 400 mg, 600 mg). Among the men, response occurred only at the highest dose level, at 600 mg daily. Among the women, the response was equal, regardless of which of the three dose regimens they were receiving. This suggests that the lowest dose – 200 mg CPZ – was sufficient to obtain good results in women. In 1980, Young and Meltzer, in a retrospective chart review, comparing placebo and low dose (200 mg CPZ equivalents) responders to conventional dose responders, discovered mostly women in the former group. This study is hard to interpret since we do not know how many were on placebo and how many on low dose. The distinction is crucial in order to subtract from neuroleptic response what may be a non-specific treatment response. It is known that acutely psychotic women respond to non-drug inpatient treatments, such as family therapy, more readily than men (Glick et al. 1990).

Chouinard and Annable (1982) reported a superior female to male response to four weeks of both pimozide and chlorpromazine. Nedopil et al. (1983) observed a superior female response on essentially all outcome measures after 20 days of neuroleptic treatment. Chouinard and Annable (1986) reported that, during an acute exacerbation of psychosis, men required higher fluspirilene doses than women in order to achieve remission. There was no sex difference in this study with respect to chlorpromazine doses. Kolakowska et al. (1985) also found superior drug response in acute first onset women.

While these studies do not directly address speed of response, they do strongly suggest that acute psychosis responds to lower neuroleptic dose in women than in men over the first month or so after an acute episode.

Studies investigating this question need to have a placebo control and to factor out premorbid functioning, which is usually found to be superior in women (Addington and Addington 1993). This is important since many investigators have been able to correlate good premorbid adjustment with early neuroleptic response (Westermeyer and Harrow 1984, Keefe et al. 1989), although not all (Straube et al. 1989).

Since there is a menstrual cycle effect on psychotic symptoms in women (Häfner et al. 1991, Hallonquist et al. 1993), it is important to preserve normal cycles in prediction studies. Neuroleptics (except clozapine) increase prolactin levels. This is dose-related and interferes with the pituitary-ovarian axis leading to cessation of menses, given a sufficiently high neuroleptic dose. If blockade of dopamine receptors by estrogens (Hruska 1986, Häfner et al. 1991) is a contributing cause to women's superior acute response, this effect will be abolished by high doses.

Hormone titers would be an important addition to prediction studies. Using the neuroleptic threshold concept (McEvoy et al. 1991), it could be predicted that, in women, improvement would take place only in a dose range *beneath* the amenorrhea-producing threshold.

Such studies would be easier to carry out with drugs like clozapine which do not affect pituitary DA receptors.

Positron emission tomography studies establishing fluctuations of DA receptor numbers over the course of the menstrual cycle may be a helpful precursor to initiating predictor studies in women.

## Tolerability

### *Extrapyramidal syndrome*

The secondary development of EPS has been linked to outcome – in both directions. For reasons which are unknown, early phase EPS predicts good outcome, whereas chronic phase EPS is associated with poor outcome (Chakos et al. 1992).

Since estrogens are synergistic with neuroleptics at DA striatal sites, pseudoparkinsonism would be expected to be greater in women than in men as long as other relevant factors (dose, rate of dose increase, drug distribution, phase of illness) were kept constant. Because of women's relative increase in cerebral blood flow, immediate effects, such as acute dystonias, might be predicted to be greatest in women.

In his classic 1960 survey of over 3.000 neuroleptic-treated patients, Ayd found that 65 % of the acute dystonias occurred in men. Swett (1975) confirmed this 2:1 ratio. A chart review study by Keepers et al. (1983) examined the effect of prophylactic anticholinergics in preventing acute dystonia in men and women over a three week hospitalization. Most (85 %) of the dystonias occurred in the first four days. This confirmed Ayd's 1960 finding that 90 % of dystonic reactions occurred within five days of initiating neuroleptic therapy. These findings suggest that dystonia results from a gradient effect on the relevant receptor balance, probably the ratio of dopamine to acetylcholine blockade. The study of Keepers et al. (1983) showed that anticholinergics effectively prevented dystonia in both sexes but that the magnitude of the prophylactic effect was most pronounced in men. This implies that the gradient effect is less steep in women, perhaps because they are prescribed lower initial doses, or because they are preferentially prescribed low potency neuroleptics. Alternatively, equivalent doses initially produce lower CNS concentrations in women due to greater drug sequestration in adipose tissue.

Chakos et al. (1992) prospectively investigated acute EPS in 70 first episode schizophrenic and schizoaffective patients, 56 % of whom were male. These were essentially drug-naive patients who were treated on a fixed dose regime. They were given 20 mg of fluphenazine daily for six weeks and, if they failed to respond, this was raised to 40 mg for another 4 weeks. Anticholinergics were not used. Over 8 weeks, 24 patients developed acute dystonia. Contrary to the sex-ratios found in free-dose surveys, more women developed dystonia – 50 % compared to 25 % of the men. The implication is that the fixed-dose strategy led to higher relative doses in women than is generally true in clinical settings, that lipid stores were saturated quickly, and that the expected synergism with estrogen did take place.

Interestingly, where surveys had shown that chronic schizophrenic women were proportionally *more* prone to parkinsonism and akathisia than men (Ayd 1960), this first episode study found roughly equivalent sex rates for parkinsonism and a higher prevalence of akathisia in men at the 8 week mark. Ayd (1960) found that parkinsonism and akathisia were not fully expressed before 72 days after initiating neuroleptic therapy, so that the 8 week mark may not have allowed for a cumulative effect of stored drug. Because of mechanisms already discussed, women may be more at risk for accumulation than men.

## *Other adverse effects*

Although EPS have been the most studied of side-effects, subjective discomfort arises just as often for patients from the many other unpleasant sequelae of neuroleptics: weight gain, sedation, hypotension, skin problems, amenorrhea, interference with sexual arousal and performance, and subtle cognitive changes. The individual meaning of such effects differs from patient to patient but, in general, it can be predicted that women are more bothered than men by effects on their appearance and feelings, while men are more bothered by effects on their function and performance (Seeman 1983a, 1989).

## Toxicity

Tardive dyskinesia, a long term sequela of neuroleptic treatment that is probably associated with neuronal cell death, may be more prevalent in women at certain ages, although this is controversial (Morgenstern and Glazer 1993). Yassa and Jeste (1992), in a recent review of the literature on this subject, discuss the many confounding factors and the possible explanations for the sex-age interplay. Important to consider is the interaction of estrogen and nerve growth factors, implicated, for example, in the neuronal cell death which accompanies Alzheimer's disease (Toran-Allerand 1990, 1991). Women are more at risk for Alzheimer's disease than men, even when longevity is taken into account. Toran-Allerand attributes this to regional brain requirements for estrogen which are unfulfilled in post-menopausal women. In men, testosterone production does not fall off as sharply and continues to be aromatized to estrogen at the cellular brain level well into old age. This may or may not have bearing on tardive dyskinesia.

Post-menopausal women are also at risk for osteoporosis and subsequent hip fracture as a consequence of falls attributable to neuroleptic-induced hypotension. They are more likely than men to be using some drugs (nonsteroidal anti-inflammatory drugs, antidepressants) and less likely to be using others (beta blockers, calcium channel blockers) all of which, by interaction, may raise neuroleptic levels to toxic thresholds.

The agranulocytosis associated with clozapine is thought to be an immune reaction and more common in women.

Behavioral toxicity (apathy, cognitive blunting, memory functions), while occuring in both sexes, may have special consequences for women in their roles as mothers and care-takers. This may have special impact on infants and young children of schizophrenic mothers (Seeman in press).

In sum, from the vantage point of predicting good neuroleptic response, tolerability and toxicity are clearly important features of the subject-drug interaction. Research designs need to take the subjective component into consideration, (Van Putten and May 1978, Hogan et al. 1985, Awad 1993), especially as it pertains to the known differences between women and men.

## Durability of effect (symptom-free remission)

Prediction of symptom-free remission during maintenance medication programs has proven virtually impossible. Retrospectively, those who sustain the fullest remissions in the sense of being relatively symptom-free, are more often women than men (Seeman 1985). This may reflect treatment adherence, premorbid competence, "natural course of illness", or true drug response, depending on the design of the study. Studies in which neuroleptic doses were systematically reduced to the lowest possible maintenance level have not reported gender difference in survival. Three dose-reduction studies were carried out in our center. The first, which attempted periodic short drug holidays, showed no gender difference (Pyke and Seeman 1981). The second looked at survivors of dose-reduction-to-relapse and found lower final doses in women until age 40, with subsequently higher doses for women (Seeman 1983b). The third, in which depot medication was reduced by 1/8 every two months in three successive steps, showed no gender difference in survival (Dale et al. in press).

In more general outcome studies, 102 of which were reviewed in 1989 by Angermeyer et al. almost all the more recent studies reported a better *female* outcome, especially with reference to hospitalization rate and total time spent in hospital. The fact that older studies, predating the neuroleptic era, did not show a female advantage (Watt et al. 1983, Seeman 1986) suggests that part of the more favourable outcome in women is attributable to neuroleptic response. Socio-economic conditions have, of course, changed markedly over this period and have affected the ascertainment of schizophrenic subjects. Diagnostic classification has also changed, so that interpretation is difficult.

An important current finding is that short-term follow-up studies of *first episode* treated patients, regardless of the dimension of outcome, almost invariably report superior outcome in women (see Table 1).

**Table 1.** First episode short-term outcome

| Study | Country | Duration | Female advantage |
|---|---|---|---|
| Salokangas and Stengard (1990) | Finland | 2 yrs | Psychosocial |
| Inoue et al. (1986) | Japan | 1–3yrs | Occupation |
| Holding et al. (1983) | Australia | 3 yrs | Psychosocial |
| Angermeyer et al. (1989) | Germany | 3 yrs | Hosp. rate<br>Length of stay |
| Pakaslahti (1992) | Finland | 5 yrs | Occupation |
| Thara and Rajkumar (1992) | India | 5 yrs | Illness variables<br>Social variables |
| Leff et al. (1992) | 8 sites | 5 yrs | Time in episode<br>Soc. impairment<br>Course pattern |
| Nyman and Jonsson (1983) | Sweden | 6–9 yrs | Soc. competence<br>Occupation<br>Symptoms |
| Goldstein (1988) | U.S. | 10 yrs | Hosp. rate; L.O.S |

For the first ten years after onset, women with schizophrenia show an outcome advantage in all outcome domains and throughout the world

When the follow-up period exceeds 10 years, this pattern begins to shift. McGlashan (1986a), in his long-term Chestnut Lodge follow-up, reports a better outcome for women for symptoms only. His follow-up period was between 2 and 32 years, with a mean of 15 years. Jonsson and Nyman (1991), who followed their original cohort for a further 8 years after their 1983 paper (14–17 years from first admission), no longer observe better outcome in women. Opjordsmoen (1991) reports on both a 10 year and a 31 year follow-up of a schizophrenia cohort in Norway. Over the 21 intervening years, there was no global change in the men, but the women *deteriorated.* As mentioned by Angermeyer et al. (1989) and in an editorial review by Lewis (1992), women's advantage disappears when follow-up studies continue into the long-term (Ciompi 1980, Lloyd et al. 1985, Harding et al. 1987, McGlashan 1988).

There may be several reasons for this. Missing from follow-up may be men who have suicided. Alternatively, the advantage afforded women by their circulating estrogens has disappeared by the end of a long follow-up period. The superior premorbid competence which accrues to women in the early years or the superior family supports available to women during the middle years may have disappeared. In addition, the stresses of aging may impinge on women more severely than on men.

In the Chestnut Lodge follow-up study, McGlashan concluded that different outcome predictor variables held for different stages of illness or follow-up periods. In the short-term, premorbid competence predicted best. In the medium-term, family support predicted best. In the long-term, family genetics was the best predictor: the more family history of schizophrenia, the worse the outcome (McGlashan 1986b).

In this context, it is important to note that course of illness is generally different in women than in men. Breier et al. (1991) have described the course of schizophrenia as being increasingly severe in the first decade, reaching and maintaining a plateau during the second decade and then gradually improving with successive years. This is a common male pattern. For women, the more prevalent course consists of a later start, a relatively even (with minor fluctuations) first decade, a very stormy second decade with worsening symptoms and more psychosocial upheaval, reaching a peak perimenopausally and then very gradually improving but never returning to the relatively good functioning of the first decade.

It is crucial that prediction studies bear these sex differences in mind. Men and women have a different long-term pattern of illness. In addition, women must be evaluated against a backdrop of menstrual fluctuations (Hallonquist et al. 1993), with a worsening premenstrually, improvement during pregnancies, and intensification post-partum and post-menopause (Seeman and Lang 1990).

## Summary of women's issues in prediction studies

In designing studies which include women as subjects, several issues have been identified as particularly significant to women. Some have been discussed above. Others are included without prior discussion because they are critically important, even though somewhat tangential to the purposes of this paper.

1. Timing of menarche may be an important predictor variable in women which may influence prediction.
2. When clinical evaluations are done, it should be noted whether or not the woman subject is menstruating regularly and at what phase of the menstrual cycle she is at the time of assessment. Hormone titers make this determination more accurate. PET studies examining receptor occupancy during the menstrual cycle can help to delineate relevant changes.
3. Pregnancy, postpartum, lactation, and menopause status should be asked about and documented clinically.
4. Whenever possible, neuroleptic dose should be kept under the amenorrhea threshold.
5. The use of contraceptives or over-the-counter drugs, such as antacids, needs to be routinely enquired about.
6. Stage of illness and the aging process need to be viewed somewhat differently in men and women.
7. Psychotic symptoms and neuroleptic side-effects are particularly important to monitor when the patient is a mother or is caring for children or ill and aging relatives.
8. Exposure to violence and victimization is a fact of life for many women. Vulnerability is increased by the condition of schizophrenia and may be further increased by the administration of neuroleptic drugs, if they result in increased passivity. The social situation of women subjects of studies is important to know about and to document.
9. For women more than for men, the therapeutic relationship with the prescriber of the medication may dramatically influence outcome. A good rapport leads to better outcome; a poor rapport may lead to a worse one. Measuring the quality of the relationship may shed light on outcome results (Frank and Gunderson 1990).
10. Because most women consider themselves to have relatively little power in important relationships, it becomes critical that women subjects in research studies feel that they have been consulted, that their opinions have been sought out and incorporated into the design of the study, that they are kept well-informed throughout the study and thoroughly debriefed afterward. This is important for all study subjects but especially so for women because they have become sensitized to power issues (Corrigan et al. 1990).
11. Attention to subjective experience, whether to symptom, side-effect, quality of the therapeutic relationship, or qualitative aspects of outcome, is of special significance in women (Awad 1992, 1993).

## References

Addington J, Addington D (1993) Premorbid functioning, cognitive functioning, symptoms, and outcome in schizophrenia. J Psychiatr Neurosci 18:18–23
Angermeyer MC, Goldstein JM, Kühn L (1989) Gender differences in schizophrenia: rehospitalization and community survival. Psychol Med 19:365–382
Awad AG (1992) Quality of life of schizophrenic patients on medications and implications for new drug trials. Hosp Commun Psychiatry 43:262–265
Awad AG (1993) Subjective response to neuroleptics in schizophrenia. Schizophr Bull 19:609–618
Ayd FJ (1960) A survey of drug induced extrapyramidal reactions. JAMA 175:1054–1060
Breier A, Schreiber JL, Dyer J, Pickar D (1991) NIMH longitudinal study of chronic schizophrenics. Arch Gen Psychiatry 48:239–246
Chakos MH, Mayerhoff DI, Loebel AD, Alvir JMA, Lieberman JA (1992) Incidence and correlates of acute extrapyramidal symptoms in first episode schizophrenia. Psychopharmacol Bull 28:81–86
Chouinard G, Annable L (1982) Pimozide in the treatment of newly admitted schizophrenic patients. Psychopharmacology 76:13–19
Chouinard G, Annable L (1986) A controlled clinical trial of fluspirilene, a long-acting injectable neuroleptic in schizophrenic patients with acute exacerbation. J Clin Psychopharmacol 6:21–26
Ciompi L (1980) The natural history of schizophrenia in the long-term. Br J Psychiatry 136:413–420
Corrigan PW, Liberman RP, Engel JD (1990) From noncompliance to collaboration in the treatment of schizophrenia. Hosp Commun Psychiatry 41:1203–1211
Dale R, Langdon M, Seeman MV (1994) Reducing the dose of depot neuroleptic in stable schizophrenia. J Psychiatr Neurosci 19 (in press)
Datz FL, Christian PS, Moore J (1987) Gender-related differences in gastric emptying. J Nucl Med 28:1204–1207
Ereshefsky l, Saklad SR, Watanabe MD, Davis CM, Jann MW (1991) Thiothixene pharmacokinetic interactions: a study of hepatic enzyme inducers, clearance inhibitors, and demographic variables. J Clin Psychopharmacol 11:296–301
Farde L, Wiesel FA, Nordstrom A, Sedvall G (1989) D1- and D2-dopamine receptor occupancy during treatment with conventional and atypical neuroleptics. Psychopharmacology 99:528–531
Fenton WF, McGlashan TH (1987) Sustained remission in drug-free schizophrenic patients. Am J Psychiatry 144:1306–1309
Frank AF, Gunderson JG (1990) The role of the therapeutic alliance in the treatment of schizophrenia: relationship to course and outcome. Arch Gen Psychiatry 47:228–238
Gaebel W, Pietzcker A (1987) Prospective study of the course of illness in schizophrenia, part II. Prediction of outcome. Schizophr Bull 13:299–306
Glick ID, Spencer JH, Clarkin JF, Haas GL, Lewis AB, Peyser J, DeMane N, Good-Ellis M, Harris E, Lestell V (1990) A randomized trial of inpatient family intervention. IV. Follow-up results for subjects with schizophrenia. Schizophr Res 3:187–200
Goldberg SC, Schooler NR, Davidson EM, Kayce MM (1966) Sex and race differences in response to drug treatment among schizophrenics. Psychopharmacologia (Berlin) 9:31–47
Goldstein JM (1988) Gender differences in the course of schizophrenia. Am J Psychiatry 145:684–689
Gur RC, Gur RE, Obrist WD, Hungerbuhler JP, Younkin D, Rosen AD, Skolnik BE, Reivich M (1982) Sex and handedness differences in cerebral blood flow during rest and cognitive activity. Science 217:659–661
Häfner H, Behrens S, De Vry J, Gattaz WF (1991) An animal model for the effects of estradiol on dopamine-mediated behavior: implications for sex differences in schizophrenia. Psychiatry Res 38:125–134
Hallonquist J, Seeman MV, Lang M, Rector N (1993) Variation in symptom severity over the menstrual cycle of schizophrenics. Biol Psychiatry 33:207–209
Harding CM, Brooks GW, Ashigaga T, Strauss JS, Breier A (1987) The Vermont longitudi-

nal study of persons with severe mental illness. II. Longterm outcome of subjects who retrospectively met DSM-III criteria for schizophrenia. Am J Psychiatry 144:727–735

Haring C, Meise U, Humpel C, Saria A, Fleischhacker WW, Hinterhumber H (1989) Dose-related plasma levels of clozapine: influence of smoking behaviour, sex and age. Psychopharmacology 99:S38–S40

Hogan TP, Awad AG, Eastwood MR (1985) Early subjective response and prediction of outcome in neuroleptic drug therapy in schizophrenia. Can J Psychiatry 30:246–248

Holding TA, Urbane S, Kay DWK (1983) Social outcome after first admission for schizophrenia in Tasmania: a study of matched pairs. Soc Psychiatry 18:145–152

Hruska RE (1986) Elevation of striatal dopamine receptors by estrogen. Dose and time studies. J Neurochem 47:1908–1915

Inoue K, Nakajima T, Kato N (1986) A longitudinal study of schizophrenia in adolescence I. The one-to three-year outcome. Jpn J Psychiatr Neurol 40:143–151

Jonsson H, Nyman AK (1991) Predicting long-term outcome in schizophrenia. Acta Psychiatr Scand 83:342–346

Kane JH, Marder SR (1993) Psychopharmacologic treatment of schizophrenia. Schizophr Bull 19:287–302

Keefe RSE, Mohs RC, Losonczy MF, Davidson M, Silverman JM, Horvath B, Davis KL (1989) Premorbid socio-sexual functioning and longterm outcome in schizophrenia. Am J Psychiatry 146:206–211

Keepers GA, Clappison VJ, Casey DE (1983) Initial anticholinergic prophylaxis for neuroleptic-induced extrapyramidal syndromes. Arch Gen Psychiatry 40:1113–1117

Kolakowska T, Williams AO, Ardern A, Reveley MA, Jambor K, Gelder MG, Mandelbrote BM (1985) Schizophrenia with good and poor outcome 1. Early clinical features, response to neuroleptics and signs of organic dysfunction. Br J Psychiatry 146:229–246

Leff J, Sartorius N, Hablensky A, Korten A, Ernberg G (1992) The International Pilot Study of Schizophrenia: five-year follow-up findings. Psychol Med 22:131–145

Lewis S (1992) Sex and schizophrenia. Vive la différence. Br J Psychiatry 161:445–450

Lloyd D, Simpson JC, Tsuang MT (1985) Are there sex differences in the long-term outcome of schizophrenia? J Nerv Ment Dis 173:643–649

Loebel AD, Lieberman JA, Alvir JMJ, Mayerhoff DI, Geisler SH, Szymanski ST (1992) Duration of psychosis and outcome in first episode schizophrenia. Am J Psychiatry 149:1183–1188

McCreadie RG, Robertson LJ, Wiles DH (1992) The Nithsdale schizophrenia surveys. IX. Akathisia, parkinsonism, tardive dyskinesia and plasma neuroleptic levels. Br J Psychiatry 161:793–799

McEvoy JP, Hogarty G, Steingard S (1991) Optimal dose of neuroleptic in acute schizophrenia: a controlled study of the neuroleptic threshold and higher haloperidol dose. Arch Gen Psychiatry 48:739–745

McGlashan TH (1986a) The prediction of outcome in chronic schizophrenia. Arch Gen Psychiatry 43:167–176

McGlashan TH (1986b) Predictors of shorter-, medium-, and longer-term outcome in schizophrenia. Am J Psychiatry 143:50–55

McGlashan TH (1988) A selective review of recent North American longterm follow-up studies of schizophrenia. Schizophr Bull 14:515–542

Morgenstern H, Glazer WM (1993) Identifying risk factors for tardive dyskinesia among long-term outpatients maintained with neuroleptic medication. Arch Gen Psychiatry 50:723–733

Nedopil N, Pflieger R, Rüther E (1983) The prediction of acute response, remission, and general outcome of neuroleptic treatment in acute schizophrenic patients. Pharmacopsychiatry 16:201–205

Niznik H, Van Tol HHM (1992) Dopamine receptor genes: new tools for molecular psychiatry. J Psychiatr Neurosci 17:158–180

Nyman AK, Jonsson H (1983) Differential evaluation of outcome in schizophrenia. Acta Psychiatr Scand 68:458–475

Opjordsmoen S (1991) Long-term clinical outcome of schizophrenia with special reference to gender differences. Acta Psychiatr Scand 83:307–313

Pakaslahti A (1992) Prediction of working disability in schizophrenia: a 5-year prospective

study of a representative cohort of first-admissons. Publications of the Social Insurance Institution, Finland, ML #119,1–102
Pyke J, Seeman MV (1981) Neuroleptic-free intervals in the treatment of schizophrenia. Am J Psychiatry 138:1620–1621
Salokangas RKR, Stengard E (1990) Gender and short-term outcome in schizophrenia. Schizophr Res 3:333–345
Seeman MV (1983a) Schizophrenic men and women require different treatment programs. J Psychiatr Treatment Evaluation 5:143–148
Seeman MV (1983b) Interaction of sex, age, and neuroleptic dose. Compr Psychiatry 24:125–128
Seeman MV (1985) Clinical and demographic correlates of neuroleptic response. Can J Psychiatry 30:243-245
Seeman MV (1986) Current outcome in schizophrenia: women vs men. Acta Psychiatr Scand 73:609–617
Seeman MV (1989) Prescribing neuroleptics for men and women. J Soc Pharmacol 3:219–236
Seeman MV (1994) The schizophrenic mother. In: Gopfert M, Webster J, Seeman MV (eds) Disturbed and mentally ill parents and their children. Cambridge University Press, Cambridge (in press)
Seeman MV, Lang (1990) The role of estrogens in schizophrenia gender differences. Schizophr Bull 16:185–194
Straube ER, Wagner W, Foerster K, Heimann H (1989) Findings significant with respect to short- and medium-term outcome in schizophrenia – preliminary report. Prog Neuropsychopharmacol Biol Psychiatry 13:185–197
Swett C (1975) Drug-induced dystonia. Am J Psychiatry 132:532–534
Thara R, Rajkumar A (1992) Gender differences in schizophrenia: results of a follow-up study in India. Schizophr Res 7:65–70
Toran-Allerand CD (1990) Interactions of estrogens with growth factors in the developing central nervous system. In: Hochberg RB, Naftolin F (eds) The new biology of steroid hormones. Raven Press, New York, pp 311–323
Toran-Allerand CD (1991) Organotypic culture of the developing cerebral cortes and hypothalamus: relevance to sexual differentiation. Psychoneuroendocrinology 16:7–24
Van Putten T, May PRA (1978) Subjective response as a predictor of outcome in pharmacotherapy: the consumer has a point. Arch Gen Psychiatry 35:477–480.
Watt DC, Katz K, Shepherd M (1983) The natural history of schizophrenia: a 5-year prospective follow-up of a representative sample of schizophrenics by means of a standardized clinical and social assessment. Psychol Med 13:663–670
Westermeyer JF, Harrow M (1984) Prognosis and outcome using broad (DSM-II) and narrow (DSM-III) concepts of schizophrenia. Schizophr Bull 10:624–637
Wode-Helgodt B, Borg S, Fryrö B, Sedvall G (1978) Clinical effects and drug concentrations in plasma and cerebrospinal fluid in psychotic patients treated with fixed doses of chlorpromazine. Acta Psychiatr Scand 58:149–173
Yassa R, Jeste DV (1992) Gender differences in tardive dyskinesia: a critical review of the literature. Schizophr Bull 18:701–715
Yonkers KA, Kando JC, Cole JO, Blumenthal S (1992) Gender differences in pharmacokinetics and pharmacodynamics of psychotropic medication. Am J Psychiatry 149:587–595
Young MA, Meltzer HY (1980) The relationship of demographic, clinical, and outcome variables to neuroleptic treatment requirements. Schizophr Bull 6:88–101

**Author's address:** Prof. Dr. M. V. Seeman, Department of Psychiatry, University of Toronto, Clarke Instiute of Psychiatry, 250 College Street, Toronto, Ontario, M5T 1R8, Canada

# Neuroleptic-psychosocial interactions and prediction of outcome*

**I. D. Glick**

Psychiatry and Behavioral Sciences, Stanford University School of Medicine, Stanford, Ca, U.S.A.

## Introduction

Over the past 3 decades, controlled studies have demonstrated the efficacy of psychotropic medications for most psychiatric disorders. Still for many patients and their families, the outcome is disappointing. A critical issue is how to increase the effectiveness of "effective" medication. In no other disorder is the challenge greater than in combining psychosocial interventions to improve neuroleptic treatment outcome for schizophrenia.

I begin with a summary of a review of the relevant literature, and then discuss the work of our group over the last two decades as well as that of the Hirsch group in London.

## Literature

Bellack and Mueser (1993) have examined in detail the progress of research on the psychological treatment of schizophrenia. As a starting point it is most appropriate to summarize their conclusions:

> "Research on psychological treatment has made significant progress over the last decade. Controlled trials of social skills training, the most widely studied intervention for individual patients, suggest some beneficial effects, although the results are mixed. Recent interest in cognitive rehabilitation or teaching patients how to manage cogni-

---

* Parts of this chapter are adapted from a study group, "Maximizing the Effectiveness of Medication for Schizophrenia and Affective Disorder." Presented at the 1991 ACNP Meeting in San Juan, and published in Psychopharmacol Bull 28:223–225 (1992)

tive deficits holds promise, but the feasibility and efficacy of these approaches remain to be demonstrated. Family intervention programs aimed at educating relatives and helping them cope more effectively with the patient's illness have shown positive effects on the course of schizophrenia, although treatment gains appear to be modest and of uncertain durability. The results of controlled research on psychological treatment suggest that intervention may improve the outcome of schizophrenia, but that many patients may require longterm treatment due to the chronic nature of the illness."

## Empirical findings

### *Short vs. long hospital treatment study*

In the late 1960s, I moved from New York to the Langley Porter Institute in California, which had a short-stay model of hospitalization (as opposed to the long-stay models predominant in the East). Was the extra time in the hospital efficacious? And if so, did it increase post-hospital compliance? To test these questions, we designed (and carried-out in the 1970s) a controlled random-assignment study of the effectiveness of two different models of hospitalization: a short-term 21–28 day model vs. a long-term, 3–4 month model (Glick and Hargreaves 1979). Contrary to the conventional wisdom of that time, our data revealed that the short-term stay was as efficacious as the long-term stay for most patients – except for two subgroups of patients, those with (1) acute schizophrenia and (2) mood disorder. The question was "why" did these latter two groups require extra time in the hospital? We speculated that there was not enough time to deliver an inpatient intervention targeted to educate the patient and family about the need for compliance with the post-hospital prescription of drug plus psychosocial therapy. In that context, we found that those patients who were hospitalized longer, received more *post-hospital* medication than those who stayed for shorter periods. In the absence of prospective data, the mechanism(s) of action of this effect was unclear.

### *Inpatient family intervention study*

Based on these results, in the 1980s we designed a study testing the notion that combining medication with a family intervention with psychoeducation might improve hospital outcome. The rationale was based also, in part, on work that had established that high "expressed emotion" was associated with an increased risk of relapse for patients with schizophrenia or with mood disorder. In addition, there had been solid evidence that treatment with family intervention in an outpatient setting decreased the risk of relapse. We initiated a controlled randomized trial of our specially designed version of an Inpatient Family Intervention (IFI). We found that in fact IFI *did* help, but not for all patients. Specifically, we found that the combination of drug plus family intervention improved post-hospital outcome for (1) females with major psychosis including schizophrenia and (2) for their families, regardless of diagnosis (Clarkin et al. 1990, Glick et al. 1990, Spencer et al. 1988). IFI did not seem efficacious for males. We speculated as to mediating variables – we found data suggested that the inpatient family intervention may have enhanced the post-hospital medication compliance and improved outcome. A key ingredient was that the IFI families showed less rejection of their patient-family member. As a result, the medication was taken in a less dissonant family context once the family had been educated about the causes of the illness and its effects (Glick et al. 1991a).

### *Effectiveness in psychiatric care studies*

In part, based on the IFI study, in the mid 1980s, we studied interactions among patients and their families, and the treatment given (or not given). We identified patients with major affective disorder in Italy, Japan, and the United States, 1 to 2 years post-hospitalization. We examined treatment delivered, treatment goals achieved, and both patient and family outcome. After interviewing patients, their families, and their doctors, separately and then *all together*, we discovered remarkably similar patterns across countries (Glick et al. 1991b). There was a significant positive association between the most important outcome measure, (i. e., the resolution of the episode) and the achievement of treatment goals for both the patient ($p<.07$) and the family ($p<.005$). Patients and families with the best resolutions received significantly more good treatment than those with the worst resolutions ($p<.02$), most notably with regard to medication ($p<.002$).

We have found an association between the amount of psychoeducation delivered and the quality of resolution of the index episode and/or better patient global outcome. Psychoeducation for significant others has been found to be associated with better outcome for schizophrenia, and more recently with mood disorder. Our data supported that literature and suggest that the mediating variables may be *delivery* of the psychoeducation, rather than with achievement of the psychoeducational goals, that is, the new knowledge that a family can reiterate at follow-up. As the raw data favored an association between outcome and achievement of the goals of the psychoeducation, an alternative explanation is that the numbers involved in analysis of the tails of the sample were too small to achieve significance. Our speculation is that working with the family empowers them to interact and join in a more collaborative (rather than adversarial) way with the patient to achieve medication and psychotherapy compliance.

Given the cognitive dysfunction in patients with acute psychiatric illness, it is possible that medication is necessary but insufficient without combining it with a family psychoeducational intervention. These suggestions are consistent with the literature suggesting the need for more active forms of medication education, such as supervised self-administration in the final days of hospitalization. Similarly, Corrigan and associates (1990) have taken this model even further by reframing compliance as a collaborative relationship in which both patient and family assume responsibility for producing a treatment regimen to which the patient can adhere.

## *Treatment strategies in schizophrenia*

Over the past decade, we have been part of the NIMH Treatment Strategies in Schizophrenia Study Group (Schooler et al. 1989), "a five-site multicenter collaborative study, investigating the efficacy of drug maintenance strategies that are designed to reduce neuroleptic medication exposure and psychoeducational family treatments in the long-term treatment of schizophrenia. Patients are identified when acutely symptomatic, randomly assigned to one of two family treatments, and enter a stabilization period that can last up to 6 months. At the end of this period they are randomly and blindly assigned to one of three drug maintenance strategies..." (Glick et al. 1989).

As reported by Keith and his colleagues, (1989), early results from this study revealed that "the initiation of family treatment with a psychoeducation workshop does substantially effect likelihood of stabilization. This may prove to be a critical component of the family management treatment program. At one site, no patient entered double-blind treatment if their family failed to attend the workshop. Whether workshop attendance represents a general measure of overall compliance or has a specific therapeutic effect is of course not possible to determine from these data.

The early implementation of the two family management approaches does not appear to distinguish those patients who stabilize from those who do not. This suggests that early in the recovery process, little outcome variance is accounted for by differences in treatment intensity when both treatments are based on the same psychoeducational model." (Keith et al. 1989). Further results bearing on medication and family interactions from this important study will be available in the near future.

## *Life events and medication*

More recently, Hirsch et al. (in press), have examined the effect of psychosocial factors on the course of schizophrenia with and without neuroleptic medication. They set out to determine whether and to what degree *life events* (independent of illness) increase the *risk of relapse in schizophrenia,* either by triggering a relapse in the following 4 weeks or by acting cumulatively over time. 71 patients fulfilling DSM-III-R criteria for schizophrenia with chronic illness were followed up for 48 weeks. Half were treated with regular neuroleptic medication and half had previously been withdrawn from medication. A sub-group was double-blindly randomized to treatment or placebo.

Using a proportional hazards regression model the only variables to have a significant effect ($p<.05$) on risk of relapse were medication status and the cumulative *life* event rate variable. No interaction between medication and events could be detected. For those of the sample exposed to the mean rate of life events during the study period it was estimated that 23 % of the relapse risk could be attributed to life events. In contrast, regular medication was associated with a reduction in risk of around 80 %. By estimating the Population Attributable Risk for those of medication, it was found that fewer than about 7 % of all relapses would habe been avoided if any life event exposure up to twice the mean rate of life events had been eliminated.

Thus they showed not only a small effect on decreasing relapse over time, but also a larger effect for drugs. In other words, the hypothesis of *interaction* was disproved, but there was *complimentarity.*

## Conclusion

The literature suggests that medication and family intervention are additive and perhaps synergistic. Each by itself covers different domains – medication for certain symptom clusters – and family-intervention for improving interpersonal skills and relationships. By extension, an assumption is that both treatments improve compliance. Given the cognitive disorder inherent in the major psychosis, family intervention and psychoeducation may be necessary to increase the effectiveness of medication. It was our clinical impression in the IFI study, that such intervention improved compliance among those who were "noncompliers" prior to hospitalization. The obvious questions that remain to be answered are "which diagnoses need which combination of therapies? in which sequences? in what doses?"

We look forward to further controlled research addressing these issues.

## References

Bellack AS, Mueser KT (1993) Psychosocial treatment for schizophrenia. Schizophr Bull 18:317–336

Corrigan PW, Liberman RP, Engel JD (1990) From noncompliance to collaboration in the treatment of schizophrenia. Hosp Commun Psychiatry 41:1203–1211

Clarkin JF, Glick ID, Haas GL, Spencer JH, Lewis, AB, Peyser JA, DeMane N, Good-Ellis M, Harris E, Lestelle V (1990) A randomized clinical trial of inpatient family intervention. V. Results for affective disorders. J Affect Disord 18:17–28

Glick ID, Clarkin JF, Haas GL et al. (1991a) A randomized clinical trial of inpatient family intervention. VI. Mediating variables and outcome. Family Process 30:85–91

Glick ID, Burti L, Suzuki K, Sacks M (1991b) Effectiveness in psychiatric care. I. A cross-national study of the process of treatment and outcomes of major depressive disorder. J Nerv Ment Dis 179:55–63

Glick ID, Hargreaves WA (1979) Psychiatric hospital treatment for the 1980s: a controlled study of short versus long hospitalization. Lexington Press, Lexington Mass

Glick ID, Jacobs M, Lieberman J, Simpson G, Schooler NR, and the Treatment Strategies in Schizophrenia Collaborative Study Group (1989) Prediction of short term outcome in schizophrenia: depressive symptoms, negative symptoms, and extrapyramidal signs. Psychopharmacol Bull 25:344–347

Glick ID, Spencer JH, Clarkin JF, Haas GL, Lewis AB, Peyser J, DeMane N, Good-Ellis M, Harris E, Lestelle V (1990) A randomized clinical trial of inpatient family intervention IV. Followup results for subjects with schizophrenia. Schizophr Res 3:187–200

Hirsch S, Bowen J, Emami J, Cramer P, Jolley A, Haw C, Dickinson M (1994) A one year prospective study of the effect of life events and medication in the aetiology of schizophrenic relapse. Arch Gen Psychiatry (in press)

Keith SJ, Bellack A, Frances A, Mance R, Matthews S, and the Treatment Strategies in Schizophrenia Collaborative Study Group (1989) The influence of diagnosis and family treatment on acute treatment response and short term outcome in schizophrenia. Psychopharmacol Bull, 25:336–339

Schooler NR, Keith SJ, Severe JB, Matthews S (1989) Acute treatment response and short term outcome in schizophrenia: first results of the NIMH Treatment Strategies in Schizophrenia study. Psychopharmacol Bull 25:331–335

Spencer JH, Glick ID, Haas GL (1988) A randomized clinical trial of inpatient family intervention III. Overall effects at followup for the entire sample. Am J Psychiatry 145:1115–1121

**Author's address:** Prof. Dr. I. D. Glick, Psychiatry and Behavioral Sciences, Stanford University School of Medicine, Stanford, Ca 94305, U.S.A.

# Pharmacokinetic aspects of neuroleptics and prediction of outcome

**S. R. Marder**

West Los Angeles Veterans Affairs Medical Center, Brentwood Division, and the Department of Psychiatry and Biobehavioral Sciences, UCLA School of Medicine, Los Angeles, Ca, U.S.A.

## Introduction

A number of characteristics of antipsychotic medications have inspired a search for early predictors of drug response. Unless a clinician has a well-documented history that a patient will respond to a particular drug or drug dose, treatment decisions will usually be made on a trial and error basis. After a decision is made to begin a trial of a particular regimen, the clinician and patient will often have to wait for weeks or even months before it is established that the treatment is successful. Moreover, if the patient fails to respond to an adequate trial of a particular drug, the clinician may be unsure if the drug was an effective one that was administered at too high or too low a dose. For these reasons, researchers have searched for pharmacokinetic indicators which can guide pharmacotherapy.

This report will not discuss pharmacodynamic predictors since they are the topics of other contributions in this book. Nevertheless, a number of pharmacodynamic predictors such as receptor occupancy as measured by Positron Emission Tomography (PET scanning), the effects of antipsychotics on the motor system (the neuroleptic threshold), subjective response, and MRI Spectroscopy are potentially important predictors which may become more useful when their associations with pharmacokinetics become more understandable.

## Conceptual and methodological comments

Antipsychotics would appear to be well-suited for pharmacokinetic monitoring. Psychotic patients demonstrate wide variation in the dose of medications that will lead to clinical improvement on the one hand and side effects on the other. Some patients with schizophrenia will only respond when their dose of haloperidol, for example, is raised to 30 or 40 mg daily. Others will demonstrate intolerable side effects when they receive 2 mg daily. Similarly, after oral administration of most antipsychotics, there is wide between-subject variability in pharmacokinetic parameters such as maximum plasma concentration ($C_{max}$) and area under the plasma concentration versus time curve extrapolated to infinite time (AUC) (Jorgensen 1986, Midha 1989). Wide between-subject variability is often a consequence of variability in first pass metabolism which in turn leads to similar variability in the percentage of drug (F%) reaching the systemic circulation intact after oral administration. It is reasonable to speculate that these differences will have clinical consequences.

Measuring plasma levels would be of little value if all schizophrenic patients responded well to a given dose of an antipsychotic. However, a substantial proportion of patients – as many as 25 % – fail to respond to an adequate medication trial. In addition, a therapeutic response will frequently occur weeks or months after a patient achieves an adequate plasma level. Therefore, dose cannot be titrated against clinical response in many individuals.

Despite the theoretical advantages of using plasma concentrations, their use has not become routine in most clinical settings. This is due in part to the failure of early studies to support their use. These studies on the relationship between plasma levels and clinical response focused on the phenothiazine antipsychotics, particularly chlorpromazine. Phenothiazines are poorly suited for plasma level measurement since some of the antipsychotic activity in the plasma may result from metabolites of the drug. Because of drug selection and methodological errors early studies failed to find a reliable relationship (May 1978).

There are also intrinsic problems with plasma level measurement that explain the relatively weak relationships that have been found in some studies (Table 1). Plasma levels of a drug may not accurately reflect the amount of drug reaching the brain. Differences between patients could result from differences in protein binding or lipophilic qualities (Cohen 1993) rather than differences in plasma concentrations. Cohen and Zubenko (1985) have also pointed out that individual differences in responsiveness to a drug level may explain differences in therapeutic

**Table 1.** Limitations of plasma levels as predictors (adapted from Cohen 1993)

1. Plasma drug concentrations do not reflect brain concentrations
2. Differences in sensitivity to an administered drug may reflect interindividual differences in responsiveness rather than drug levels
3. Drug metabolites may contribute to therapeutic activity
4. Actions of drugs at receptors lead to a complex cascade of effects
5. Sensitivity to a drug level may change over time

outcome. This is clearly an important factor since a substantial proportion of patients who have an adequate plasma concentration of a drug will nevertheless fail to respond (Van Putten et al. 1991a). Moreover, sensitivity to a particular drug level may change over time.

A number of antipsychotic medications, particularly the phenothiazines, undergo extensive metabolism (Jorgensen 1986). Circulating metabolites may have substantial antipsychotic activity and may cause side effects that differ from those of the parent compounds. As a result, measuring only the parent compound may provide an inaccurate estimate of the drug's antipsychotic activity.

## Empirical findings

### *Prediction of response in acute treatment*

Recent studies on the usefulness of plasma levels have benefitted from improved methodology and have provided more promising results. Haloperidol is the drug that has been most widely studied. Van Putten et al. (1991b) recently reviewed ten studies of haloperidol plasma levels and clinical response which they considered to have fulfilled their criteria for an adequate design. The most important factor considered was the assignment of patients to fixed doses of haloperidol. (This is considered vital since clinicians will tend to treat poor drug responders with higher drug doses. This can result in patients with high plasma concentrations having the poorest responders – the inverted U-shaped curve.) Five of these studies suggested a "therapeutic window" between plasma concentration and therapeutic response (see Table 2). There is remark-

**Table 2.** Haloperidol plasma levels and clinical response

| Study | N | Dose | Range (ng/ml) |
|---|---|---|---|
| Bleeker (1985) | 29 | 5 or 10 mg/day | None |
| Bigelow (1985) | 19 | .40 mg/kg | None |
| Rimon (1981) | 12 | 60 and 120 mg/day | None |
| Wistedt (1984) | 10 | .2 mg/kg | Linear |
| Itoh (1984) | 11 | 6 mg/day | None |
| Linkowski (1984) | 20 | 30 mg/day | None |
| Potkin (1985) | 43 | .40 or .15 mg/kg | 4–26 |
| Smith et al. (1984) | 27 | 10, 20, or 25 mg/day | 7–17 |
| Mavroidis et al. (1983) | 14 | 6, 12, or 24 mg/day | 4.7–11 |
| Santos et al. (1989) | 30 | 10, 15, or 30 mg/day | 12–55 |
| Van Putten et al. (1992) | 69 | 5, 10, or 20 mg/day | 5–12 |

able consistency regarding the lower end of the therapeutic range with most studies pointing to a threshold of 4 to 5 ng/ml. On the other hand, there is a lack of consistency regarding the upper end with results varying from 11–55 ng/ml. Van Putten's study (1992) includes data which may reconcile these differences. Many patients who tolerated higher doses did well with higher plasma concentrations. On the other hand, patients who did poorly in their therapeutic range of 5 to 12 ng/ml did not improve when their levels were raised. Also, individuals who did poorly and had levels above 12 ng/ml tended to improve when their levels were lowered. The author's impression was that poor response at higher levels was associated with adverse side effects. This was supported by their finding that 69 % of the patients with levels above 12 ng/ml had disabling side effects. Six studies failed to find a therapeutic relationship. Three of these studies (Bigelow 1985, Itoh 1984, Rimon 1981) used patients who were previously poor responders to antipsychotics which makes it less likely that a therapeutic relationship could be found. Also, three of the studies used relatively low doses of haloperidol (Itoh 1984, Bleeker 1984, Wistedt 1984) making it difficult to define an upper part of the therapeutic window.

Three studies (Bigelow 1985, Rimon 1981, Linkowski 1984) used relatively high doses which would result in few patients having levels near a therapeutic threshold. Volavka and his co-workers (1992) randomized 176 acutely ill schizophrenic patients to one of three plasma ranges of haloperidol: low (2 to 13 ng/ml); medium (13.1 to 24); and high (24.1 to 35). This is an innovative design which permits clinicians to evaluate the usefulness of targeting a particular plasma concentration. Overall, the three groups had approximately the same rate of response, although there was a suggestion that higher levels were associated with less improvement.

Taken as a group, the studies which were most carefully designed and executed were able to define a therapeutic window, although the exact values of the window differed somewhat among the positive studies. Nevertheless, they provide guidance to clinicians who are interested in using plasma levels for patients receiving haloperidol.

We have located five studies which focused on the relationship between fluphenazine levels and outcome. Most of the studies were relatively small, making it difficult to find statistically significant relationships. The studies by Van Putten et al. (1991a) and Levinson et al. (1993), however, are of sufficient size for interpretation.

Van Putten used logistic regression to model the relationship between plasma fluphenazine concentration (as measured by a sensitive radio-immuno-assay) and both clinical improvement and disabling side effects. There was a significant relationship between plasma concentration and both outcome measures. The two curves are very close together indicating that levels of fluphenazine that result in clinical improvement are close to the levels that result in substantial side effect. Therefore, at a fluphenazine concentration of 1 ng/ml, about 60 % of patients would de-

**Table 3.** Fluphenazine plasma levels and clinical response

| Study | N | Dose | Range (ng/ml) |
|---|---|---|---|
| Dysken (1981) | 29 | 5, 10, 20 mg/day | .2–2.8 |
| Mavroidis (1984) | 19 | 5, 10, 20 mg/day | .13–.70 |
| Hitzemann (1986) | 15 | 5, 10, 20 mg/day | None |
| Van Putten (1991a) | 72 | 5, 10, 20 mg/day | .4–.8[1] |
| Levinson et al. (1993) | 49 | 10, 20, 30 mg/day | .4–2.0 |

[1] Patients improved at higher levels, but patients experienced disabling side effects

monstrate a substantial antipsychotic effect, but more than 40 % would have disabling side effects. For the clinician, this means that a high proportion of patients will suffer serious discomforts from sedation, stiffness, tremor, restlessness, and other effects at the doses that are required for adequately treating their schizophrenia. Patients with levels in the range of 0.4–0.8 ng/ml were most likely to show improvement without disabling side effects.

Levinson's findings were consistent with Van Putten's in that they also found that maximal symptom reduction occurred at levels between 1 and 2 ng/ml, but side effects increased from moderate to more severe within this range. They found that patients with levels of 0.5 to 0.8 ng/ml would improve with minimal or mild EPS. Taken together, these studies suggest that one of the potential uses of plasma level measurement for acute treatment is to optimize the treatment of patients who are sensitive to side effects. Given the relatively narrow range where there is a reasonable beneficial effect to side effect ratio, the clinician could use a plasma level to make dosage adjustments.

### *Prediction of response in maintenance treatment*

Plasma level measurement for antipsychotic drugs may also be useful for long-term maintenance treatment. During this stage, the goal of treatment is to prevent relapse in stabilized patients. One of the problems of maintenance treatment is that clinicians are unable to titrate drug dose against clinical response in patients who already stable. Moreover, this is a time when treating patients with the lowest effective drug dose may be particularly important since EPS – particularly akathisia and akinesia – may cause substantial personal discomfort and may also interfere with rehabilitation efforts. In addition, there is some evidence that higher maintenance doses may be associated with poorer compliance (Marder 1987).

A recent study (Marder et al. 1991) suggests that measuring plasma concentrations of fluphenazine may be useful for monitoring patients who are receiving fluphenazine decanoate. In this study plasma concentrations were measured after 6 months on an assigned dose when patients had reached a stable steady state. The rates of relapse (or psychotic exacerbations as the authors called it) were relatively low above fluphenazine levels of 0.8 or 0.9 ng/ml suggesting that this is a reasonable plasma level for maintenance. However, very few patients with levels above 1.2 ng/ml exacerbated suggesting that if the clinician had given a priority to preventing relapse and was less concerned about side effects, then this higher level might be preferable. On the other hand, patients with plasma levels that are lower than 0.9 ng/ml may be on the linear part of the curve and would benefit from a dosage increase. It is interesting to note that the relationships between fluphenazine levels and both clinical improvement and side effects were similar to those found for acute treatment.

This study suggests that monitoring plasma concentrations may be helpful for the routine monitoring of maintenance patients, particularly when dosage reduction is being considered. It will important to determine if these relationships can be confirmed with other antipsychotics that are used for maintenance treatment.

## Future research recommendations

The meaning of pharmacokinetic predictors will be more apparent as pharmacodynamic factors become more accessible to researchers. Positron Emission Tomography (PET) is a potentially powerful tool for pharmacodynamic monitoring. There is strong evidence that activity at $D_2$ receptors explains the properties of standard antipsychotics. A number of studies have found that the clinical activity of these drugs as well as their tendency to cause EPS is closely related to their affinity for $D_2$ receptors (Creese et al. 1976, Seeman et al. 1976). Recent studies using PET have found that 70 to 80 % of $D_2$ receptors are occupied when conventional antipsychotics are administered at therapeutic doses (Farde et al. 1992). Wolkin and co-workers (1989) have reported that there is maximal occupancy of $D_2$ receptors in humans when haloperidol is administered at what is considered to be a therapeutic plasma concentration of haloperidol (6–10 ng/ml). These studies indicate the potential for studying relationships between plasma concentrations and activity at receptor sites in the brain.

## Conclusions

The initial hope that the treatment of schizophrenia could be improved by providing pharmacokinetic information to clinicians has not as yet been fulfilled. The obstacles have included inadequate clinical research data as well as the intrinsic complexity of the pharmacokinetics of these drugs. Nevertheless, recent studies using drugs such as haloperidol and fluphenazine suggest that in the near future there will be circumstances when clinical decision-making will be aided by plasma level measurement. The use of plasma levels for improving maintenance treatment is particularly promising.

## References


Bigelow LB, Kirch DG, Braun T, Korpi BT (1985) Absence of relationship of serum haloperidol concentration and clinical response in chronic schizophrenia: a fixed-dose study. Psychopharmacol Bull 21:66–68

Bleeker JAC, Dingemans PM, Frohn-De Winder ML (1984) Plasma level and effect of low-dose haloperidol in acute psychosis. Psychopharmacol Bull 20:317–319

Cohen BM, Waternaux C (1993) Neuroleptic plasma levels: limitations and values. In: Marder SR, Davis JM, Janicak PG (eds) Clinical use of neuroleptic plasma levels. American Psychiatric Press, Washington DC London, pp 1–15

Cohen BM, Zubenko GS (1985) Relevance of genetic variability to clinical psychopharmacology. Psychopharmacol Bull 21:641–650

Creese I, Burt DR, Snyder SH (1976) Dopamine receptor binding predicts clinical and pharmacologic potencies of antischizophrenic drugs. Science 192:481–483

Dysken MW, Javaid JI, Chang SS et al. (1981) Fluphenazine pharmacokinetics and therapeutic response. Psychopharmacol (Berl) 73:205–210

Farde L, Nordstrom A-L, Wiesel FA et al. (1992) Positron emission tomographic analysis of central $D_1$ and $D_2$ dopamine receptor occupancy in patients treated with classical neuroleptics and clozapine. Arch Gen Psychiatry 49:538–544

Hitzemann RJ, Garver DL, Mavroidis M et al. (1986) Fluphenazine activity and antipsychotic response. Psychopharmacol (Berl) 90:270–273

Itoh H, Yagi G, Fuji Y et al. (1984) The relationship between haloperidol blood levels and clinical responses. Prog Neuropsychopharmacol Biol Psychiatry 8:285–292

Jorgensen A (1986) Metabolism and pharmacokinetics of antipsychotic drugs. In: Bridges JW, Chasseaud LF (eds) Progress in drug metabolism. Taylor and Francis, London Philadelphia, pp 111–174

Levinson DF, Simpson GM, Lo ES, Cooper TB (1993) Fluphenazine plasma levels, dosage and acute treatment response In: Marder SR, Davis JM, Janicak PG (eds) Clinical use of neuroleptic plasma levels. American Psychiatric Press, Washington DC London, pp 45–61

Linkowski P, Hubain P, von Frenckell R et al. (1984) Haloperidol plasma levels and clinical response in paranoid schizophrenics. Eur Arch Psychiatry Neurol Sci 234:231–236

Marder SR, Midha KK, Van Putten T, Aravagiri M, Hawes EM, Hubbard JW, McKay G, Mintz J (1991) Plasma levels of fluphenazine in patients receiving fluphenazine decanoate: relationship to clinical response. Br J Psychiatry 158:658–665

Marder SR, Van Putten T, Mintz J, Lebell M, McKenzie J, May PRA (1987) Low and conventional dose maintenance therapy with fluphenazine decanoate: two year outcome. Arch Gen Psychiatry 44:518–521

Mavroidis ML, Kanter DR, Hirschozitz J et al. (1983) Clinical response and plasma haloperidol levels in schizophrenia. Psychopharmacology 81:354–356

Mavroidis ML, Kanter DR, Hirschozitz J et al. (1984) Fluphenazine plasma levels and clinical response. J Clin Psychiatry 45:370–373

May PRA, Van Putten T (1978) Plasma levels of chlorpromazine in schizophrenia: a critical review of the literature. Arch Gen Psychiatry 35:1081–1087

Midha KK, Hawes EM, Hubbard JW, Korchinski ED, McKay G (1989) Intersubject variation in the pharmacokinetics of chlorpromazine in healthy men. J Clin Psychopharmacol 9:48

Potkin SG, Shen Y, Zhou D et al. (1985) Does a therapeutic window for plasma haloperidol exist? – Preliminary Chinese data. Psychopharmacol Bull 21:59–61

Rimon R, Averbuch I, Rozick P et al. (1981) Serum and CSF levels of haloperidol by radioimmunoassay and radioreceptor assay during high-dose therapy of resistant schizophrenic patients. Psychopharmacology 73:197–199

Santos JL, Cabranes JA, Almoguere I (1989) Clinical implications of determination of plasma haloperidol levels. Acta Psychiatr Scand 79:348–354

Seeman P, Lee T, Chau-Wong M, Wong K (1976) Antipsychotic drug doses and neuroleptic/dopamine receptors. Nature 261:717–719

Smith RC, Baumgartner R, Misra CH (1984) Haloperidol plasma levels and prolactin response as predictors of clinical improvement in schizophrenia: chemical vs radioreceptor plasma level assay. Arch Gen Psychiatry 41:1044–1049

Van Putten T, Aravagiri M, Marder SR, Wirshing WC, Mintz J, Chabert N (1991a) Plasma fluphenazine levels and clinical response in newly admitted schizophrenic patients. Psychopharmacol Bull 27:91–96.

Van Putten T, Marder SR, Mintz J, Poland RE (1992) Haloperidol plasma levels and clinical response: a therapeutic window relationship. Am J Psychiatry 149:500–505

Van Putten T, Marder SR, Wirshing WC, Aravagiri M, Chabert N (1991b) Neuroleptic plasma levels. Schizophr Bull 17:197–216

Volavka J, Cooper T, Czobor P et al. (1992) Haloperidol blood levels and clinical effects. Arch Gen Psychiatry 49:354–361

Wistedt B, Johanidesz G, Omerhodzic M et al. (1984) Plasma haloperidol levels and clinical response in acut schizophrenia. Nordisk Psychiatrik Tidsskrift 1:9–13

Wolkin A, Brodie JD, Barouche F et al. (1989) Dopamine receptor occupancy and plasma haloperidol levels. Arch Gen Psychiatry 46:482–483

**Author's address:** Prof. Dr. S. R. Marder, Psychiatry Service (116A), West Los Angeles Veterans Affairs Medical Center, 11301 Wilshire Boulevard, Los Angeles, CA 90073, U.S.A.

# Extrapyramidal side-effects and prediction of neuroleptic treatment response*

**W. W. Fleischhacker**

Department of Biological Psychiatry, Innsbruck University Clinics, Innsbruck, Austria

## Introduction

When antipsychotics were introduced into clinical psychiatry in the 1950's extrapyramidal motor side effects (EPS) were felt to be an integral part of their profile of action. The propensity to induce EPS in animal models was an important part of the screening procedures in the development of antipsychotics. The term "neuroleptic" that was coined to characterize this new class of drugs had to do with their impact on motor functions. It wasn't until the development of clozapine that psychopharmacologists realized that antipsychotic efficacy is not necessarily linked to EPS.

In 1974 Van Putten published a landmark paper on the correlation between antipsychotic induced EPS and non-response. Since then this notion has been picked up by various research groups and will be discussed in more detail later.

Each type of EPS will be discussed separately because the pathophysiology as well as the clinical implications of parkinsonism, akathisia and tardive dyskinesia show relevant differences.

## Neuroleptic-induced akathisia (NIA)

Early akathisia is the side effect which was most often studied in terms of prediction of treatment response. After Van Putten (1974) originally reported his observation about the influence of drug induced dysphoria and NIA on compliance, the same group (Van Putten et al. 1984) published their study in which they looked at NIA incidence rates in patients treated with haloperidol and thiothixene. They found a high frequency

---

* This paper is dedicated to the memory of Theodore van Putten, M.D.

of NIA after both drugs and suggested that especially NIA produced by haloperidol demonstrated a considerable tendency to become treatment resistant. The diagnosis of treatment resistance was based on a non-responsivity of NIA to anticholinergics. For the group of patients with haloperidol-induced treatment resistant akathisia a statistically significant negative correlation was found between NIA and the total change score of the Brief Psychiatric Rating Scale (BPRS) suggesting that a good outcome was somewhat less likely in these patients.

Levinson et al. (1990) have also explored the impact of extrapyramidal motor side effects on treatment outcome. NIA was clearly associated with worse outcome in their study. This was irrespective of whether akathisia responded to benztropine treatment or not. Interestingly there was a good correlation between fluphenazine dose and acute EPS but dose did not predict the occurence of NIA.

Similar results were obtained by McEvoy et al. (1991) who found that "observed restlessness" during treatment with haloperidol coincided with poor treatment response. Unfortunately, although they have assessed it, the authors provide no information about the impact of "reported restlessness", which apparently refers to the subjective component of NIA on treatment outcome. Although not specifically stated, it appears that haloperidol dose had no influence on the results.

The fact that NIA is a poor diagnostic indicator for treatment outcome is also mentioned in passing in Cohen's et al. (1991) report on clozapine-induced akathisia.

In the most recent report, Chakos et al. (1992) deal with the incidence of acute EPS in first episode schizophrenic patients. In contrast to the work cited above their analysis showed that patients with acute akathisia had a more substantial improvement than others. Remission was categorized by operationalized criteria derived from changes on rating scales scores. In addition to a better outcome, patients developing acute akathisia and/or dystonia also had a reduced time to remission than patients without these side effects.

## Acute dystonia and parkinsonism

Some of the very early studies (Hollister et al. 1960, Goldmann 1961, Bishop et al. 1965) have already claimed that acute EPS have no direct influence on treatment outcome. This view is only partially supported by the more recent literature. While Levinson et al. (1990) did not detect an influence of acute EPS on treatment response, and these side effects also did not explain a significant amount of the outcome variance in the regression analysis conducted by McEvoy et al. (1991), acute dystonia was shown to be correlated with a better treatment outcome in the report by Chakos et al. (1992). In a study focusing on the subjective response to neuroleptics and outcome, Hogan and Awad (1992) also investigated the influence of EPS. These authors demonstrated a strong correlation between early dysphoria and poor drug response. Although early EPS was not related to subjective response, dysphoric patients showed more EPS by the end of the observation period (3 weeks) compared to non-dysphorics.

## Tardive dyskinesia (TD)

The influence of tardive dyskinesia on the course of schizophrenia is highlighted in two studies. It needs to be pointed out, that both studies do not really attempt to predict response but rather focus on the prediction of relapse in remitted patients. The results of these reports are controversial. While Lieberman et al. (1987) found that TD, next to other variables predicted relapse following neuroleptic withdrawal, Buchanan et al. (1992) were not able to confirm this.

## Discussion

A review of the literature on the influence of extrapyramidal motor side effects on antipsychotic drug response in schizophrenia reveals equivocal results.

The first striking observation in reviewing the literature is the vast variation in design of the studies reported as well as the different statistical approaches and hypotheses tested. The fact that different studies evaluated different populations has also to be emphasized. The Hillside Study (Chakos et al. 1992) for instance reported on first episode schizophrenic patients who had no or only little neuroleptic preexposure. With the evidence increasing that this group of patients is easier to treat than chronic multiepisode patients, the notion that these patients also differ from others in terms of developing EPS is not unlikely. This might be one of the reasons why these first episode patients were the only ones where akathisia and dystonia actually had a positive influence on treatment response. Chakos et al. (1992) have hypothesized, that first episode patients have a different pharmacologic responsivity than others where the course of schizophrenia and/or extensive pharmacologic preexposure might have altered the functional state of the dopaminergic system.

Compliance is an issue poorly controlled for in many of the available studies. We do not think, that one can make definitive statements on the relationship between EPS and drug response without taking the possibility of noncompliance into account. One of the likeliest explanations for the negative influence of EPS on subsequent response could indeed be the suggestion that patients who develop EPS are poor compliers, as it has been shown in various studies (Fleischhacker et al. 1994), and therefore have no chance to respond to a drug since they are simply not taking enough of it. Since plasma levels are really the only reasonably reliable measure of assessing compliance, these need to be analyzed.

Different types of EPS appear to have a different pathophysiology. Acute dystonia for instance is said to be more the consequence of an increased dopaminergic transmission, probably induced due to feedback mechanisms following the acute blockade of postsynaptic dopamine receptors at the very beginning of antipsychotic treatment. Parkinsonism and NIA on the other hand are the result of a reduced dopaminergic tone. While parkinsonism is associated with the nigrostriatal system, NIA has been suggested to be a consequence of dopaminergic blockade in DA10 neurons originating in the ventral tegmental area and projecting to limbic and cortical structures. This would also explain why NIA apparently has a different effect on treatment outcome than parkinsonism.

It is interesting to note that in a second report on the same study McEvoy et al. (1991a) demonstrated that good responders to haloperidol have shown a significantly higher EPS induced drop out rate. This finding can be put into perspective with Chakos' et al. (1992) suggestion that acute dystonia is a positive indicator of subsequent treatment response.

Lastly, given the heterogeneity of the reported data the likelihood of a mere chance finding cannot be completely disregarded. Therefore we await results from large scale studies that include the evaluation of plasma levels and a concise and differentiated assessment of extrapyramidal motor side effects. Until then, the question of their influence on drug response in schizophrenia cannot be answered definitively.

## References


Bishop MP, Gallant DM, Sykes TF (1965) Extrapyramidal side effects and therapeutic response. Arch Gen Psychiatry 13:155–162

Buchanan RW, Kirkpatrick B, Summerfelt A, Hanlon TE, Levine J, Carpenter Jr WT (1992) Clinical predictors of relapse following neuroleptic withdrawal. Biol Psychiatry 32:72–78

Chakos MH, Mayerhoff DI, Loebel AD, Alvier JM, Lieberman JA (1992) Incidence and correlates of acute extrapyramidal symptoms in first episode of schizophrenia. Psychopharmacol Bull 28:81–86

Cohen BM, Keck PE, Satlin A, Cole JO (1991) Prevalence and severity of akathisia in patients on clozapine. Biol Psychiatry 29:1215–1219

Fleischhacker WW, Meise U, Günther V, Kurz M (1994) Compliance with antipsychotic drug treatment: influence of side effects. Acta Psychiatr Scand 89 [Suppl 382]:11–15

Goldman D (1961) Parkinsonism and related phenomena from administration of drugs: their production and control under clinical conditions and possible relation to therapeutic effect. Rev Can Biol 20:549–560

Hogan TP, Awad AG (1992) Subjective response to neuroleptics and outcome in schizophrenia: a re-examination comparing two measures. Psychol Med 22:347–352

Hollister LE, Chaffey EM, Klett CJ (1960) Abnormal symptoms, signs and laboratory tests during treatment with phenothiazine derivatives. Clin Pharmacol Ther 1:284–293

Levinson DF, Simpson GM, Singh H, Yadalam K, Jain A, Stephanos J, Silver P (1990) Fluphenazine dose, clinical response, and extrapyramidal symptoms during acute treatment. Arch Gen Psychiatry 47:761–768

Lieberman JA, Kane JM, Sarantakos S, Gadaleta D, Woerner M, Alvir J, Ramos-Lorenzi J (1987) Prediction of relapse in schizophrenia. Arch Gen Psychiatry 44:597–603

McEvoy JP, Schooler NR, Wilson WH (1991) Predictors of therapeutic response to haloperidol in acute schizophrenia. Psychopharmacol Bull 27:97–101

McEvoy JP, Hogarty GE, Steingard S (1991a) Optimal dose of neuroleptic in acute schizophrenia. Arch Gen Psychiatry 48:739–745

Van Putten T (1974) Why do schizophrenic patients refuse to take their drugs? Arch Gen Psychiatry 31:67–72

Van Putten T, May PRA, Marder SR (1984) Akathisia with haloperidol and thiothixene. Arch Gen Psychiatry 41:1036–1039

**Author's address:** Prof. Dr. W. W. Fleischhacker, Department of Biological Psychiatry, Innsbruck University Clinics, Anichstrasse 35, A-6020 Innsbruck, Austria

# Subjective effects of neuroleptics predict compliance

**D. Naber, A. Walther, T. Kircher, D. Hayek,** and **R. Holzbach**

Department of Psychiatry, University of Munich, Federal Republic of Germany

## Summary

The low compliance of long-term neuroleptic treatment might be explained not only by extrapyramidal motor side effects (EPMS) but also by other subjective effects, hardly measurable by usual clinical rating scales. Therefore, a self-rating scale to measure subjective well-being on neuroleptics (SWN) was developed; first analyses indicate good practicability, reliability, validity and sensitivity. As the acute psychosis subsides, schizophrenic patients are able to fill out the questionnaire in 15–20 minutes.

Data, obtained from 216 remitted patients, showed that SWN correlates with psychiatrist's ratings (PANSS), self-ratings of mood states (POMS, SDS, BfS) and EPMS; but variables explained only 19–47% of SWN variance. A repeated application after 3 months in 53 patients did not show any altered SWN in those with constant neuroleptic medication. Marked alterations were noted if dosage or drug was changed. SWN in 28 patients, treated with clozapine because of therapy resistance or major side-effects, was despite of the negative selection, significantly better ($t=2.34$, $p=.02$) than in 38 patients under classical neuroleptics. Moreover, already at discharge, patients who 4–6 months later were non-compliant ($n=14$), differed significantly ($t=2.31$, $p=.02$) in SWN, but not in BPRS or PANSS from those who remained compliant ($n=34$).

These data agree with clinical experience and show that SWN is a useful tool to investigate a hitherto neglected psychopathological dimension. The early detection of major subjective effects of neuroleptics might be helpful in identifying patients at risk of noncompliance. In these patients, strategies such as depot-injection, reduction of dosage or change of medication should be considered.

One major predictor of neuroleptic treatment outcome is certainly the response to a rather simple question: Does the patient regularly take his/her neuroleptic drug? For the majority, the answer is no; only 40–55% of schizophrenic patients under neuroleptic maintenance treatment are compliant (Axelrod and Wetzeler 1989, Johnson 1977, van Putten 1974). Side-effects are suggested to cause noncompliance (Hogan et al. 1983), but only the study by van Putten (1974) found a significant relation with motor side-effects, particularly with akathisia. Some side-effects might be too subtle to be detected by objective examination, but nevertheless of major relevance. This assumption about the importance of the subjective effects of neuroleptics has been supported by impressive descriptions of psychiatrists after self-administration of antipsychotic drugs (Belmaker and Wald 1977, Ernst 1954, Heimann and Witt 1955). However, despite of the increasing interest in this issue (Awad 1993, Brenner et al. 1986, Windgassen 1992), there are only a few studies in which the clinical relevance of subjective effects of neuroleptics was systematically investigated (Jaeger et al. 1990, Liddle and Barnes 1988, Selten et al. 1993, van Putten et al. 1981).

Although effects in normal volunteers are hardly comparable to those in patients, many authors have described similar reactions in schizophrenic patients: a reduction of a.o. emotionality, will power and spontaneity, named "pharmacogenic depression" (Helmchen and Hippius 1969), "post-remissive exhaustion" (Heinrich 1967), "akinetic depression" (Rifkin et al. 1975, van Putten and May 1978), "neuroleptic-induced anhedonia" (Wise 1991), and "neuroleptic dysphoria" (Emerich and Sanberg 1991). These authors, particularly Heinrich (1967), emphasized the difficulty in differentiating the etiology. Aside from the neuroleptic drugs, there are two other main factors to consider: the illness, schizophrenia itself, particularly if negative symptoms prevail and the (psychogenic) reaction of the patient having experienced psychosis. It should be stressed that these investigations on dysphoric or anhedonic effects of neuroleptics pertain to long-term treatment. They are by no means similar to studies which revealed that in acutely psychotic patients, depressive syndromes decrease under neuroleptic therapy (Knights and Hirsch 1981, Möller and v. Zerssen 1981). For example, a recent long-term study showed that drug-free schizophrenic patients were less depressed than those treated with neuroleptics (Bandelow et al. 1992). Johnson (1981) described in chronic schizophrenic patients that depression was more common in those on higher doses of neuroleptics.

In the present investigation, a recently developed self-rating scale to measure subjective well-being under neuroleptic treatment (Naber et al. in preparation) was used to address the following questions:

1. Is self-rating by schizophrenic patients practicable, valid, sensitive and reliable?
2. What are the relationships between self-rated well-being and objective psychopathology and motor side-effects of neuroleptics, respectively?
3. Do compliant and noncompliant schizophrenic patients differ regarding their subjective well-being?

## Scale to measure subjective well-being under neuroleptic treatment (SWN)

The Likert scale with 6 classifications had originally 54 statements such as "I am full of energy and life", "I feel very comfortable in my body", "I feel powerless and exhausted" and "My thinking is difficult and slow", pertaining to patients' status during the last 7 days. This version was completed by 64 remitted schizophrenic patients. Patients were also asked to rate the importance of the item/statement for their individual well-being.

The examination of item-scale-correlation, variance and subjective importance led to a reduction of 38 statements, (20 positive, 18 negative). A confirmatory scale-structure analysis with a multi-trait analysis program revealed 5 subfactors (Table 1).

**Table 1.** SWN subscales and reliability

| | Items | Floor % | Ceiling % | Scale fit % | Cronbach's α |
|---|---|---|---|---|---|
| Emotional regulation | 8 | 0,0 | 1,3 | 67,5 | .77 |
| Self-control | 6 | 0,4 | 1,3 | 76,7 | .73 |
| Mental functioning | 8 | 0,0 | 1,3 | 87,5 | .88 |
| Social integration | 8 | 0,0 | 1,7 | 85,0 | .81 |
| Physical functioning | 7 | 0,4 | 1,3 | 91,4 | .86 |
| Total score | 38 | 0,0 | 0,0 | 81,6 | .95 |

## Methods

The revised version was completed by 216 schizophrenic patients (32 +/- 9 years, duration of illness 6 +/- 7 years), either in-patiens, 1–2 days prior to discharge (n=127) or out-patients (n=89). They were all able to complete the scale in 15–20 minutes.
Subgroups of these 216 patients also completed other self-ratings, either the Profile of Mood-Scales (POMS) (n=112), the self-rating depression-scale (SDS) (n=34) or the "Befindlichkeits-scale" (BFS) (n=32). For another subgroup of 120 patients, a psychiatric examination was performed. Objective psychopathology was rated by means of the BPRS and the PANSS, extra pyramidal symptoms were rated by the Simpson-Angus-scale.
53 patients completed the scale a second time 3–4 months after discharge from in-patient treatment, another 42 patients 4–6 months after dismissal.

## Results

### *Relationships of SWN to other self-rating-scales and objective psychopathology*

All subfactors of SWN are significantly correlated with the POMS, the SDS and BFS. However, these variables explained only 19–47 % of SWN variance.

**Table 2.** Relationships between SWN (5 subfactors, total score) and objective psychopathology (PANSS) as well as extrapyramidal motor side-effects (EPMS)

| | Social integration | Self control | Mental functioning | Physical functioning | Emotional regulation | Total score |
|---|---|---|---|---|---|---|
| Positive symptoms | –.13 | –.17 | –.09 | –.19[1] | –.06 | –.14 |
| Negative symptoms | –.405 | –.35[5] | –.33[5] | –.29[4] | –.33[5] | –.37[5] |
| General symptoms | –.38[5] | –.37[5] | –.33[5] | –.38[5] | –.25[3] | –.37[5] |
| EPMS | –.14 | –.15 | –.15 | –.20[1] | –.17[1] | –.23[2] |

Pearson's correlation coefficient, [1]$p<.05$, [2]$p<.01$, [3]$p<.005$, [4]$p<.001$, [5]$p<.0005$

Regarding the relationships to objective psychopathological variables, rated by the psychiatrists, and extrapyramidal motor symptoms, SWN correlates significantly with mostly schizophrenic negative symptoms and also, but only slightly, to the Simpson-Angus-score (Table 2).

### *Stability over time, sensitivity*

3–4 months after discharge from in-patient treatment, 53 out-patients completed the scale a second time. In 37 patients, neuroleptic medication was constant, in 16, either dosage or drug was changed. For patients with constant medication, there were no significant differences in SWN, but highly significant correlations ($r = .75 - .89$).
Only patients with changed neuroleptic treatment showed marked differences on all 5 subfactors.

28 patients under clozapine (180 +/– 110 mg/day) were compared with 38 patients under conventional neuroleptics (haloperidol, flupenthixol 195 +/- 110, chlorpromazine-equivalents mg/day). Both groups did not differ in clinical variables such as age, duration of illness, severity of illness or DSM-III-R subtype. However, clozapine patients had previously reacted to classical neuroleptics with either therapy-resistance or severe motor side-effects. Despite of the negative selection, the total score as well as all 5 subfactors showed that patients rated their well-being significantly better under clozapine than under typical neuroleptics (student's t-test; $t = 1{,}68 - 2{,}34$, $p = .02 - .05$).

### *Relationship to compliance*

48 schizophrenic patients completed the scale a second time 4–6 months after discharge from in-patient treatment. Moreover, the physician, responsible for out-patient treatment was asked for information about compliance ("Does your patient regularly take his/her neuroleptic drug?"). 14 patients were described as noncompliant, 34 as compliant. At discharge, there was no significant difference regarding objective psycho-

pathology (PANSS, BPRS), but already at that point of time, patients who 4–6 months later turned out to be noncompliant, had significantly worse SWN on total score (student's t-test, $t = 2{,}31$, $p = .02$) and on 3 of the 5 subfactors ($t = 1{,}23 - 1{,}88$, $p<.05$) than the compliant 34 patients.

## Discussion

These preliminary data indicate that at least most remitted or no more acutely psychotic schizophrenic patients are able to rate their subjective well-being. This is in agreement with numerous studies which showed that 63–95 % of mostly remitted schizophrenic patients could complete self-ratings to measure affective states (Bandelow et al. 1990, Brown et al. 1979, Craig and van Natta 1976, Hogan et al. 1983, Maurer and Dittrich 1979). The major differences between self- and observer-rating, found in most of these studies, might indicate that some parts of the affective state are barely measurable by an expert rating and underline the relevance of self-ratings.

There are several other attempts to measure the "subjective experience of deficits" or "negative symptoms" in schizophrenic patients (Jaeger et al. 1990, Liddle and Barnes 1988, Welten et al. 1993). The scales used in these studies were not "pure" self-rating scales, but an "interview-based self-rating-instrument" (Liddle and Barnes 1988, Selten et al. 1993) or "for the most part a self-report instrument with a minimum of rater input" (Jaeger et al. 1990). According to the authors, these rating instruments can be used even for the majority of severely disturbed schizophrenic patients. Similar to the data in the present study, subjective well-being correlated significantly with objective psychopathology, mostly with negative symptoms, but correlation coefficients were only in the .20–.50 range (Jaeger et al. 1990, Liddle and Barnes 1988). The relationship between "subjective experience of deficits" and neuroleptic dosage was investigated only by Liddle and Barnes (1988), who found "no substantial evidence for an association".

In contrast to the scale by Hogan and co-workers (1983), in which patients are asked to differentiate between the effect of neuroleptic drugs and the illness, the scale used in this study does not require patients' distinction between pharmacogenic or morbogenic components. Our impression is that such a differention in a cross-sectional study is impossible, for the psychiatrist as well as for the patient.

Despite the rather low number of patients in both groups and the negative selection of clozapine patients, there was a significant difference in self-rated well-being between patients treated with the atypical neuroleptic and those under conventional clinical neuroleptics. This data confirm clinical experience (Naber et al. 1992) and a study on 20 patients treated either with perazine or clozapine. Clozapine patients rated themselves significantly higher on scores of "spontaneity", "activity" and "mood" (Gebhardt 1972).

A significant relationship between motor side-effects and affective symptoms or the degree of depression has been found by Johnson (1981) and by Barnes and co-workers (1989), but not in other studies (Bandelow et al. 1990, 1992, Craig et al. 1985, Prosser et al. 1987). The present study found relationships of only marginal significance which might be due to the fact that no patient had severe motor side-effects.

There are several investigations, indicating the clinical relevance of subjective response to antipsychotic drugs (Awad 1993); but mostly on short-term treatment. Van Putten and co-workers (1987, 1981) reported twice that an initial dysphoric response is a powerful predictor of immediate treatment outcome. They suggested that subjective effects associated with neuroleptic administration might also predict long-term treatment compliance. These preliminary data support that assumption. Subjective effects of neuroleptics are measurable, affect patients' quality of life (Awad and Hogan 1994, Diamond 1985) and should be considered more thoroughly in clinical routine as well as in clinical trials of potential neuroleptic drugs. SWN might be a useful tool in detecting patients at risk for noncompliance. For those patients with major subjective effects, strategies such as depot-injection, reduction of dosage or change of neuroleptic drug should be considered.

## References


Awad AG (1993) Subjective response to neuroleptics in schizophrenia. Schizophr Bull 19:609–618

Awad AG, Hogan TP (1994) Subjective response to neuroleptics and quality of life – implications for treatment outcome. Acta Psychiatr Scand 89 [Suppl 380]:27–32

Axelrod S, Wetzler S (1989) Factors associated with better compliance with psychiatric aftercare. Hosp Commun Psychiatry 40:397–401

Bandelow B, Müller P, Gaebel W, Köpcke W, Linden M, Müller-Spahn F, Pietzcker A, Reischies FM, Tegeler J (1990) Depressive syndromes in schizophrenic patients after discharge from hospital. Eur Arch Psychiatry Clin Neurosci 140:113–120

Bandelow B, Müller P, Frick U, Gaebel W, Linden M, Müller-Spahn F, Pietzcker A, Tegeler J (1992) Depressive syndromes in schizophrenic patients under neuroleptic therapy. Eur Arch Psychiatry Clin Neurosci 141:291–295

Barnes TR, Curson DA, Liddle PF, Patel M (1989) The nature and prevalence of depression in chronic schizophrenic in-patients. Br J Psychiatry 154:486–491

Belmaker RH, Wald D (1977) Haloperidol in normals. Br J Psychiatry 131:222–223

Brenner HD, Böker W, Rui C (1986) Subjektive Neuroleptikawirkung bei Schizophrenen und ihre Bedeutung für die Therapie. In: Hinterhuber H, Schubert H, Kulhanek F (Hrsg) Seiteneffekte und Störwirkungen der Psychopharmaka. Schattauer, Stuttgart, S 97–107

Brown SL, Sweeney DR, Schwarz GE (1979) Differences in self-reported and observed pleasure in depression and schizophrenia. J Nerv Ment Dis 167:410–415

Craig TJ, Van Natta PA (1976) Recognition of depressed affect in hospitalized psychiatric patients: staff and patient perceptions. Dis Nerv Syst 37:561–566

Craig TJ, Richardson MA, Pass R, Bregman Z (1985) Measurement of mood and affect in schizophrenic inpatients. Am J Psychiatry 142:1272–1277

Diamond R (1985) Drugs and the quality of life: the patient's point of view. J Clin Psychiatry 46:29–35

Emerich DF, Sanberg PR (1991) Neuroleptic dysphoria. Biol Psychiatry 29:201–203

Ernst K (1954) Psychopathologische Wirkungen des Phenothiazin-Derivates "Largactil" (="Megaphen") im Selbstversuch und bei Kranken. Arch Psychiat Z Neurol 192:573–90
Gebhardt R (1972) Veränderungen der subjektiven Befindlichkeit psychotischer Patienten unter neuroleptischer Therapie. Pharmakopsychiat 5:295–300
Hare EH, Willcox DRC (1967) Do psychiatric inpatients take their pills? Br J Psychiatry 113:1435–1439
Heimann H, Witt PN (1955) Die Wirkungen einer einmaligen Largactilgabe bei Gesunden. Monatsschr Psychiat Neurol 129:104–128
Heinrich K (1967) Zur Bedeutung des postremissiven Erschöpfungs-Syndroms für die Rehabilitation Schizophrener. Nervenarzt 38:487–491
Helmchen H, Hippius H (1969) Pharmakogene Depressionen. In: Hippius H, Selbach H (Hrsg) Das depressive Syndrom. Schattauer, München, S 443–448
Hogan TP, Awad AG, Eastwood R (1983) A self report scale predictive of drug compliance in schizophrenics: reliability and discriminative validity. Psychol Med 13:177–183
Jaeger J, Bitter I, Czobor P, Volavka J (1990) The measurement of subjective experience in schizophrenia: the subjective deficit syndrome scale. Comp Psychiat 31:216–226
Johnson DAW (1977) Practical considerations in the use of depot neuroleptics for the treatment of schizophrenia. Br J Hosp Med 17:564–569
Johnson DAW (1981) Studies of depressive symptoms in schizophrenia. The prevalence of depression and its possible causes. Br J Psychiatry 139:89–101
Knights A, Hirsch SR (1981) 'Revealed' depression and drug treatment for schizophrenia. Arch Gen Psychiatry 38:806–811
Liddle PF, Barnes TRE (1988) The subjective experience of deficits in schizophrenia. Comp Psychiat 29:157–164
Maurer Y, Dittrich A (1979) Vergleich von Selbst- und Fremdbeurteilung bei schizophrenen Patienten. Pharmakopsychiat 12:375–382
Möller HJ, v. Zerssen D (1981) Depressive Symptomatik im stationären Behandlungsverlauf von 280 schizophrenen Patienten. Pharmacopsychiat 14:172–179
Naber D, Holzbach R, Perro C, Hippius H (1992) Clinical management of clozapine patients in relation to efficacy and side-effects. Br J Psychiatry 160[Suppl 17]:54–59
Prosser ES, Csernansky JG, Kaplan J, Thiemann S, Becker TJ, Hollister LE (1987) Depression, parkinsonian symptoms, and negative symptoms in schizophrenics trated with neuroleptics. J Nerv Ment Dis 175:100–105
Rifkin A, Quitkin F, Klein DF (1975) Akinesia. A poorly recognized drug-induced extrapyramidal behavioral disorder. Arch Gen Psychiatry 32:672–674
Selten JP, Sijben NES, van den Bosch RJ, Omloo-Visser J, Warmerdam H (1993) The subjective experience of negative symptoms: a self-rating scale. Comp Psychiat 34:192–197
Van Putten T (1974) Why do schizophrenic patients refuse to take their drugs? Arch Gen Psychiatry 31:67–72
Van Putten T, May PR (1978) 'Akinetic depression' in schizophrenia. Arch Gen Psychiatry 35:1101–1107
Van Putten T (1978) Subjective response as a predictor of outcome in pharmacotherapy. Arch Gen Psychiatry 35:477–480
Wilson JD, Enoch MD (1967) Estimation of drug rejection by schizophrenic inpatients with analysis of clinical factors. Br J Psychiatry 113:209–211
Windgassen K (1992) Treatment with neuroleptics: the patient's perspective. Acta Pychiatr Scand 86:405–410
Wise RA (1991) Neuroleptic-induced anhedonia. Recent studies. In: Tamminga CA, Schulz SC (eds) Advances in neuropsychiatry and psychopharmacology, vol I. Schizophrenia research. Raven Press, New York, pp 323–331

**Authors' address:** Prof. Dr. D. Naber, Department of Psychiatry, University of Munich, Nußbaumstrasse 7, D–80336 Munich, Federal Republic of Germany

## Appendix: Scale to measure subjective well-being under neuroleptic treatment (SWN)

---

Please note:
All statements refer to the past 7 days.
Please mark the appropriate response.

---

| | |
|---|---|
| 1. I am full of energy and life | ❍ not at all<br>❍ a little<br>❍ somewhat<br>❍ noticeably<br>❍ much<br>❍ very much |
| 2. I feel safe and secure. | ❍ not at all<br>❍ a little<br>❍ somewhat<br>❍ noticeably<br>❍ much<br>❍ very much |
| 3. I feel powerless and not in control of myself. | ❍ not at all<br>❍ a little<br>❍ somewhat<br>❍ noticeably<br>❍ much<br>❍ very much |
| 4. I am filled with sensations and emotions. | ❍ not at all<br>❍ a little<br>❍ somewhat<br>❍ noticeably<br>❍ much<br>❍ very much |
| 5. I feel very comfortable with my body. | ❍ not at all<br>❍ a little<br>❍ somewhat<br>❍ noticeably<br>❍ much<br>❍ very much |
| 6. I feel indifferent towards my relatives, friends and colleagues. | ❍ not at all<br>❍ a little<br>❍ somewhat<br>❍ noticeably<br>❍ much<br>❍ very much |

<u>Please note:</u>
All statements refer to the past 7 days.
Please mark the appropriate response.

| | |
|---|---|
| 7. I find it easy to think. | ❍ not at all<br>❍ a little<br>❍ somewhat<br>❍ noticeably<br>❍ much<br>❍ very much |
| 8. I have no hope for the future. | ❍ not at all<br>❍ a little<br>❍ somewhat<br>❍ noticeably<br>❍ much<br>❍ very much |
| 9. I can easily realize my thoughts and ideas. | ❍ not at all<br>❍ a little<br>❍ somewhat<br>❍ noticeably<br>❍ much<br>❍ very much |
| 10. All of my thoughts and emotions feel strange to me. | ❍ not at all<br>❍ a little<br>❍ somewhat<br>❍ noticeably<br>❍ much<br>❍ very much |
| 11. My body feels familiar. | ❍ not at all<br>❍ a little<br>❍ somewhat<br>❍ noticeably<br>❍ much<br>❍ very much |
| 12. I am very shy about getting to know people. | ❍ not at all<br>❍ a little<br>❍ somewhat<br>❍ noticeably<br>❍ much<br>❍ very much |

<u>Please note:</u>
All statements refer to the past 7 days.
Please mark the appropriate response.

| | |
|---|---|
| 13. I am imaginative and full of ideas. | ❍ not at all<br>❍ a little<br>❍ somewhat<br>❍ noticeably<br>❍ much<br>❍ very much |
| 14. My environment seems friendly and familiar to me. | ❍ not at all<br>❍ a little<br>❍ somewhat<br>❍ noticeably<br>❍ much<br>❍ very much |
| 15. My thoughts always revolve around the same things. | ❍ not at all<br>❍ a little<br>❍ somewhat<br>❍ noticeably<br>❍ much<br>❍ very much |
| 16. I feel weak and exhausted. | ❍ not at all<br>❍ a little<br>❍ somewhat<br>❍ noticeably<br>❍ much<br>❍ very much |
| 17. I feel lost and alone. | ❍ not at all<br>❍ a little<br>❍ somewhat<br>❍ noticeably<br>❍ much<br>❍ very much |
| 18. I do what I want to do and know how to assert myself. | ❍ not at all<br>❍ a little<br>❍ somewhat<br>❍ noticeably<br>❍ much<br>❍ very much |

Please note:
All statements refer to the past 7 days.
Please mark the appropriate response.

| | |
|---|---|
| 19. My emotions and sensations are dull. Nothing matters to me. | ❍ not at all<br>❍ a little<br>❍ somewhat<br>❍ noticeably<br>❍ much<br>❍ very much |
| 20. I am happy and satisfied with my sex life. | ❍ not at all<br>❍ a little<br>❍ somewhat<br>❍ noticeably<br>❍ much<br>❍ very much |
| 21. I do not care what happens around me. I am only interested in myself. | ❍ not at all<br>❍ a little<br>❍ somewhat<br>❍ noticeably<br>❍ much<br>❍ very much |
| 22. I have meaningful relationships with relatives, friends and colleagues. | ❍ not at all<br>❍ a little<br>❍ somewhat<br>❍ noticeably<br>❍ much<br>❍ very much |
| 23. My thinking is difficult and slow. | ❍ not at all<br>❍ a little<br>❍ somewhat<br>❍ noticeably<br>❍ much<br>❍ very much |
| 24. I find it easy to organize my ideas and I can think systematically. | ❍ not at all<br>❍ a little<br>❍ somewhat<br>❍ noticeably<br>❍ much<br>❍ very much |

<u>Please note:</u>
All statements refer to the past 7 days.
Please mark the appropriate response.

---

25. My feelings and behavior are inappropriate to situations. I get upset over small things, important ones hardly affect me.
❍ not at all
❍ a little
❍ somewhat
❍ noticeably
❍ much
❍ very much

---

26. I feel as though my body does not really belong to me.
❍ not at all
❍ a little
❍ somewhat
❍ noticeably
❍ much
❍ very much

---

27. I find it easy to keep in touch with people around me.
❍ not at all
❍ a little
❍ somewhat
❍ noticeably
❍ much
❍ very much

---

28. I lack imagination and ideas.
❍ not at all
❍ a little
❍ somewhat
❍ noticeaby
❍ much
❍ very much

---

29. My emotions are steady and balanced.
❍ not at all
❍ a little
❍ somewhat
❍ noticeably
❍ much
❍ very much

---

30. I perceive my environment as being changed, strange and threatening.
❍ not at all
❍ a little
❍ somewhat
❍ noticeably
❍ much
❍ very much

---

<u>Please note:</u>
All statements refer to the past 7 days.
Please mark the appropriate response.

---

31. Many different things are interesting and accessible for me.

❍ not at all
❍ a little
❍ somewhat
❍ noticeably
❍ much
❍ very much

---

32. I find it easy to draw a line between myself and others.

❍ not at all
❍ a little
❍ somewhat
❍ noticeably
❍ much
❍ very much

---

33. My body is a burden to me.

❍ not at all
❍ a little
❍ somewhat
❍ noticeably
❍ much
❍ very much

---

34. My thoughts are flightly and undirected. I find it difficult to think clearly.

❍ not at all
❍ a little
❍ somewhat
❍ noticeably
❍ much
❍ very much

---

35. I am interested in what is happening around me, and it is important to me.

❍ not at all
❍ a little
❍ somewhat
❍ noticeably
❍ much
❍ very much

---

36. My feelings and behavior are appropriate in the particular situation.

❍ not at all
❍ a little
❍ somewhat
❍ noticeably
❍ much
❍ very much

---

Please note:
All statements refer to the past 7 days.
Please mark the appropriate response.

| | |
|---|---|
| 37. My thoughts and ideas remain unfulfilled. I am unable to realize them. | ❍ not at all<br>❍ a little<br>❍ somewhat<br>❍ noticeably<br>❍ much<br>❍ very much |
| 38. I am full of confidence. Everything will be allright. | ❍ not at all<br>❍ a little<br>❍ somewhat<br>❍ noticeably<br>❍ much<br>❍ very much |

## Scoring instructions

For the total score as well as the 5 subscores, the following items have to be reversed: **3, 6, 8, 10, 12, 15, 16, 17, 19, 21, 23, 25, 26, 28, 30, 33, 34, 37**.

Item 20 ("I am happy and satisfied with my sex life") was not highly significantly correlated with any of the 5 subscales. All other 37 items belong to one of the following 5 subscales.

| | |
|---|---|
| Emotional regulation (8 items): | **4, 8, 19, 21, 29, 31, 35, 38** |
| Self-control (6 items): | **3, 10, 15, 25, 32, 36** |
| Mental functioning (8 items): | **7, 9, 13, 23, 24, 28, 34, 37** |
| Social integration (8 items): | **2, 6, 12, 14, 17, 22, 27, 30** |
| Physical functioning (7 items): | **1, 5, 11, 16, 18, 26, 33** |

# Neuropsychological prediction of treatment response and outcome in schizophrenia

**R. M. Bilder** and **J. A. Bates**

Hillside Hospital Division, Long Island Jewish Medical Center, Glen Oaks, NY, and Long Island Campus, Albert Einstein College of Medicine, U.S.A.

## Introduction

Despite decades of experience using antipsychotic medications, we still have a very limited capacity to predict who among our patients will benefit, how much they will benefit, and the extent to which they are likely to suffer disabling side effects from treatment. The contributions to this volume reflect increasing insight into a range of factors that may influence treatment response and outcome, but it is ironic that we can repeat the lament of Philip May and his colleagues in that the situation today has advanced little since 1964 (May 1966, May et al. 1976). Investigators continue to comment that the best predictor of antipsychotic treatment response is a prior history of response to the same treatment (May and Goldberg 1978, Awad 1989). In the era when only "typical" neuroleptic treatments were available, this lack of predictive power may have made less difference to clinicians, but the rapid development of new antipsychotic agents prompts a need to enhance our capacity to predict who will benefit, and who may be at increased risk from different treatments. One goal for current research is determining how neuropsychological (NP) methods may help both in the prediction and the definition of outcome. The key advantages of neuropsychology in these contexts include: (a) the possibility that NP methods may distinguish reliably between reversible state effects and more persistent trait effects; and (b) the possibility that NP methods may offer more valid indices of integrity or compromise within the specific functional brain systems that are the targets of antipsychotic drug treatments. To the extent that NP indices of specific neuropsychopharmacologic system functions can be validated, there are new opportunities to develop targeted treatment strategies, which could include rational selection of treatments based on NP profiles, and titration of ongoing treatments using changes in NP function as the key dependent measures.

There is an increasing appreciation that NP measures may be useful in predicting or serving directly as measures of outcome. This may be part of a more general increase in the sensitivity of clinicians and researchers to a broader range of treatment response and outcome variables, which in turn seems to have followed revisions in conceptualizing the salient dimensions of psychopathology in schizophrenia. While older concepts of schizophrenia emphasized principally the florid or positive psychotic symptoms, newer models have pointed to the salience of negative symptoms and the deficit syndrome, and to symptoms of conceptual disorganization that may persist despite "optimal" treatment (Bilder et al. 1985, Liddle 1987, Arndt et al. 1991), and these persistent symptoms may mark a less favorable long term course and outcome (rev. by Lieberman and Sobel 1993). Accompanying awareness of these persistent symptom syndromes, there is an increased awareness that residual neuropsychological dysfunction is a central feature of long-term disability in the schizophrenia syndrome. This shift in focus may be attributed in part to the success of typical antipsychotic treatments in the control of florid delusions and hallucinations in many patients. The negative and conceptual disorganization symptom domains, and residual NP deficits may have greater persistence, and be particularly disabling features of the illness, despite "successful" treatment of the positive psychotic symptoms. There has also been an increase in sensitivity to patients' quality of life following different interventions, which in some instances may alter the criteria for treatment success.

NP studies face many of the problems common to other methods. One central problem is distinguishing between optimal treatment response and complete normalization of function. Although we all hope for complete recovery of functional deficits when treating patients with schizophrenia, our expectations must be realistic to avoid the risks of treatments that may cause more harm than good. How high should dosage of a specific compound be escalated, how long should the treatment continue before trying alternative compounds, and how many adjunctive agents should be considered before we can conclude rationally that there will not be further benefit? Clinical researchers recognize that there are absolute and relative criteria for treatment response, and while many of the criteria widely used to assess efficacy involve degrees of reduction in key symptoms, it can be argued that the optimal treatment is that which restores the patients most fully to their premorbid (or precurrent episode) level of function, even though this condition may be marked by substantial impairment. It is generally acknowledged that effective treatment with antipsychotic medications yields at best limited normalization of neuropsychological function, and this is clearly also true for a variety of other outcome measures, including social adjustment and capacity to work (Bilder et al. 1992b). A challenge to research therefore involves identifying the real (and realistic) goals of treatment, which in turn depends on identifying the appropriate functional "baseline" from which the illness or a specific episode have emerged. We look forward to the development of new treatments that show more than limited normalization of function, at which point these concepts will have to be refined.

Defining an appropriate functional "baseline", which can then serve as a target for successful treatment, is complicated by the difficulty of determining when the morbid process began. In some cases, it is clear that functional abilities were compromised from early in life, while in others, a deteriorative process is apparent. In either of these courses of illness and cognitive development, it is difficult to tell whether current deficits should be considered part of the pathologic process that also underlies psychosis, or may reflect a coincidental abnormality. Regardless, NP methods offer among the best validated indices of premorbid capacity, and of possible deterioration from those premorbid levels (Bilder et al. 1992a), and therefore the NP methods may be most useful in defining treatment targets. The NP methods that are better at defining these premorbid functional levels may do so precisely because they index relatively stable, trait-like aspects of brain function, that persist through episodes of illness and into recovery. These can be distinguished from the state-dependent dysfunctions that accompany acute episodes of illness, and also may respond relatively well to treatment.

Acknowledging these basic points, it can be argued that neuropsychological methods may be useful in several aspects of prediction:

1 by offering sets of predictor variables, including those that may be relevant to the specific putative mechanisms of action of different treatments;
2 by offering sets of outcome measures, and particularly by simultaneously considering multiple independent dimensions of outcome, including those that may index capacity for occupational and vocational success;
3 by offering sets of moderating variables, which may enhance prediction by accounting for unexplained variance due to a range of factors, such as heterogeneity of baseline functioning, or interactions with adverse cognitive or motor effects.

While this summary of the *potential* of NP methods appears rosy, optimism must unfortunately be tempered by gaps in current knowledge. Despite a few promising leads, the following review of literature reveals that we still know little about the overall predictive power of NP methods, still less about the relative sensitivity and specificity of different NP methods in prediction, and almost nothing that offers insight into the specific mechanisms of action of antipsychotic drugs. While this may be sobering, we emphasize that applying NP methods in prediction of treatment response and outcome comprises an extremely promising, and so far under-utilized, opportunity to contribute to the successful treatment of severe mental disorders.

## Empirical findings

We reviewed 14 studies in which "neuropsychological" methods were used to predict treatment response and/or outcome measures. This review is not systematic, since we found that standard structured methods for literature search (i. e., keyword searches through bibliographic databases) yielded fewer citations than those of which we were aware. The studies are summarized briefly in Table 1.

There are several striking features of these studies, most of which are methodologic limitations. First, with the exception of Weaver and Brooks (1964), sample size was relatively small (all were less than 65; mean N=29). Given the difficulty in adequately quantifying the predictive power of different measures, it is unfortunate that larger-scale screening efforts have not been conducted more often. Second, sufficient details about sample characteristics are often difficult to discern from the published reports, despite the importance of these characteristics in the prediction process. Inspection of the table reveals a diversity of diagnostic practices, inclusion/exclusion criteria, treatment received, and outcome measures; sometimes even basic information (i. e., sex distribution) is missing. In general, however, the studies have focused most on patients suffering from chronic schizophrenia, with acute exacerbations of illness. Third, treatment methods vary considerably, and most studies report results of uncontrolled trials. Fourth, few studies have examined both short-term treatment response and long-term outcome measures, thus limiting our knowledge of the relationship between these indexes of treatment success. It is acknowledged that few investigators may have the resources to conduct long-term longitudinal follow-up studies; it still seems unfortunate that more studies have not attempted to provide longer-term outcome measures, or even short-term indexes of functional outcome. Finally, a limited set of NP measures have been used across studies, and few investigators have sought to examine the relative predictive power of multiple NP measures within any single study. In fact, it is not clear that many investigators have attempted to define and assess specific NP constructs. Even when NP constructs have been defined, these usually have not been defined with special relevance to the presumed mechanism of action of treatment.

Given these limitations, it is impressive that the studies have shown relatively consistent capacity of NP measures to predict certain aspects of treatment response, and a more robust tendency for the NP measures to predict measures of longer-term outcome, including key measures of "rehabilitation potential," service utilization, and course of illness. Among the successes of NP prediction are the studies attempting to predict long-term outcome using measures of service utilization as an index of outcome. This application of NP methods may become increasingly important as managed care impacts more heavily on patterns of service delivery, and efforts are made to determine more accurately how limited resources may be best deployed. In fact, this was a central element of ra-

**Table 1.** Neuropsychological prediction of treatment response and outcome in schizophrenia

| Study | Sample | Predictor measure and condition | Outcome measure and condition | Comment |
|---|---|---|---|---|
| Weaver and Brooks (1964) | Chronic schizophrenic in-patients, N=248 | RT, tapping test, serial reaction test, pegboard and pursuit rotor task | Hospital status/rehabilitation potential at 2 year follow-up | Measures of motor speed and coordination were predictive |
| Cancro et al. (1971) | Recently hospitalized schizophrenic males, sr. staff dx. N=30 | Simple and cross-modal RT tasks given during a pre-medication period | Total nights in any mental institution over the next 3 years | Simple RT was a significant predictor (avg. $R^2=.25$). RT added 17 % var. to thought disorder as a predictor, for overall $R^2>.60$ |
| May et al. (1976) | Schizophrenics, N=11 | Subjective response measures, finger tapping speed and Kornetsky's continuous performance test, 4 hours after test-dose | Global assessment ratings at end of treatment | Subjective response, attention and perception measures predicted eventual outcome ($R^2=.30$–$.46$) |
| Kay and Singh (1979) | "Unequivocal" schizophrenia (Slater & Roth criteria) N=50 | Developmental tests of cognitive style, Span of Attention Test, sleeplessness rating scale, and pulse; during drug free placebo baseline | Therapeutic outcome rating (sx remission, return to premorbid fxn) assessed by ward psychiatrist after 12–14 wks of neuroleptic treatment | Randomness of response improved more than defects in conceptual style; favorable clinical response associated with resolution of attention deficit; better outcome associated with greater initial attentional and arousal disturbance |
| Zahn and Carpenter (1978) | DSM II-CATEGO acute schizophrenics with good premorbid adjustment, N=46 | Reaction time after a 3 week drug free pre-treatment period | Global ratings; pts. classified as "definitely improved" (n=18), vs "not improved" (n=17) after 3–4 mos. hospitalization | Reaction time predicted improvement, independent of clinical state at baseline |

(continued)

**Table 1.** (continued)

| Study | Sample | Predictor measure and condition | Outcome measure and condition | Comment |
|---|---|---|---|---|
| Asarnow and MacCrimmon (1982) | ICD8 schizophrenics, N=10 | Forced choice span of apprehension (SOA) 1 week after hospitalization, receiving "stabilized conventional doses of phenothiazines" | Freedom from distraction after 12 weeks of tx (Rattan-Chapman Test) | Residual thought disorder predicted by 10 letter SOA |
| Pogue-Geile and Harrow (1983) | In-patient RDC schizophrenia, N=10 | Digit Symbol Substitution Test of WAIS-R | Overall functioning and Strauss-Carpenter Scales during one year following hospitalization | Digit Symbol predicted overall and work functioning ($R^2$=.07–.13) |
| Marder (1984) | DSM III schizophrenia, out-patients, N=31 (13 acute, 18 outpatients) | Initial improvement on SOA task before and after 1 wk of tx. | Reduction in schizophrenic thought disturbances in response to drug treatment (haloperidol) 14 days later | SOA improvement predicts the amount of unusual thought content at day 14 ($R^2$=.60), and SCL-90 psychoticism at day 14 ($R^2$=.63) |
| Marder et al. (1988) | DSM III schizophrenia (N=36) | SOA at baseline (div. pts. into high and low span groups), following 4 wks drug discontinuation | Survival without clinical worsening; by BPRS decrease > 3 on thought disorder or paranoia cluster scores during subsequent 2 yrs. on 5mg (low dose) or 25mg (high dose) fluphenazine decanoate | Prediction only in high dose group; paradoxically, high span survival = 21 %, low span survival = 86 % |
| Mueser et al. (1991) | Recently admitted acute exacerbation DSM III-R schizophrenia (N=34), schizoaffective (N=21), and major affective (N=22) | WMS verbal, visual, concentration, raw score and MQ during pre-treatment phase | Symptom (BPRS) and social skills assessment after 2 wks of tx, 1 month follow-up after discharge | Memory predicted social skills improvement ($R^2$=.26) for schizophrenia and schizoaffective, but not major affective disorders; baseline demographic and clinical measures not predictive |

(continued)

**Table 1.** (continued)

| Study | Sample | Predictor measure and condition | Outcome measure and condition | Comment |
|---|---|---|---|---|
| Jaeger and Douglas (1992) | First episode RDC schizophrenia and schizoaffective N=19 | Wisconsin Card Sorting Test perseverative errors and NP scale scores at baseline (i. e. within 12 months of onset of treatment) | SAS global scores: instrumental role, household, and social functioning, social adjustment, at retest 18 months after initial testing | WCST predicted SAS global scores ($R^2$=.16–.32); attentional, executive and motor scales also predicted outcome variables |
| Smith et al. (1992) | RDC Schizophrenia (N=18) or schizoaffective (N=6) | Luria-Nebraska pathognomonic subscale (PATH), Trail Making, Seashore Rhythm Test after minimum 1 wk drug free period | Sx. improvement 3 wks predischarge, rated by BPRS and the New Haven Schizophrenia Index | PATH and trail making were significant predictors ($R^2$=.15–.28) |
| Kern et al. (1992) | Chart Dx:10 schizophrenics, 3 schizoaffective, 2 bi-polar, 1 psychotic NOS, total N=16 | Backward Masking, Degraded-Stimulus Continuous Performance Test, Digit Span Distractibility, Wisconsin Card Sorting Test, Rey AVLT, Rey-Osterreith Complex figure, PPVT, Pin Test; at baseline | Skills training ability (Symptom Management or Medication Management); on-task behavior, and change during approx. 16 mos. | Rey AVLT, Digit Span Distractibility, and Degraded-Stimulus Continuous Performance Test variables predicted outcome measures. Measures of distractibility predicted on-task behavior, vigilance predicted change |
| Wykes and Dunn (1992) | Mixed psychiatric patients PSE/CATEGO schizophrenia (N=28), other dx. (N=21) | Reaction time/response processing | Usage of psychological hospital services during 6 yr follow-up | The RT/response processing task predicted use among schizophrenia group ($R^2$=.17–30 |

*RT* reaction time; $R^2$ variance explained

tionale for the landmark study of Weaver and Brooks (1964), which showed that simple measures of motor speed and coordination could identify which patients would go on to have the best chances of rehabilitation success. The study of Cancro et al. (1971) also showed that simple reaction time (RT) measures could predict utilization of hospital services over a three year period, with the RT measures explaining about 17 % of total variance. Wykes and Dunn (1992) also found that simple measures of RT and "response processing" could predict service utilization, with the RT measures accounting for 17–30 % of the variance in outcome over a six year period. Jaeger and Douglas (1992) found 16–32 % of variance in long-term social/vocational outcome could be explained by a single measure (Wisconsin Card Sorting Test perseverative errors) obtained in a first-episode sample after 6 months of treatment.

Prediction of shorter-term treatment response variables generally has been less impressive, and there are reports of findings that appear paradoxical. For example, Kay and Singh (1979) found complex relations between initial NP state and antipsychotic treatment response; in fact, patients with more severe initial attentional dyscontrol tended to improve more during treatment. Marder et al. (1984) also found a somewhat surprising association of poorer attention span with lower rates of relapse during treatment. These paradoxical findings seem to reflect that patients with the most acute disturbances of attentional control (which may be correlated with florid psychotic symptoms) may show the greatest gains with treatment. In contrast, other patients who have more persistent defects in NP function may benefit less from treatment, and thus show less change in either symptoms or NP test scores, although they have longer-term patterns of severe disability. There are, however, reports that NP test performance predicts short-term treatment response, even among groups of patients with comparable levels of initial symptomatology. For example, the study of Zahn and Carpenter (1978) showed not only that RT measures could predict improvement during a 3–4 months' hospital stay, but also that the predictive power of the RT measures was independent of patients' clinical state at baseline. Similar findings were reported by Mueser et al. (1991), who found that memory test performance accounted for 26 % of variance in social skills improvement, while demographic and clinical symptom measures were not significant predictors.

Among the variety of possible study designs, the test-dose and early treatment-effects strategies appear to be under-utilized. These paradigms attempt to enhance predictive validity by assessing acute effects of specific treatments on NP functions before or near the beginning of treatment. The test-dose strategy using either dopamine agonists or antagonists has been usefully applied in predicting patients' survival free from relapse, but symptoms or pituitary hormone levels have most often been used as dependent measures (rev. by Lieberman 1993), and use of NP measures has not yet had much impact. May et al. (1976) reported preliminary results using a 200mg chlorpromazine test-dose, and found that poorer finger tapping speed and CPT performance 4 hours after the test-dose accounted for 30–46 % of variance in post-treatment global assessment ratings. While the predictive validity was good, these findings of association between poorer performance and better outcome are difficult to interpret. For the finger tapping results, adverse impact on motor speed may have marked those subjects with higher bioavailability of the drug. For the CPT both pre-test-dose and post-test-dose scores predicted outcome, so it may be that patients with greater attentional deficit at baseline were more responsive to treatment (as was hypothesized for the study of Kay and Singh 1979, and Marder et al. 1984, above). We are not aware of other studies that have attempted to use either test-dose or initial treatment change in NP function to predict the longer-term treatment response or outcome.

The range of NP measures used to predict subsequent treatment response or outcome has been limited, and there has been little systematic attention to selection of NP measures that are relevant either to clinical prediction, or to the putative psychopharmacological mechanisms of the compounds under study. In the earlier studies, measures of RT and "attention" predominated; more recently other measures of memory and executive functions have been included as predictors. Both old and new patterns of test selection appear to reflect more the dominant experimental zeitgeists than efforts to focus on key psychopharmacologic actions. Kay and Singh (1979) were unique in selecting measures that they considered theoretically important indices of "neuroleptic reversible" and "neuroleptic resistant" forms of deficit. Even at the behavioral level, investigators have most often failed to examine the *differential* validity of NP measures as predictors of different aspects of treatment response and/or outcome. A noteworthy exception was the study of Kern et al. (1992), who pointed out that measures of distractibility appeared more important in predicting "on-task behavior", while vigilance performance appeared more influential as a predictor of change during skills training.

## Conceptual and methodological comments

Despite some relatively robust findings, use of NP methods to predict treatment response and outcome is still in an early stage of development. NP methods have demonstrated substantial validity especially in the prediction of long-term outcome. Given the extensive variability in measures on both sides of the prediction equation, it is surprising that the NP methods have routinely accounted for between 15–30 % of variance in outcome. The clinical utility of the NP methods in predicting outcome is significant, particularly since methods that rely on assessment of symptoms (which remain the standard of behavioral assessment in psychopharmacologic studies), have such poor predictive validity. NP prediction of acute treatment response has been less successful, although there are some promising leads. Several studies have shown "paradoxical" effects, in which patients with initially poorest performance, especially on tests of attention, appear to make the greatest clinical gains. These findings suggest that certain NP measures may tap treatment-reversible processes that merit further study. In general, the literature supports the conclusion that NP methods are good at measuring traits present during both periods of symptom exacerbation and remission: these traits may do a reasonable job of predicting outcome precisely because they remain detectable in the midst of "noise" contributed by the psychotic state. In contrast, NP markers of treatment-reversible state abnormalities have been harder to define.

## Future research recommendations

The existing literature on NP prediction of treatment response and outcome offers several promising avenues for future research. First, better defining the NP trait characteristics that remain stable through periods of exacerbation and remission, will help provide clearer functional (or dysfunctional) baselines. The global functioning of patients may show acute deviations from this baseline due to state-related perturbations, but adequate treatment should target restoration of this level as a minimal outcome criterion. Second, the nature of potentially reversible state changes should be better characterized. What specific aspects of attention and other NP functions are improved by antipsychotic drug treatment? Can these state abnormalities be better quantified, especially *relative* to more enduring trait characteristics, so that the clinician has a clear idea of precisely what dysfunction is likely to be ameliorated, and in which patients? Third, fresh approaches to prediction need to consider the possibility of developing probes more relevant to the specific mechanisms of action of antipsychotic treatments. The test-dose strategy may be capitalized on to distinguish treatment-sensitive functions, and to better characterize the relation of acute to longer-term treatment effects. Furthermore, future efforts should aim to bridge the gap between clinical and preclinical studies. It seems surprising that behavioral methods used widely in preclinical drug evaluation are not adapted for use in clinical studies. There have been efforts in recent years to develop NP methods more closely in line with the body of animal research, where the specific component structure of tasks is typically more clearly dissected (Bilder et al. 1992b). By adapting these methods to the study of antipsychotic treatment effects, there is hope that we will both advance our understanding of the specific behavioral loci of drug action, and enhance our capacity to predict the course and outcome of treatment. Finally, if NP methods sensitive to specific drug treatment effects are validated, these methods may be used to monitor the course of treatment, and offer sets of behavioral targets that may be more reliable than the measurement of symptoms, which remain the method of choice today. Application of these NP strategies holds the promise that both treatment selection and dose-titration will someday have more specific and sensitive behavioral targets, and that these may supplement and complement methods for quantifying other aspects of treatment (such as receptor occupancy).

## Conclusions

NP methods are increasingly used to predict outcome, or to serve as outcome measures themselves. Substantive progress has been made in identifying NP markers of long-term disability; some of these features may be measured reliably even in acute symptomatic states, and comprise useful predictors of outcome. Less progress has been made in defining and characterizing the dimensions of treatment-reversible deficits, although this area holds promise both in basic and applied studies. As our choice of treatments expands, so does the importance of prediction. Advances in the application of NP methods should contribute to this process, and simultaneously increase our understanding of the basic mechanisms underlying antipsychotic treatment response and outcome.

## References


Arndt S, Alliger RJ, Andreasen NC (1991) The distinction of positive and negative symptoms: the failure of a two-dimensional model. Br J Psychiatry 158:317–322

Asarnow RF, MacCrimmon DJ (1982) Attention/Information processing, neuropsychological functioning, and thought disorder during the acute and partial recovery phase of schizophrenia: a longitudinal study. Psychiatry Res 7:309–319

Awad AG (1989) Drug therapy in schizophrenia – Variability of outcome and prediction of response. Can J Psychiatry 34:711–720

Bilder RM, Mukherjee S, Rieder RO, Pandurangi AK (1985) Symptomatic and neuropsychological components of defect states. Schizophr Bull 11:409–418

Bilder RM, Lipschutz-Broch L, Reiter G, Geisler SH, Mayerhoff DI, Lieberman JA (1992a) Intellectual deficits in first-episode schizophrenia: evidence for progressive deterioration. Schizophr Bull 18:437–448

Bilder RM, Turkel E, Lipschutz-Broch L, Lieberman JA (1992b) Antipsychotic medication effects on neuropsychological functions. Psychopharmacol Bull 4:353–366

Cancro R, Sutton S, Kerr J, Sugerman A (1971) Reaction time and prognosis in acute schizophrenia. J Nerv Ment Dis 151:351–359

Jaeger J, Douglas E (1992) Neuropsychiatric rehabilitation for persistent mental illness. Psychiatr Q 63:71–94

Kay SR, Singh MM (1979) Cognitive abnormality in schizophrenia: a dual-process model. Biol Psychiatry 14:155–176

Kern RS, Green MF, Satz P (1992) Neuropsychological predictors of skills training for chronic psychiatric patients. Psychiatry Res 43:223–230

Liddle PF (1987) The symptoms of chronic schizophrenia: a re-examination of the positive-negative dichotomy. Br J Psychiatry 151:145–151

Lieberman JA, Sobel SN (1993) Predictors of treatment response and course of schizophrenia. Curr Opin Psychiatry 6:63–69

Lieberman JA (1993) Prediction of outcome in first-episode schizophrenia. J Clin Psychiatry 54 [Suppl 3]:13–17

Marder SR, Asarnow RF, Van Putten T (1984) Information processing and neuroleptic response in acute and stabilized schizophrenic patients. Psychiatry Res 13:41–49

Marder SR, Asarnow RF, Van Putten (1988) Information processing and maintenance dose requirements in schizophrenia. Psychopharmacol Bull 24:247–250

May PRA (1966) Prediction in neuropsychopharmacology – a summary. In: Wittenborn JR, May PRA (eds) Prediction of response to pharmacotherapy. Charles C Thomas, Springfield Illinois, pp 201–215

May PRA, Van Putten T, Yale C, Potepan P, Jenden DJ, Fairchild MD, Goldstein MJ, Dixon WJ (1976) Predicting individual responses to drug treatment in schizophrenia: a test dose model. J Nerv Ment Dis 162:177–183

May PRA, Goldberg SC (1978) Prediction of schizophrenic patients' response to pharmacotherapy. In: Lipton MA, DiMascio A, Killam KF (eds) Psychopharmacology: a generation of progress. Raven Press, New York, pp 1139–1153

Mueser KT, Bellack AS, Douglas MS, Wade JH (1991) Prediction of social skill acquisition in schizophrenic and major affective disorder patients from memory and symptomatology. Psychiatry Res 37:281–296

Pogue-Geile MF, Harrow M (1983) The longitudinal study of negative symptoms in schizophrenia: psychomotor retardation. Annual Meeting of the American Psychological Association, Anaheim, CA, August 1983 (Abstract)

Smith RC, Largen J, Vroulis G, Ravichandran GK (1992) Neuropsychological test scores and clinical response to neuroleptic drugs in schizophrenic patients. Compr Psychiatry 33:139–145

Weaver LA, Brooks GW (1963) The use of psychomotor tests in predicting the potential of chronic schizophrenics. J Neuropsychiatry 5:170–180

Wykes T, Dunn G (1992) Cognitive deficit and the prediction of rehabilitation success in a chronic psychiatric group. Psychol Med 22:389–398

Zahn TP, Carpenter WT (1978) Effects of short-term outcome and clinical improvement on reaction time in acute schizophrenia. J Psychiatr Res 14:59–68

**Authors' address:** Dr. R. M. Bilder, Hillside Hospital, Long Island Jewish Medical Center 75–59 263rd Street, Glen Oaks, NY 11004, U.S.A.

# Neurochemical and neuroendocrine measures and prediction of outcome to neuroleptic therapy

**F. Müller-Spahn, C. Hock,** and **G. Kurtz**

Psychiatric Department, Ludwig-Maximilians-University, München, Federal Republic of Germany

## Introduction

The early discrimination between responders and non-responders would be of substantial clinical relevance in optimizing neuroleptic therapy. Identification of early predictors of outcome to neuroleptic treatment would be useful for avoiding unnecessary treatment of refractory patients (Harvey et al. 1991). Despite the numerous studies performed to find "markers" of neuroleptic response in acute psychotic patients getting "the right drug for the right patient" has remained an unsolved problem. Although the biological basis of schizophrenia is unknown so far, there is much evidence of an abnormal dopamine (DA) activity being an important factor in schizophrenia. In a recent study, Seeman et al. (1993) reported a sixfold elevation in the density of dopamine D4 receptors in schizophrenia. The dopamine hypothesis, primarily based on the

**Table 1.** Prediction of outcome to neuroleptic therapy – neurochemical and neuroendocrine measures

| Dopaminergic system | Noradrenergic system | Immunological function | Hypothalamic pituitary-thyroid axis |
|---|---|---|---|
| HVA | MHPG | T-cells | TSH response to TRH |
| ($^3$H)-Spiperone binding | ($^3$H)-Clonidine binding | T-cell-subgroups | |
| | Clonidine-test | | |
| DBH | | | |
| Apomorphine-test | | | |

*CSF* Cerebrospinal fluid, *HVA* Homovanillic acid, *DBH* Dopamine $\beta$-hydroxylase, *MHPG* 3-Methoxy-4-hydroxyphenylglycol, *TRH* Thyrotropinreleasing hormone, *TSH* Thyroid-stimulating hormone fact that neuroleptics block dopamine receptors and that their ability to displace dopamine antagonists in vitro, correlates significantly with their clinical antipsychotic potencies (Seeman et al. 1976). Although recent advances in biochemical research suggest that several neurotransmitter systems are involved in the pathophysiology of schizophrenia, dysfunctions in the dopaminergic and noradrenergic system are a matter of great significance. This paper will review studies addressing neurochemical and neuroendocrine measures associated with drug response in schizophrenia (Table 1).

## Empirical findings

### *Dopaminergic system*

Plasma free homovanillic acid (HVA), the major metabolite of dopamine, can reflect brain turnover of dopamine (Pickar et al. 1986, Davilla et al. 1988), thus making it a potentially useful tool for studying the pharmacologic action of antipsychotic drugs (Lieberman and Koreen 1993). It has been reported that only about 17 percent of pHVA is of brain origin reflecting neuroleptic-induced elevations in midbrain dopaminergic metabolism; the major contributor of pHVA is the peripheral nervous system (Lambert et al. 1991). Changes in pHVA correlated with change in CSF HVA following neuroleptic treatment (Sharma et al. 1989). There is much evidence that pHVA is elevated in acute psychotic schizophrenics (Bowers et al. 1984, Pickar et al. 1986, Mazure et al. 1987, 1991). After an initial increase in pHVA following acute neuroleptic treatment a subsequent decrease of metabolite concentration has been demonstrated (Davilla et al. 1988, Mazure et al. 1991).

Elevated pretreatment pHVA levels and the subsequent decline have been associated with improvement in positive symptoms (Bowers et al. 1984, Chang et al. 1988, Mazure et al. 1991, Davidson et al. 1991). In most studies (Table 2) baseline pHVA or the pattern of pHVA in response to neuroleptic therapy has been shown to be a useful clinical predictor of treatment outcome (review Lieberman and Koreen 1993). Chang et al. (1988, 1990), Bowers et al. (1989), Davidson et al. (1991) and Mazure et al. (1991) have reported higher pHVA baseline levels in the good response group. Moreover, Chang et al. (1988) have found a differential pHVA response between good and poor outcome schizophrenic patients following a six week haloperidol treatment. Within the group of good responders pretreatment pHVA was higher followed by a significant decline over time. In contrast a different response pattern with a 14-day-level significantly higher than the baseline level, was seen in the poor responder group, a decrease towards pretreatment values was found after 3 weeks. Those patients who had the greatest change in pHVA showed the most improvement.

Davilla et al. (1988) reported a significant correlation between an in-

**Table 2.** Prediction of outcome to neuroleptic therapy. Studies of plasma HVA concentrations in schizophrenic patients

| Author | Year | Subjects | Drug<br>Treatment period | Results |
|---|---|---|---|---|
| Chang et al. | 1988 | 24 SCZ (DSM-III) | Haloperidol<br>42 days | baseline pHVA increased in R, initial increase and then substantial decrease in pHVA |
| Davilla et al. | 1988 | 14 SCZ (DSM-III) | Haloperidol<br>28 days | baseline pHVA not correlated with improvement, pattern of pHVA in response to therapy has prognostic value |
| Sharma et al. | 1988 | 11 SCZ (RDC) | Trifluoperazine<br>35 days | no relationship between CSF HVA and pHVA pre- and post-treatment |
| Bowers et al. | 1989 | 37 nonorganic psychotic patients (DSM-III) | Haloperidol<br>Perphenazine<br>10 days | early response correlated with pre-treatment pHVA |
| van Putten et al. | 1989 | 22 SCZ (DSM-III) | Fluphenazine<br>42 days | pHVA at week 1 is a predictor of outcome at 4–6 weeks |
| Alfredsson and Wiesel | 1990 | 24 SCZ (DSM-III-R) | Sulpiride<br>42 days | baseline pHVA not different in R and NR, pattern of pHVA response to therapy has prognostic value |
| Chang et al. | 1990 | 33 SCZ (DSM-III) | Haloperidol<br>42 days | baseline pHVA increased in R, pattern of pHVA in response to therapy has prognostic value |
| Davidson et al. | 1991 | 20 SCZ (DSM-III-R) | Thioridazine<br>35 days | pHVA decreased in R but not in NR, baseline pHVA increased in R |
| Mazure et al. | 1991 | 37 acutely nonorganic psychotic patients (DSM-III-R) | Perphenazine<br>10 days | baseline pHVA significantly correlated with good response |
| Koreen et al. | 1994 | 41 SCZ | Fluphenazine<br>28 days | baseline and week 1 pHVA greater in R than in NR |

*R* Responder, *NR* Nonresponder, *RDC* Research Diagnostic Criteria, *DSM-III* Diagnostic and Statistical Manual of Mental Disorders, *SCZ* Schizophrenics crease in pHVA concentration on day 4 or a decrease from day 4 to day 28 and the degreee of improvement after a 4 weeks therapy with haloperidol, thus indicating that the pattern of pHVA in response to neuroleptic therapy predicted outcome whereas the baseline pHVA level did not correlate with clinical improvement confirming results by Davis et al. (1985). In their report Davis et al. (1985) haven't found any significant correlations between clinical improvement after 10 mg of haloperidol for 4 weeks and baseline pHVA, thus indicating little prognostic value.

In another study we carried out sex differences in the pHVA pretreatment levels of schizophrenic patients have been found (unpublished data). Baseline pHVA was significantly higher in females and decreased over time in both sexes following uncontrolled neuroleptic therapy with a statistical significance in women after 7 days. The pHVA decrease was paralleled by the clinical improvement (Fig. 1).

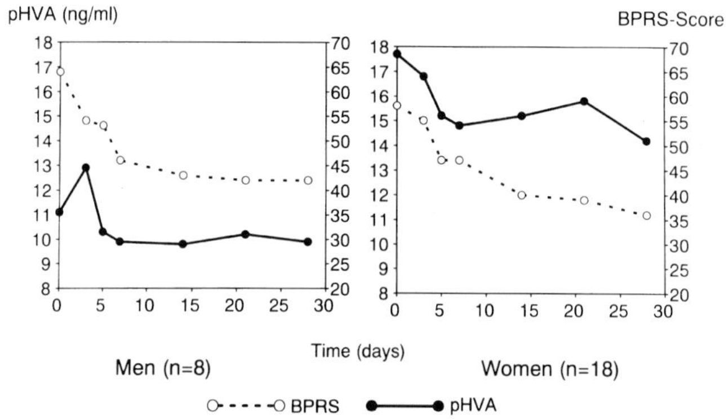


**Fig. 1.** Mean plasma homovanillic acid (pHVA) levels and changes of BPRS-scores during 4 weeks of neuroleptic treatment

Although pHVA is influenced by many factors like prior neuroleptic therapy, activity, diet, and renal clearance, it has remained the most reliable and least invasive method to evaluate brain dopamine activity (Lieberman and Koreen 1993) by means of a peripheral measure.

In accordance with the dopamine hypothesis of schizophrenia, a large number of dopamine receptor binding studies have been performed. Increases in ($^3$H)-spiperone binding sites in unmedicated and medicated schizophrenics on intact lymphocytes have been reported by several investigators (Lefur et al. 1983, Bondy et al. 1984). There is substantial evidence for a correlation between spiperone binding studies in brains of schizophrenic patients and spiperone binding studies on lymphocytes although the latter are pharmacologically different from those in the central nervous system (Fleminger et al. 1982, Grodzicki et al. 1990). Grodzicki et al. (1990) have found considerable differences between treatment-responsive and non-responsive schizophrenic patients, compared to controls the responders showed a significantly higher maximal spiperone binding capacity ($B_{max}$) whereas the level of spiperone binding in the non-responsive group was only slightly elevated.

## Dopamine β-Hydroxylase (DBH)

The enzyme DBH catalyses the synthesis of norepinephrine from dopamine. Variations in the enzymes of synthesis or metabolism have been suggested to be a possible source of alterations in dopaminergic and noradrenergic functions. It has been speculated that low CSF DBH levels reflecting low brain DBH activity, thus indicating high DA activity might be a risk factor for psychosis and that these patients might substantially benefit from neuroleptic therapy (Sternberg et al. 1982, Arató et al. 1983). In a small group of schizophrenic patients, Sternberg et al. (1983) have found low levels of CSF DBH activity being significantly related to good prognosis and excellent clinical response to neuroleptic therapy.

In another study Bartkó et al. (1990) examined a set of 22 putative predictor variables in 98 schizophrenic patients. They have found significant correlations between 10 of 22 variables from different data levels and neuroleptic response. The combination of the best 5 predictors including absence of disturbances of premorbid adjustment, severe positive symptoms at admission, absence of family history of schizophrenia, working ability without restriction during the year before admission, and reduced serum DBH activity have explained 29 % of outcome variance.

Most studies, however, show that DBH acitivity – especially assayed in serum but also in CSF – in schizophrenic patients did not provide consistent findings (Goldstein et al. 1974, Sapir et al. 1989, Van Kammen 1991) thus indicating that serum as well as CSF DBH activity is no useful predictor of neuroleptic drug response.

## Stimulant challenge tests

Other procedures to investigate relationships between dopaminergic and noradrenergic receptor activity and clinical response to neuroleptic therapy comprise stimulant challenge tests with amphetamine and apomorphine. D-amphetamine is an indirect DA agonist that increases DA and NE release and block uptake (van Kammen 1991), apomorphine is a direct $DA_2$ agonist. Angrist et al. (1981) have reported that transient psychopathological worsening after amphetamine correlated inversely with apomorphine emesis sensitivity and predicted a favourable outcome after neuroleptics, whereas lack of response to amphetamine predicted a poor one. Sensitivity to apomorphine emesis did not correlate significantly with treatment change.

Van Kammen et al. (1982) examined the hypothesis whether the amphetamine challenge test was able to predict an impending relapse or to know when a patient could stop taking neuroleptics in 13 schizophrenic patients. Six patients who had shown an acute psychotic exacerbation with d-amphetamine relapsed within 3 months after pimozide withdrawal.

There are, however, only few studies involving small groups of patients with a different state of psychosis that investigated the behavioural response to stimulant challenge tests.

Summarizing these data, stimulant challenge tests assessing psychotic behaviour are more likely to evaluate clinical instability with a subsequent higher risk for relapse than to have predictive potency for short-term neuroleptic treatment outcome.

## Neuroendocrine strategy

The neuroendocrine strategy for predictor research used the apomorphine-induced growth hormone (GH) response to assess central DA receptor activity in psychotic patients. It has been hypothesized that psychotic symptoms according to the dopamine hypothesis are associated with increased DA receptor activity and that they should most rapidly respond to the DA receptor blocking effects of neuroleptics (Zemlan et al. 1986). The centrally acting DA agonist apomorphine has been suggested to serve as a limited model for the mesolimbic and mesocortical DA receptor activity (Creese et al. 1978, Zemlan et al. 1986). According to this idea, patients with an elevated GH-response after stimulation with apomorphine reflecting an increased DA receptor activation in the tuberoinfundibular system are expected to have a favorable response to neuroleptics. Zemlan et al. (1986) reported that a subgroup of acutely psychotic schizophrenic patients with elevated thought disorder cluster scores also had elevated GH responses to apomorphine. Those patients with thought disorders and auditory hallucinations responded rapidly to a treatment with a fixed dose of 10 mg haloperidol/day.

In opposition to these findings another study directly investigating the predictive value of the apomorphine test to neuroleptic treatment outcome has found no substantial relationships (Müller-Spahn 1991). 21 male schizophrenic patients with predominant paranoid delusions and hallucinations were stimulated with 0.006 mg apomorphine per kg body weigth and then treated with different neuroleptics over 42 days. Apomorphine-induced GH and prolactin levels were not correlated to psy-

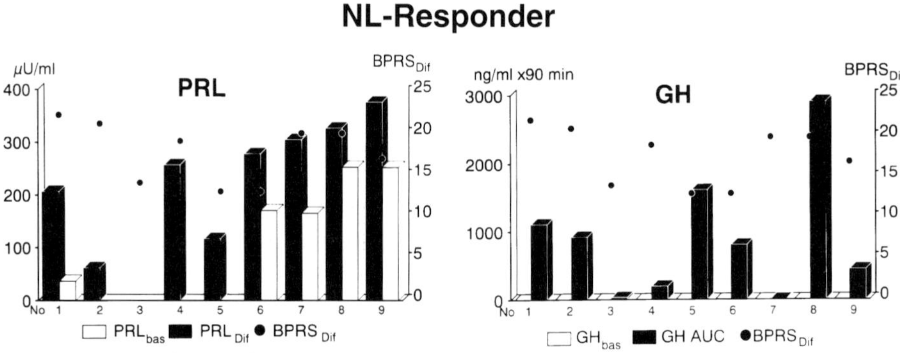


**Fig. 2.** Apomorphine-induced prolactin (PRL)- and growth hormone (GH)-levels in the good outcome group (responder: difference of BPRS-syndrome scores 3–5 before and after 4 weeks of neuroleptic treatment at least 40%)

chopathological changes. The differentiation between clinical responders (Fig. 2) and non-responders has not shown any relevant effects.

Studies investigating the predictive value of the apomorphine test show inconsistent results. This may be at least partly explained by the biological heterogeneity of schizophrenic subgroups and the fact that the GH response to apomorphine reflects tuberoinfundibular DA activity and not primarily mesolimbic or mesocortical DA receptor activity.

## *Noradrenergic system*

The role of norepinephrine (NE) in the pathophysiology of schizophrenia has been studied in numerous investigations. Only few clinical studies have, however, clearly demonstrated abnormal NE activity in schizophrenia (Lieberman and Koreen 1993). Studies assessing plasma 3-methoxy-4-hydroxyphenylglycol (MHPG), the major metabolite of NE, have not provided consistent results concerning its predictive potency for treatment outcome. Bowers et al. (1989) have reported that early responders to neuroleptic therapy showed a tendency to higher plasma MHPG levels prior to treatment whereas the simultaneously assessed pretreatment free pHVA was significantly higher.

In contrast, Mazure et al. (1991) have found that only elevated pretreatment pHVA but not MHPG was significantly associated with good response. Responders, however, showed a significant decrease in MHPG from pretreatment to posttreatment suggesting that the response pattern is of higher significance than a single MHPG value prior to therapy.

### $^{3}$H-clonidine binding

$^{3}$H-clonidine binding in platelets has been investigated (Pandey et al. 1989) in order to examine the hypothesis that $\alpha 2$-adrenergic receptor function is increased in schizophrenia. There is substantial evidence that many neuroleptics have also potent $\alpha 2$-adrenergic receptor blocking properties. Schizophrenics with hyperactive $\alpha 2$-adrenergic receptors are speculated to benefit from neuroleptics with $\alpha 2$-adrenergic receptor blocking properties. Baseline $B_{max}$ in schizophrenic patients was significantly correlated with the decrease in Brief Psychiatric Rating Scale Scores after treatment with trifluoperazine (Pandey et al. 1989) suggesting that $\alpha$-adrenergic binding sites may predict clinical response in schizophrenic patients.

Van Kammen et al. (1989) have reported that responders to clonidine treatment had a diagnosis of paranoid schizophrenia and a higher pretreatment GH response to clonidine challenge.

At present, the few studies dealing with this topic and the inconsistent findings concerning alterations in $\alpha 2$-adrenergic receptor function do not permit final conclusions about its predictive value.

### T-cells and T-cell subgroups

Schizophrenics and patients with a schizoaffective psychosis have been studied (Müller et al. 1991, 1993, McAllister et al. 1989) in order to evaluate the possible influence of neuroleptic therapy on immune parameters. Müller et al. (1993) have found no correlations between the psychopathology and the elevated $CD3^+$ and $CD4^+$ cells at admission. Neuroleptic therapy was reported to have no substantial effect on these neuroimmune measures suggesting that neuroleptic therapy does not "downregulate" the increased cell numbers.

### The hypothalamic-pituitary-thyroid (HPT) axis

Recent results investigating the response of thyrotropin to TRH (see review by Lieberman and Koreen 1993) are relatively inconsistent. They show no differences between basal or peak TSH between controls and schizophrenic patients (Baumgartner et al. 1988, Roy et al. 1989) on one hand and a significantly less blunted TSH response in schizophrenics (Kiriike et al. 1988) on the other hand.

Only few studies used the TRH test to evaluate the HPT function in schizophrenic patients and its predictive value to neuroleptic outcome (Langer et al. 1986, Baumgartner et al. 1988, Beasley et al. 1988). It has been hypothesized that rapid neuroleptic responders with diminished $\Delta$ $TSH_{max}$ have either increased postsynaptic pituitary dopamine receptor sensitivity or elevated CNS presynaptic dopamine activity (Beasley et al. 1988).

Langer et al. (1986) have reported that a blunted TSH response at admission was associated with recovery after nine weeks treatment with haloperidol. These data suggested that the TRH-test might be a possible predictor of treatment outcome. Beasley et al. (1988) have found similar results. A reduced TSH response was associated with affective disorder and was a significant predictor of a favourable rapid response to neuroleptic treatment. On the other hand Baumgartner et al. (1988) could not confirm these findings. At present the TRH-test has not been proven as a predictor of therapeutic response or outcome.

## Conceptual and methodological comments

Quality and success of biological research in schizophrenia depend decisively on the level of its clinical investigation methods (Gaebel and Maier 1993). Currently the biological basis of schizophrenia is not clarified. Biochemical and neuroendocrine data do not provide clear and consistent support for the etiopathogenesis of schizophrenia (Lieberman and Koreen 1993). The function of the dopaminergic system is, however, suggested to play an important role.

There is some evidence that schizophrenia is characterized by abnormally low prefrontal dopamine activity inducing increased dopamine activity in mesolimbic neurons (Davis et al. 1991). Positive symptoms have been associated with increased, negative symptoms with reduced dopaminergic activity.

Much attention has been focused on neuroleptic drug actions in different biological systems. As neuroleptics primarily act by blocking DA receptor activity in the mesolimbic area (antipsychotic effects), metabolites of dopamine and neuroendocrine challenge tests with DA2-receptor agonists have been investigated to clarify possible relationships to treatment outcome. The results derived from these studies are not always convincing and only few were replicated. This is attributed to the following methodological problems:

1. Subject selection with insufficient evaluation of affective, positive and negative symptoms as well as age of onset and course of illness (first-episode vs. chronic); 2. Controls were frequently not sufficiently matched; 3. Sample sizes were too small; neuroleptic drug treatment was frequently not controlled and not comparable with regard to dosage, pharmacological properties and length of therapy; 4. Insufficient correlation between peripheral and central measures, e.g. plasma HVA is primarily of peripheral origin, CSF HVA collected by lumbar puncture is the result of different dopaminergic CNS regions; 5. There is more than one neurotransmitter system involved in the pathogenesis of schizophrenia, not all schizophrenics show the same biochemical dysfunctions; 6. Neurochemical and neuroendocrine "markers" do not offer the specificity required to clarify the heterogeneity within psychoses (Garver et al. 1988); 7. The assumption, that investigation of the hypothalamic-pituitary axis reflects the putative pathophysiology of those brain regions involved in psychotic symptomatology has never been proved" (Lieberman and Koreen 1993).

Regarding these critical points, the heterogeneity of the biochemical and neuroendocrine data is not surprising. Despite these problems the investigation of the DA metabolite HVA in controlled studies seems to be the only putative predictor of neuroleptic outcome so far.

## Future research recommendations

Future research recommendations should on the one hand focus on the elimination or the limitation of such methological problems mentioned above, on the other hand it ought to emphasize methodological progress.

Promising strategies include in vivo neuroimaging techniques using specific ligands, the identification of gene polymorphisms of the various neurotransmitter receptor subtypes, and the use of multivariate quantitative analysis of biological specimens with large patient samples to increase statistical power (Lieberman and Koreen 1993). The cloning of the $D_1$, $D_2$ and $D_4$ receptor would help to clarify the role of dopamine and of neuroleptics in schizophrenia and its individual value as useful clinical predictor of response.

## Conclusions

New strategies on biochemical predictor research of neuroleptic treatment outcome should focus on a comprehensive and methodologically outstanding elaboration of the study design concerning patient selection, assessment of psychopathology, sample sizes, matching of control groups, multivariate quantitative analysis of different biological specimens as well as on advances of molecular biology.

## References

Alfredsson G, Wiesel F (1990) Relationships between clinical effects and monoamine metabolites and aminoacids in sulpiride-treated schizophrenic patients. Psychopharmacology 101:324–331

Angrist B, Peselow E, Rotrosen J, Gershon S (1981) Relationships between responders to dopamine agonists, psychopathology, neuroleptic treatment response, and need for neuroleptic maintenance in schizophrenic subjects. In: Angrist G, Burrows C, Lader M, Lingjaerde O, Sedvall G, Wheatley D (eds) Recent advances in neuropsychopharmacology. Pergamon Press, Oxford New York Toronto Sidney Paris Frankfurt, pp 49–54

Arató M, Bagdy G, Blümel F, Perenyi A, Rihmer Z (1983) Reduced serum dopamine-$\beta$-hydroxylase activity in paranoid schizophrenics. Pharmacopsychiatry 16:19–22

Bartkó G, Frecska E, Horvath S, Zádor G, Arató M (1990) Predicting neuroleptic response from a combination of multilevel variable in acute schizophrenic patients. Acta Psychiatr Scand 82:408–412

Baumgartner A, Gräf K, Kürten I, Meinhold H (1988) The hypothalamic-pituitary-thyroid axis in psychiatric patients and healthy subjects: parts 1–4. Psychiatry Res 24:271–331

Beasley C, Magnusson M, Garver D (1988) TSH response to TRH and haloperidol response latency in psychoses. Biol Psychiatry 24:423–431

Bondy B, Ackenheil M, Birzle W, Elbers R, Fröhler M (1984) Catecholamines and their receptors in blood: evidence for alterations in schizophrenia. Biol Psychiatry 19:1377–1393

Bowers M, Swigar M, Jatlow P, Goicoechea N (1984) Plasma catecholamine metabolites and early response to haloperidol. J Clin Psychiatry 45:248–251

Bowers M, Swigar M, Jatlow P, Hoffmann F (1989) Plasma catecholamine metabolites and treatment response at neuroleptic steady state. Biol Psychiatry 25:734–738

Chang W, Chen T, Lee C, Hung J, Hu W, Yeh E (1988) Plasma homovanillic acid levels and subtyping of schizophrenia. Psychiatry Res 23:239–244

Chang W, Chen T, Lin S, Lung F, Lin W, Hu W, Yeh E (1990) Plasma catecholamine metabolites in schizophrenics: evidence for the two subtype concept. Biol Psychiatry 27:510–518

Creese I, Burt D, Snyder S (1978) Biochemical actions of neuroleptic drugs: focus on the dopamine receptor. In: Iversen S, Snyder S (eds) Handbook of psychopharmacology 10. Plenum Press, New York, pp 37–89

Davidson M, Kahn R, Knott P, Kaminsky R, Cooper M, DuMont K, Aptu S, Davis K (1991) Effects of neuroleptic treatment on symptoms of schizophrenia and plasma homovanillic acid concentrations. Arch Gen Psychiatry 48:910–913

Davilla R, Manero E, Zumarraga M, Andia I, Schweitzer J, Friedhoff A (1988) Plasma homovanillic acid as a predictor of response to neuroleptics. Arch Gen Psychiatry 5:564–567

Davis K, Davidson M, Mohs R, Kendler K, Davis B, Johns L, DeNigris Y, Horvath T (1985)

Plasma homovanillic acid concentration and the severity of schizophrenic illness. Science 227:1601–1602

Davis K, Kahn R, Ko G, Davidson M (1991) Dopamine in schizophrenia: a review and reconceptualization. Am J Psychiatry 148:1474–1486

Fleminger S, Jenner P, Marsden C (1982) Are dopamine receptors present on human lymphozytes? J Pharm Pharmacol 34:658–663

Gaebel W, Maier W (1993) Neurobiological determinants of schizophrenic illness. Concept strategy and method of a research program. Nervenarzt 64:415–426

Garver D, Kelly K, Fried K, Magnusson M, Hirschowitz J (1988) Drug response patterns as a basis of nosology for the mood-incongruent psychoses (the schizophrenias). Psychol Med 18:873–885

Goldstein M, Freedman L, Ebstein R (1974) Studies on dopamine-$\beta$-hydroxylase in mental disorders. J Psychiatr Res 11:205–210

Grodzicki J, Pardo M, Schved G, Schlosberg A, Fuchs S, Kanety H (1990) Differences in ($^{3}$H)-spiperone binding to peripheral blood lymphozytes from neuroleptic responsive and nonresponsive schizophrenic patients. Biol Psychiatry 27:1327–1330

Harvey P, Davidson M, Powchik P, Schmeidler J, McQueeney R, Kaminsky R, Davis K (1991) Time course and clinical predictors of treatment response in schizophrenia. Schizophr Res 5:161–166

Kiriike N, Izumiya S, Nishiwaki Y, Maeda T, Nagata T, Kawakita Y (1988) TRH test and DST in schizoaffective mania, mania and schizophrenia. Biol Psychiatry 24:415–422

Koreen A, Lieberman J, Alvir J, Mayerhoff D, Loebel A, Chakos M, Amin F, Cooper T (1994) Plasma homovanillic acid in first-episode schizophrenia: psychopathology and treatment response. Arch Gen Psychiatry (in press)

Lambert G, Eisenhofer G, Cox H, Horne M, Kaliff V, Kelly M, Jennings G, Esker M (1991) Direct determination of homovanillic acid release from the human brain: an indicator of central dopaminergic activity. Life Sci 49:1061–1072

Langer G, Koinig G, Hatzinger R, Schönbeck G, Resch F, Aschauer H, Keshavan M, Sieghart W (1986) Response of thyrotropin to thyrotropin-releasing hormone as predictor of treatment outcome. Arch Gen Psychiatry 43:861–868

Lefur G, Zarifian E, Phan T (1983) ($^{3}$H)-spiperidol binding on lymphozytes: changes in two different groups of schizophrenic patients and effect of neuroleptic treatment. Life Sci 32:249–255

Lieberman JA, Koreen A (1993) Neurochemistry and neuroendocrinology of schizophrenia: a selective review. Schizophr Bull 19:371–429

Mazure C, Bowers M, Hoffmann F, Miller K, Nelson J (1987) Plasma catecholamines in subtypes of major depression. Biol Psychiatry 22:1469–1472

Mazure C, Nelson J, Jatlow P, Bowers M (1991) Plasma free homovanillic acid (HVA) as a predictor of clinical response in acute psychosis. Biol Psychiatry 30:475–482

McAllister C, Rapaport M, Pickar D, Paul S (1989) Effect of short-term administration of antipsychotic drugs on lymphozyte subsets in schizophrenic patients. Arch Gen Psychiatry 46:956–957

Müller N, Ackenheil M, Hofschuster E, Mempel W, Eckstein R (1991) Cellular immunity in schizophrenic patients before and during neuroleptic treatment. Psychiatry Res 37:147–160

Müller N, Hofschuster E, Ackenheil M, Eckstein R (1993) T-cells and psychopathology in schizophrenia: relationships to the outcome of neuroleptic therapy. Acta Psychiatr Scand 87:66–71

Müller-Spahn F (1991) Neuroendokrinologie und Schizophrenieforschung. Monographien aus dem Gesamtgebiete der Psychiatric, Bd. 64. Springer, Berlin Heidelberg New York

Pandey G, Janicak P, Javoid J, Davis J (1989) Increased $^{3}$H-Clonidine binding in platelets of patients with depressive and schizophrenic disorders. Psychiatry Res 28:73–88

Pickar D, Labarca R, Doran A, Wolkowitz O, Roy A, Breier A, Linnoila M, Paul S (1986) Longitudinal measurement of plasma homovanillic acid levels in schizophrenic patients. Arch Gen Psychiatry 4:669–679

Roy A, Wolkowitz O, Doran A, Pickar D (1989) TRH test in schizophrenic patients and controls. Biol Psychiatry 25:523–526

Sapri M, Rao B, Chanuabasavanna S (1989) Serum dopamine-$\beta$-hydroxylase activity in clinical subtypes of depression. Acta Psychiatr Scand 80:474–478

Seeman P, Lee T, Chau Wong M, Wong K (1976) Antipsychotic drug doses and neuroleptic/dopamine receptors. Nature 261:717–719

Seeman P, Guan H, Van Tol H (1993) Dopamine D4 receptors elevated in schizophrenia. Nature 365:441–445

Sharma R, Javaid J, Janicak P, Comaty J, Davis J, Faull K (1988) Effect of trifluoperazine on CSF and plasma HVA levels in schizophrenic subjects. Am J Psychiatry 145:1480–1481

Sternberg D, Kammen D, Lerner P, Bunney W (1982) Dopamine-β-hydroxylase and treatment response. Science 216:1432–1435

Sternberg D, van Kammen D, Lerner P, Ballenger J, Marder S, Post R, Bunney W (1983) CSF dopamine-β-hydroxylase in schizophrenia. Arch Gen Psychiatry 40:743–747

Van Kammen D, Docherty J, Bunney W (1982) Prediction of early relapse after pimozide discontinuation by response to d-amphetamine during pimozide treatment. Biol Psychiatry 17:233–242

Van Kammen D, Peters J, van Kammen W, Rosen J, Yao J, McAdam D, Linnoila M (1989) Clonidine treatment of schizophrenia: can we predict treatment response? Psychiatry Res 27:297–311

Van Kammen (1991) The biochemical basis of relapse and drug response in schizophrenia: review and hypothesis. Psychol Med 21:881–895

Van Putten T, Marder S, Aravagiri M, Chabert N, Mintz J (1989) Plasma homovanillic acid as a predictor of response to fluphenazine treatment. Psychopharmacol Bull 1:89–91

Zemlan F, Hirschowitz J, Sautter F, Garver D (1986) Relationships of psychotic symptom clusters in schizophrenia to neuroleptic treatment and growth hormone response to apomorphine. Psychiatry Res 18:239–255

**Authors' address:** Prof. Dr. F. Müller-Spahn, Psychiatric Department, LM-University of Munich, Nußbaumstrasse 7, D–80336 München, Federal Republic of Germany

# Prediction of clinical response to neuroleptics and positron emission tomography in schizophrenia

**M. S. Buchsbaum** and **C. T. Luu**

Department of Psychiatry, Mount Sinai School of Medicine, New York, N.Y., U.S.A.

## Introduction

Every clinician knows that some schizophrenics show marked improvement in symptoms when treated even with low doses of neuroleptics and others show little improvement or even worsening when medication is given (Carpenter et al. 1981, Brown et al. 1989, Garver et al. 1988). This diversity in treatment response may be especially marked in university research programs where patients who are having their first psychotic episode as well as those who are chronically ill and especially medication resistent may appear. The variation in clinical effects of typical antipsychotic drugs may be explained by the density, affinity, and pharmacological class of receptors with which they interact. Furthermore, individual differences in the pharmacokinetics of antipsychotic drugs, biological heterogeneity in schizophrenia and the particular cerebral regions whose functions are altered directly or indirectly by their administration will play a role on the clinical outcome. Imaging is an insightful pathway into understanding and unraveling some of these variations. The imaging of regional cerebral metabolism can provide information about the initial state of the patient's brain and the functional consequences of neuroleptic administration throughout the brain.

Conflicting positron emission tomographic (PET) studies using radioligands for the dopamine receptor have found elevated (Wong et al. 1986, Tune et al. 1993) or normal (Farde et al. 1986) values. However, these studies have not taken into account the large individual variation in clinical response to dopamine-blocking neuroleptics discussed above, nor considered possible multitransmitter hypotheses of schizophrenia (Bunney 1988, 1990, Carlsson and Carlsson 1990).

It is possible that only neuroleptic responders have elevated radioligand binding consistent with hyperdopaminergia, and that division of patient groups on this potential indicator of dopamine function is critical to understanding ligand imaging results so far. It is also possible that the dynamic activity of the dopamine system rather than the static receptor numbers are important for assessing diagnosis. Metabolic rate measurement with fluorodeoxyglucose (FDG) may reveal functional differences less apparent when only relatively fixed indices related to receptor number are imaged. Lastly, if two neurotransmitter system interaction hypotheses of the schizophrenic pathophysiology are considered, including dopamine/glutamate and dopamine/serotonin balances, local metabolic rate differences may be greater markers of diagnosis than any one single neurotransmitter binding study. Direct or indirect effects on the cortex might well also appear and in fact be crucial for understanding the action of neuroleptics – effects, so far, not detectable with reliance solely on PET D2 receptor ligand studies which poorly image regions with less concentrated D2 receptors than the striatum. For these reasons, we chose to image glucose metabolic rate to explore differences between neuroleptic responders and nonresponders.

Most human PET studies have shown greater effects of dopaminergic drugs on the metabolism of the striatum than on the cortex. We initially found a significant increase in both relative and micromole metabolic rate in the putamen in eight schizophrenics scanned both on and off neuroleptics (Buchsbaum et al. 1987). Increases in striatum metabolic rate with neuroleptics were also found by five others (Buchsbaum 1993). All but one of the previously reported trials scanned subjects during the course of clinical treatment, with confounding of order effects, patient medication responsiveness, and a variety of doctor's choice neuroleptic medications and doses as well as a lack of placebo-controlled, blinded ratings. Both our study and the recent study by Bartlett et al. (1991) show the problems of the use of several medications with the demonstration of differences between thiothixene and other neuroleptics. In our current design (Buchsbaum et al. 1992), all patients received medication treatment in a random order. The dosage was titrated to the patient's own optimal clinical effect. The behavioral rating data was obtained entirely separate from medication status.

We hypothesized that patients with abnormally low metabolic rates in the striatum might be receiving excessive inhibitory dopaminergic input from the ventral tegmental area and substantia nigra and therefore would have function normalized by the dopaminergic blockade of neuroleptics (Bunney 1988, 1990, Carlsson and Carlsson 1990). By contrast, individual patients without this inhibition would be expected to show normal metabolic rates in the striatum and therefore demonstrate little change either in regional metabolism or clinical symptoms with haloperidol treatment.

## Empirical findings

### *Prediction of neuroleptic response*

*Patients.* Twenty-five patients with schizophrenia (21 men, 4 woman, mean age 34.8, SD=8.7, range 20–54) entered this trial (reported in additional detail in Buchsbaum et al. 1992). The 18-item BPRS (Overall and Gorham 1962) was obtained on all subjects at weekly intervals and had a mean value of 39.1 (SD=8.6), at the time of the off-medication PET scan. Patients were recruited from the research programs of the University of California at Irvine (UCI) and San Diego (UCSD), the UCI Emergency Room, and chronic care facilities of Metropolitan State Hospital to achieve heterogeneity in medication responsiveness. Fourteen were outpatients and 11 were inpatients.

*Design.* Patients entered a 10-week, double-blind crossover trial. Patients on stable oral medication entered the study after screening. All subjects received either haloperidol and then placebo or placebo and then haloperidol for weeks 1–5 and weeks 6–10. PET scans were obtained during weeks 5 and 10. This was done to control effects of previous medication and order effects. Four patients had never received neuroleptic medication at the time they entered the trial. Thus half of the patients (haloperidol first) were off medication five weeks when receiving their placebo period scan; the other half were off a median of 5 weeks (placebo first) with 2 never previously medicated and one off four years.

Patients were clinically assessed using the BPRS at weekly intervals by trained raters. The same rater was used for weeks 5 and 10.

The research psychiatrists (SP, BS, JL), who were blind to drug assignment, ordered capsules on a flexible dosage schedule, beginning at 4 mg, according to their clinical judgment. Increases in dosage were continued until the achievement of marked therapeutic effect on the BPRS, until the appearance of dose-limiting side effects, or until a maximum of five capsules (20 mg/day when haloperidol). The mean dose used was 11.0 mg haloperidol. Benztropine (2 mg bid) was given with haloperidol (0 mg with placebo) for extrapyramidal side-effects and was stopped 24 hours before the PET scan to minimize the effects.

*Uptake and scanning.* All subjects did the continuous performance test (CPT) during the uptake of fluorodeoxyglucose (FDG) (Nuechterlein et al. 1983). This task has been widely reported to show poor performance in patients with schizophrenia and in their offspring (Cornblatt et al. 1989). The subject observed a series of blurred digits on a display and was required to press a button to the target number "0", which occured 25 % of the time. Since the task requires sustained vigilance, the FDG method which integrates cerebral metabolic activity over a 30 minute period is especially suitable. Imaging of shorter intervals of activity, for example with 015 blood flow method, could not assess the maintenance of vigilance over time which has been hypothesized to be a core deficit in schizophrenia.

Subjects were moved to the scanner 32–45 minutes after FDG injection. An individually molded, thermoplastic headholder was made for each subject to minimize head movement and to allow the subject's accurate repositioning on the second scan.

The scans were performed with in-plane resolution of 7.6 mm and resolution of 10.9 mm in the axial dimension. Scan raw count images to glucose metabolic rate as done elsewhere (Buchsbaum et al. 1984, 1989) are reported in micromoles glucose/100 grams/minute. Subcortical structures were assessed using stereotaxic coordinates derived from a standard neuroanatomical atlas (Matsui and Hirano 1978). The caudate and putamen were measured using the same atlas and a sterotaxic atlas method as described elsewhere (Siegel et al. 1993). All subcortical regions were 3 by 3 pixel squares and were validated with magnetic resonance imaging (MRI) in 20 normal controls as described elsewhere (Buchsbaum et al. 1991). Regions of interest were analyzed as mean metabolic rate for all structures. Values were also expressed as relative metabolic rate for the cortex, as metabolic rate/whole brain metabolic rate, and for subcortical regions of interest as metabolic rate/whole slice metabolic rate.

*Haloperidol response.* Patients were divided into responders (n = 12) and nonresponders (n = 13) based on the difference between the mean of weeks 4 and 5 BPRS ratings for placebo and active compound; this division was independent of any PET analysis. Responders had improvement (median -7.5 point BPRS drop) and nonresponders had worsening (median 5 point BPRS increase). The haloperidol dose did not differ between groups (responders 11.8, SD=5,9; nonresponders 10.1, SD=6,3; t=0.68, p=NS). Responders were somewhat older (39 ± 9.4 years) than nonresponders (31 ± 7.2 years), but total BPRS scores at baseline did not differ in the two groups (responders = 42 ± 7.9; nonresponders = 36 ± 9.7, p=NS). Responders had significantly lower relative metabolic rates in the striatum when off medication in the placebo period (1.18 ± 0.26) than nonresponders did (1.27 ± 0.27, F=4.92, df=1,23, p=.037 (Fig. 1)). For both relative and absolute data, responder-nonresponder differences were greater for the ventral putamen (28% slice) than for the dorsal putamen (42% slice); this gradient was less marked in the caudate (ANOVA in Table 1; Buchsbaum et al. 1992).

Haloperidol increased relative metabolic rate in the striatum (placebo 1.23, SD=.28 vs haloperidol 1.29, SD .29, F=5.88, df=1,23, P=.02). Responders also had significantly larger increases in relative metabolic rate on haloperidol than did nonresponders, who showed high levels of activity on placebo that did not change appreciably with haloperidol treatment. Medication effects were greater in the right than the left hemisphere for the caudate, but not the posterior putamen.

Multiple discriminant analysis (BMDP 7M) (Dixon 1982) identified metabolic activity in the right inferior putamen (28% slice) and the left caudate (41% slice) on placebo as the best predictors of response to haloperidol, with 78.3% of subjects identified correctly (F=5.9, df=2,20, P<.01); jackknifed classification had same percentage correct.

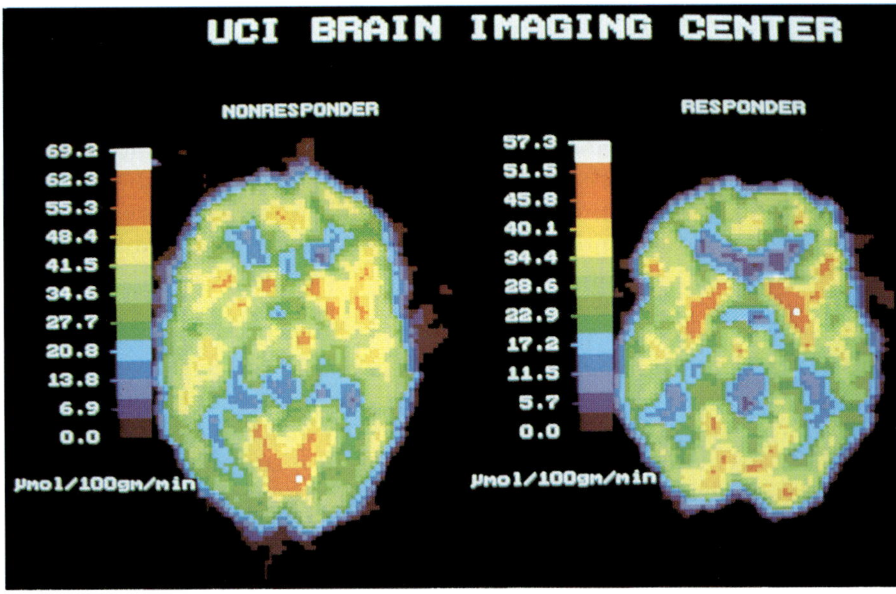


**Fig. 1.** Positron emission tomography scans of patients off medication for five weeks in randomized, double-blind crossover comparison of haloperidol and placebo. A typical clinical nonresponder to haloperidol is shown on the left and a responder on the right. Note the relatively low metabolic rate in the basal ganglia of the responder. In contrast, the nonresponder has a higher metabolic rate in the basal ganglia on placebo. Scans are presented with a metabolic rate scale in micromoles of glucose/100g brain/min. with red and yellow indicating high metabolic rate and blue and purple indicating low metabolic rate

**Table 1.** Ventral putamen glucose metabolic rate

| | LEFT | | RIGHT | |
|---|---|---|---|---|
| | Mean | SD | Mean | SD |
| Responder | 1.12 | .09 | 1.03[3] | .29 |
| Nonresponder | 1.27 | .18 | 1.36 | .22 |
| Normal controls | 1.13 | .14 | 1.20 | .17 |
| Schizophrenics | 1.12 | .19 | 1.14 | .17 |
| Quads | 1.22 | .10 | 1.28[a] | .10 |
| Normal controls | 1.22 | .10 | 1.09 | .04[b] |

[a] Significantly different from nonresponders, $p<0.05$; [b] variance significantly smaller than quads, $p<0.05$

*Correlations between change in metabolic rate and symptoms.* As observed earlier (Buchsbaum et al. 1992) patients who showed the greatest increases in relative metabolic rate in the striatum tended to have the greatest symptomatic improvement. This was strongest for the 28 % slice level where correlations between total BPRS improvement score and caudate, anterior putamen and posterior putamen for both right and left hemisphere were all in the predicted direction, and the correlation for the right putamen reached statistical significance (-.43, $P<.05$). Exploration of this relationship with individual subscales of the BPRS revealed that the correlation did not appear to have its origin in motor retardation or uncooperativeness (which had only positive correlations at the most dorsal level) but more in blunted affect, somatic concern, emotional withdrawal, guilt feelings, and suspiciousness, all having significant negative correlations at the ventral level.

### *Neuroleptic response in identical quadruplets*

*Case history.* The patients were four 51 year old identical quadruplets. Nora, Iris, Myra and Hester (in birth order) all received the diagnosis of schizophrenia by the age of 24. Nora, Iris, and Myra graduated from high school, but Hester had withdrawn from school in 11th grade because of emotional problems. Nora and Iris became ill within a few months of each other, about two years after graduation, and both were hospitalized for "schizophrenic reaction, catatonic type" in 1951–1952. Myra and Hester had their first hospital admission at the National Institute of Mental Health (NIMH) in 1955, but had had major psychiatric symptoms between 1951 and 1955. The quadruplets' birth, childhood, and initial NIMH studies in 1955 are described elsewhere (Rosenthal 1963) and presented in tabular form in the reports from their 1981–1982 NIMH studies (DeLisi et al. 1984). Lifetime psychiatric diagnoses using the Research Diagnostic Criteria were made on each patient in 1982 (Nora: Schizophrenia, chronic undifferentiated; Iris: Schizophrenia, chronic; Myra: Schizoaffective Disorder, schizophrenia residual type; Hester: Schizophrenia, chronic undifferentiated). Neurochemical, attentional, social, and historical data are presented elsewhere (Buchsbaum et al. 1984, DeLisi et al. 1984, Mirsky et al. 1984). Six adult normal controls served as a comparison group.

*Neuroleptic response.* The quadruplets differential response to neuroleptics was noteworthy. Nora and Hester had modest clinical response, Iris had minimal response, and Myra was actually worse on medication and was discharged off medication (DeLisi et al. 1984).

*Positron emission tomography.* Cerebral glucography was obtained in 1981 at the Intramural Research Program of the National Institute of Mental Health, Bethesda, Maryland, with PET scanning as described elsewhere (Buchsbaum et al. 1982). The reduced metabolic rates in the frontal lobe shown by the quadruplets and the familial effects are reported using analytic methods matching our recent studies (Buchsbaum 1993). The subjects sat in a darkened room with their eyes closed. $^{18}$F-deoxyglucose (3–5 mCi) was injected intravenously. Subjects remained still during the 35-minute radiotracer uptake period to match our six concurrent normal controls and eight patients with schizophrenia. After the uptake period, the subjects were moved to our ECAT scanner where six to eight horizontal planes were obtained with in-plane resolution of 15mm. Scans were reprocessed for this report using exactly the same stereotaxic approach as described for our current anatomical approach.

*Striatal metabolic rate.* All four quadruplets tended to have higher metabolic rate in the striatum than our normal controls. This reached statistical significance for the right caudate at the 34 % level and right putamen at the 28 % level (Matsui and Hirano 1978), except for the dorsal caudate values, which were low in comparison to higher resolution scans (0.98 in quads, .84 in normals, t=1.44, p=ns), putamen values tended to be even higher in the quads than in current normals (Table 1). We also contrasted the variance within the quads and within the normals. The quads were generally more variable as a group than normal controls, and this was significant for dorsal caudate and ventral putamen (Table 1). Thus metabolic rate variability seemed to match the drug response heterogeneity observed. Comparing the metabolic rates in the right infe-

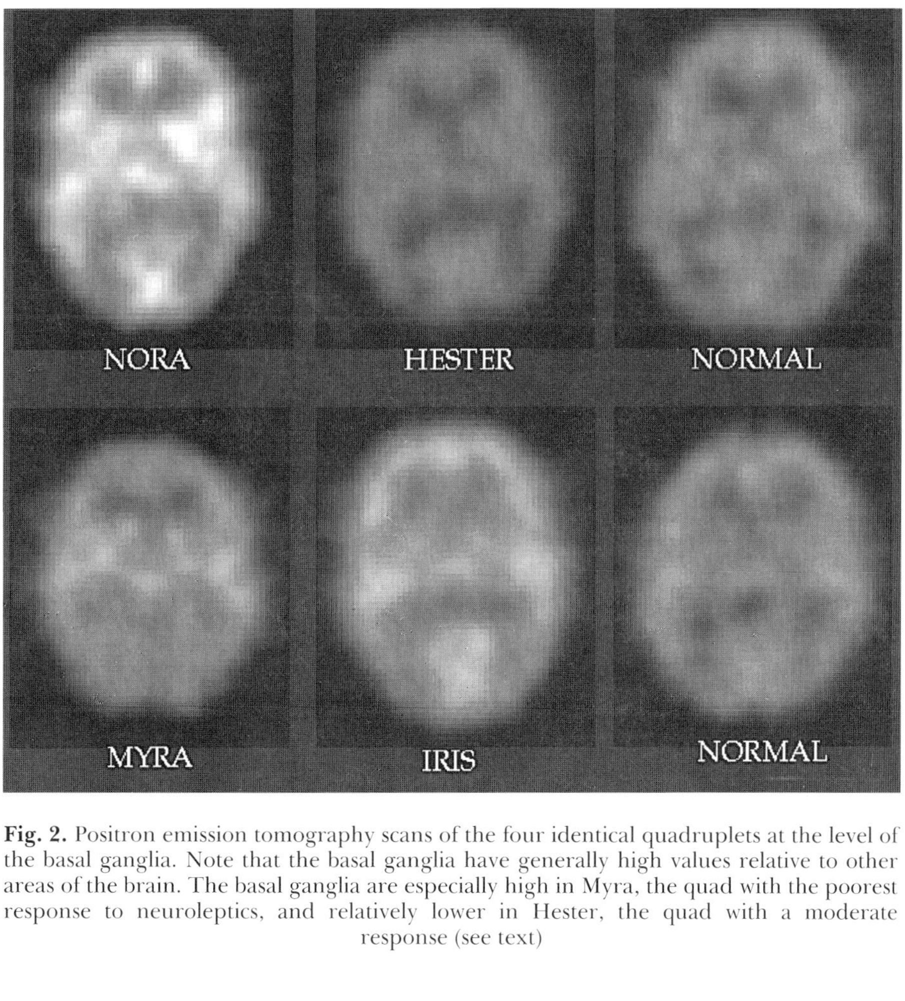


**Fig. 2.** Positron emission tomography scans of the four identical quadruplets at the level of the basal ganglia. Note that the basal ganglia have generally high values relative to other areas of the brain. The basal ganglia are especially high in Myra, the quad with the poorest response to neuroleptics, and relatively lower in Hester, the quad with a moderate response (see text)

rior putamen, selected in our current sample of 25 schizophrenics (Buchsbaum et al. 1992) as the best predictor of neuroleptic response, the quads showed values for Nora (1.17), Iris (1.25), Myra (1.41), and Hester (1.22) that paralleled individual differences in drug response (DeLisi et al. 1984). Myra, the quad with the highest value showed the poorest response (worse on medication) and Nora, the quad with the lowest value, showed the best neuroleptic response (Fig. 2).

## Discussion

Our data suggest that the relative metabolic rate in the striatum, more than that in any other structure, is related to clinical response to neuroleptics. The striatum shows the largest and most consistent changes with haloperidol, and patients who respond clinically show the lowest values on placebo. Not only do a number of studies show that dopamine antagonists increase striatal metabolic rate (Buchsbaum et al. 1993), but dopamine agonists appear to lower metabolic rate (Cleghorn 1991, Wolkin 1987). Thus, metabolic rate appears to be a useful measure for assessing striatal activity. Thalamic areas, including the anterior thalamus, also show some decreases, and cortical decreases in the inferior frontal and middle temporal gyrus are at trend levels. Limbic structures, including the hippocampus and amygdala, may be affected, but other limbic structures such as the cingulate gyrus showed no changes (Buchsbaum et al. 1992). Taken together, this pattern of effects in descending order, striatum, thalamus, and cortex, might be related to the circuits linking striatum and cortex described by Alexander et al. (1986). They viewed the basal ganglia as a mechanism to concentrate information from the cortex and provide a cortical-basal ganglia-thalamus-cortex regulatory loop. Haloperidol might work at least partly by diminishing abnormally active VTA and substantia nigra dopaminergic pathways inhibiting the basal ganglia. If this were so, we might expect the metabolic effects to be greatest in the striatum and then diminished and diffused in successively later stages of the circuit. These authors stress the separate motor and association circuits, and propose a lateral-orbitofrontal pathway with ventromedial striatum and anterior and medial dorsal thalamus possibly linked to attentional performance and the maintenance of attentional set. This set of structures seems to fit our data the best, consistent both with our previous findings of low inferior frontal and ventral striatal values in never-medicated schizophrenics (Buchsbaum et al. 1990, 1992), as well as with the current pattern of successively diminished effects in basal ganglia, thalamus and cortex. Components of the motor loop, including the supplementary motor area and ventrolateral thalamus, were neither different between normal subjects and schizophrenics nor affected by haloperidol. The attenuated effects in the frontal lobe and/or lack of effect on the motor loop may be consistent with the minimal effects of haloperidol on CPT performance. Interestingly, Iyo et al. (1993) using

N-methylspiperone found that the ratio of binding availability in the striatum to that in the frontal cortex differentiated subjects who had experienced methamphetamine psychosis, while data from the two regions independently did not differentiate the groups. This is consistent with the importance of frontal/striatal connection.

The greater difference between responders and nonresponders off medication (placebo baseline) in the ventral than the dorsal putamen and the apparent relation of the ventral striatum to medication response within identical quadruplets is of interest. It suggests that ventral striatal activity might relate to the functional state of the neuroleptic response system rather than to trait-like or genetic features of schizophrenia. These functional states could be the result of previous neuroleptic history or be episode rather than diathesis markers. The association between ventral medial regions of the striatum and the limbic system has been discussed above. Further, patients with schizophrenia had a much greater increase in D2 receptor density in the ventral putamen than in dorsal regions when compared to normal controls (Joyce et al. 1988).

While resolution of dorsal/ventral differences is within the capabilities of the scanner used in collection of this data, it is clear that the lower portions of the striatum are complex in structure and are close to the bottom of the brain. Accurate matching with MRI templates at higher PET resolution (Cohen et al. 1992, Harris and Pearlson 1993) will be advantageous in further understanding of the metabolic correlates of neuroleptic response and differences between new neuroleptics. Large clinical samples will be needed in further studies to better understand the relationship of episode, medication induced change and underlying genetic heterogeneity.

## Acknowledgements

This research was supported by grants from the National Institute of Mental Health (MH40071 to Dr. Buchsbaum, The Neuroscience Center for Research in Schizophrenia, MH 44188 to Dr. Bunney, and MH45962 to Dr. Potkin. At Mount Sinai, J. Spiegel provided computer systems assistance. In California, The Brain Imaging Commitee and the Irvine Health Foundation also provided support. D. Harvey and M. Sleek provided administrative assistance, A. Peterson, H. Bair, C. Tang, S. Tang, C. Reynolds, and L. La Casse technical assistance, and M. Rose and K. Fox nursing support. P. Jerabek and A. Najafi produced FDG.

## References

Alexander GE, DeLong MR, Strick PL (1986) Parallel organization of functionally segregated circuits linking basal ganglia and cortex. Ann Rev Neurosci 9:357–81

Bartlett EJ, Wolkin A, Brodie JD, Laska EM, Wolf AP (1991) Importance of pharmacologic control in PET studies: effects of thiothixene and haloperidol on cerebral glucose utilization in chronic schizophrenia. Psychiatry Res: Neuroimaging 40:115–124

Brown WA, Herz LR (1989) Response to neuroleptic drugs as a device for classifying schizophrenia. Schizophr Bull 15:123–129

Buchsbaum MS (1993) Critical review of psychopathology in twins: structural and functional imaging of the brain. In: Bouchard TJ Jr, Propping P (eds) Twins as a tool of behavioral genetics. John Wiley, Sussex, pp 257–271

Buchsbaum MS, Gillin JC, Wu J, Hazlett E, Sicotte N, DuPont RM (1989) Regional cerebral glucose metabolic rate in human sleep assessed by positron emission tomography. Life Sci 45:1349–1356

Buchsbaum MS, Haier RJ, Potkin SG, Nuechterlein K, Bracha S, Lohr J, Wu J, Lottenberg S, Jerabek PA, Trenary M, Tafalla R, Reynolds C, Bunney WE Jr (1992) Fronto-striatal disorder of cerebral metabolism in never-medicated schizophrenics. Arch Gen Psychiatry 49:935–942

Buchsbaum MS, Ingvar DH, Kessler R, Waters RN, Cappelletti J, van Kammen DP, King AC, Johnson JJ, Manning RG, Flynn RM, Mann LS, Bunney WE, Sokoloff L (1982) Cerebral glucography with positron tomography in normals and in patients with schizophrenia. Arch Gen Psychiatry 39:251–259

Buchsbaum MS, Mirsky AF, DeLisi LE, Morihisa J, Karson CN, Mendelson WB, King AC, Johnson J, Kessler R (1984) The Genain quadruplets: electrophysiological, positron emission and X-ray tomographic studies. Psychiatry Res 13:95–108

Buchsbaum MS, Nuechterlein KH, Haier RJ, Wu J, Sicotte N, Hazlett E, Asarnow R, Potkin S, Guich S (1990) Glucose metabolic rate in normals and schizophrenics during the continuous performance test assessed by positron emission tomography. Br J Psychiatry 156:216–227

Buchsbaum MS, Potkin SG, Marhall JF, Lottenberg S, Tang CY, Heh CW, Tafalla R, Reynolds C, Abel L, Plon L, Bunney WE Jr (1992) Effects of clozapine and thiothixene on glucose metabolic rate in schizophrenia. Neuropsychopharmacology 6(3):155–163

Buchsbaum MS, Potkin SG, Siegel BV, Lohr J, Katz M, Gottschalk LA, Gulasekaram B, Marshall JF, Lottenberg S, Teng CY, Abel L, Plon L, Bunney WE (1992) Striatal metabolic rate and clinical response to neuroleptics in schizophrenia. Arch Gen Psychiatry 49:966–974

Buchsbaum MS, Siegel BV (1994) Neuroimaging and the aging process in psychiatry. Int Rev Psychiatry 6:109–118

Buchsbaum MS, Tafalla RJ, Reynolds C, Trenary M, Burgwald L, Potkin S, Bunney WE Jr (1991) Drug effects on brain lateralization in the basal ganglia of schizophrenics. In: Willner P, Scheel-Kruger J (eds) The mesolimbic system: from motivation to action. John Wiley, Sussex, pp 529–538

Buchsbaum MS, Wu JC, DeLisi LE, Holcomb HH, Hazlett E, Cooper-Langston K, Kessler R (1987) Positron emission tomography studies of basal ganglia and somatosensory cortex neuroleptic drug effects: differences between normal controls and schizophrenic patients. Biol Psychiatry 22:479–494

Bunney WE Jr (1988) A view of the neurosciences and psychopharmacology of the major psychoses – present and future. CINP, Munich, Germany (Abstract)

Bunney WE Jr (1990) Dopamine glutamate interactions in schizophrenia. American College of Neuropsychopharmacology (ACNP), San Juan, Puerto Rico, December 10–14, p 44 (Abstract)

Carlsson M, Carlsson A (1990) Schizophrenia: a subcortical neurotransmitter imbalance syndrome? Schizophr Bull 16:425–432

Carpenter WT Jr, Heinrichs DW (1981) Treatment-relevant subtypes of schizophrenia. J Nerv Ment Dis 169:113–119

Cleghorn JM, Szechtman H, Garnett ES, Nahmias C, Brown GM, Kaplan RD, Szechtman B, Franco S (1991) Apomorphine effects on brain matabolism in neuroleptic-naive schizophrenic patients. Psychiatry Res: Neuroimaging 40:135–153

Cohen G, Andreasen NC, Allinger R, Arndt S, Kuan J, Yuh W, Ehrhardt J (1992) Segmentation techniques for the classification of brain tissue using magnetic resonance imaging. Psychiatry Res: Neuroimaging 45:33–51

Cornblatt BA, Lenzenweger MF, Ertenmeyer-Kimting L (1989) The continuous performance test, idential pairs version. II. Contrasting attentional profiles in schizophrenic and depressed patients. Psychiatry Res 29:65–85

Dixon WJ (1982) BMD Biomedical computer programs. University of California Press, Berkeley Ca

DeLisi LE, Mirsky AF, Buchsbaum MS, van Kammen DP, Berman KF, Caton C, Kafka MS, Ninan PT, Phelps BH, Karoum F, Ko GN, Korpi EN, Linnoila M, Scheinin M, Wyatt RJ (1984) The Genain quadruplets 25 years later: a diagnostic and biochemical follow up. Psychiatry Res 13:59–76

Farde L, Hall H, Ehrin E, Sedvall G (1986) Quantitative analysis of $D_2$ dopamine receptor binding in the living human brain by PET. Science 231:258–261

Garver DL, Kelly K, Fried KA, Magnusson M, Hirschowitz J (1988) Drug response patterns as a basis of nosology for the mood-incongruent psychoses (the schizophrenias). Psychol Med 18:873–885

Harris GJ, Pearlson GD (1993) MRI-guided region of interest placement on emission computed tomograms. Psychiatry Res: Neuroimaging 50:57–63

Iyo M, Nishiro M, Itoh T, Fukuda H, Suzuki K, Yamasaki T, Fukui S, Tateno Y (1992) Dopamine $D_2$ and serotonin$_2$ receptors in susceptibility to methamphetamine psychosis detected by positron emission tomography. Psychiatry Res: Neuroimaging 50(4):217–231

Joyce JN, Lexow N, Bird E, Winokur A (1988) Organization of dopmaine D1 and D2 receptors in human striatum: receptor autoradiographic studies in huntington's disease and schizophrenia. Synapse 2:546–557

Matsui T, Hirano A (1978) An atlas of the human brain for computerized tomography. Igaku-Shoin, Tokyo

Mirksy AF, DeLisi LE, Buchsbaum MS, Quinn OW, Schwerdt P, Siever LJ, Mann L, Weingartner H, Zec R, Sostek A, Alterman I, Revere I, Dawson SD, Zahn TP (1984) The Genain quadruplets: psychological studies. Psychiatry Res 13:77–93

Nuechterlein KH, Parasuraman R, Jiang Q (1983) Visual sustained attention: image degradation produces rapid decrement over time. Science 220:327–329

Overall JE, Gorham DR (1962) The Brief Psychiatric Rating Scale. Psychol Rep 10:799–812

Rosenthal D (1963) The Genain quadruplets. Basic Books, New York

Siegel BV, Buchsbaum MS, Bunney WE, Gottschalk LA, Haier RJ, Lohr JB, Lottenberg S, Najafi A, Nuechterlein KH, Potkin SG, Wu JC (1993) Cortical-striatal-thalamic circuits and brain glucose metabolic activity in 70 unmedicated male schizophrenic. Am J Psychiatry 150:1325–1336

Tune LE, Wong DF, Pearlson G, Strauss M, Young T, Shaya EK, Dannals RF, Wilson AA, Ravert HT, Sapp J, Cooper T, Chase GA, Wagner HN Jr (1993) Dopamine $D_2$receptor density estimates in schizophrenia: a positron emission tomography study with $^{11}$C-N-methylspiperone. Psychiatry Res 49(3):219–237

Wolkin A, Angrist B, Wolf A, Brodie J, Wolkin B, Jaeger J, Cancro R, Rotrosen J (1987) Effects of amphetamine on local cerebral metabolism in normal and schizophrenic subjects as determined by positron emission tomography. Psychopharmacology 92:241–246

Wong DF, Wagner HN Jr, Tune LE, Dannals RF, Pearlson GD, Links JM, Tamminga CA, Broussolle EP, Ravert HT, Wilson AA, Toung TJK, Malat J, Williams JA, O'Tuama LA, Snyder SH, Kuhar MJ, Gjedde A (1986) Positron emission tomography reveals elevated $D_2$ dopamine receptors in drug-naive schizophrenics. Science 234:1558–1563

**Authors' address:** Prof. Dr. M. S. Buchsbaum, Department of Psychiatry, Mount Sinai School of Medicine, Box 1505, 1 Gustave Levy Place, New York, NY 10029, U.S.A.

# Brain morphology and prediction of neuroleptic treatment response in schizophrenia

**P. Falkai**[1] and **B. Bogerts**[2]

[1]Department of Psychiatry, University of Düsseldorf, and
[2]Department of Psychiatry, University of Magdeburg,
Federal Republic of Germany

## Summary

Since the introduction of computed tomography into schizophrenia research, many studies were performed to correlate brain morphology with neuroleptic treatment response. CT measures like the VBR, third ventricular size, cerebral asymmetry and cortical enlargement yielded equivocal results. As temporal and frontal lobe structures are involved in the pathophysiology of schizophrenia, a CT scan study with 143 schizophrenic responders and non-responders after 4 weeks of haloperidol treatment was performed using 12 different measures focussing on frontal and peritemporal cerebrospinal fluid spaces. Beside a significantly enlarged basotemporal, a trendwise enlarged parasagittal cerebrospinal fluid space, and a significantly reduced frontal lobe asymmetry in non-responders, none of the other measures helped to predict short-term neuroleptic response. Methodological problems of this study and future perspectives of brain morphology in treatment prediction research are discussed.

## Introduction

The attempt to correlate brain morphology and prediction of neuroleptic treatment response in schizophrenic patients goes back nearly 30 years ago, when Cazzullo (1963) published the striking observation that schizophrenics who had enlarged ventricles as assessed by pneumoencephalography had relatively poorer response to antipsychotic treatment than did patients who had no signs of enlargement of CSF (= cerebral spinal fluid) spaces. He reported that those patients who had abnormal pneumoencephalograms (PEG), had poorer prognosis for antipsychotic medication response. Since the introduction of computertomography (CT) into schizophrenia research (Johnstone et al. 1976), several studies supported this finding, but others did not.

We reviewed 18 studies which compared *VBR* (ventricle to brain ratio = maximal area of the lateral ventricles in percent of the adjacent whole brain area) and other lateral ventricular parameters with treatment response to D2-(dopamine-2-receptor) blocking agents. 9 authors found a significantly *enlarged VBR* in **neuroleptic non-responders** (DeQuardo et al. 1988, Gattaz et al. 1988, Luchins et al. 1983, Nasrallah et al. 1980, Pandurangi et al. 1989, Schulz et al. 1983, Smith et al. 1985, Smith and Maser 1983, Weinberger et al. 1980), while 9 studies (Boronow et al. 1985, Kling et al. 1983, Losonczy et al. 1986, Nasrallah et al. 1983a, Nimgaonkar et al. 1988, Ninan et al. 1989, Panduarangi et al. 1986, Shelton et al. 1988, Silverman et al. 1987) did not support this finding.

Reanalysis of the data of Weinberger et al. (1980), Jeste et al. (1982) concluded, that patients with a VBR outside the normal range (> 2 standard deviations) of the control subjects were always non-responders. On the other hand patients within the normal range could not clearly be classified as being treatment refractory or not. This finding was replicated in two subsequent studies (Luchins et al. 1983, Schulz et al. 1983).

None of the 7 studies examining the *size of the third ventricle* and *neuroleptic non-response*, found a correlation between these two parameters (Boronow et al. 1985, Kaiya et al. 1989, Kaplan et al. 1990, MacDonald et al. 1989, Naber et al. 1985, Ninan et al. 1989, Shelton et al. 1988).

One study (Smith and Maser 1983) described an association between neuroleptic treatment outcome and a medium sized enlargement of the cortical sulci, while specifically narrow or wide sulci were correlated with non-response. 8 studies found no connection between *cortical atrophy* and non-response (Boronow et al. 1985, Buckman et al. 1990, MacDonald et al. 1989, Naber et al. 1985, Nasrallah et al. 1983b, Ninan et al. 1989, Shelton et al. 1988, Smith et al. 1987).

Some studies revealed an inversion of the *normal cerebral asymmetry* in schizophrenia (Luchins et al. 1979, 1982, Luchins and Meltzer 1986, Tsai et al. 1983). In the CT scans of right handed control subjects the right frontal lobe is bigger than the left one and the left occipital lobe bigger than the right counterpart (LeMay and Kido 1978, Weinberger et al. 1982, Zatz et al. 1982). This loss of cerebral asymmetry in schizophrenia however showed no correlation to neuroleptic treatment outcome (Luchins and Meltzer 1983, Smith et al. 1987).

In a metaanalysis of 33 CT scan studies, Friedman et al. (1992) could not support the notion that structural brain abnormalities in general predict antipsychotic response. However, age, illness duration, and age of onset of the patient cohort, the percentage of patients with marked structural abnormalities included in the study overall, the duration of treatment and the degree of symptom improvement were significant predictors of antipsychotic treatment response, while date of study, gender and presence of washout period were unrelated.

In summary the literature provides equivocal results on the significance of CT scan brain morphology and neuroleptic treatment outcome in schizophrenic patients. The heterogeneity of the results presented may be a result of variable definitions of outcome to neuroleptic therapy. In addition, diverging morphometric criteria and the heterogeneity of schizophrenia itself may have also contributed to the inconsistency of results.

In the present study focussing on frontal and temporo-limbic spinal fluid spaces, the CT scans of haloperidol responders were compared with haloperidol non-responders with the help of a recently introduced delineation method (Bogerts et al. 1987).

## Demographic characteristics of patients and control subjects

143 schizophrenic patients of the Department of Psychiatry, University of Düsseldorf, took part in dose-response studies with haloperidol (mean dosage 15mg/day) over a period of 4 weeks. Based on clinical global impression (CGI) they were classified into patients improving markedly (= responders), marginally or not improving at all (non-responders). 75 patients classified as responders (20 males, 55 females; mean age 36), and 68 as non-responders (24 males, 44 females; mean age 33) were included into the study. Mean age, sex ratio and mean duration of illness was not significantly different in both groups. For further details see Table 1.

**Table 1.** Group characteristics of 143 schizophrenic responders and non-responders

| | Responders | Non-responders |
|---|---|---|
| Number | 75 | 68 |
| Sex (m/f) | 20/55 | 24/44 |
| Mean age (years) | 36 | 33 |
| Mean duration of illness (years) | 5.3 | 6.6 |

### *Morphometric methods*

From each brain 10 transversal standard sections (15 % to the orbitomeatal line, 9 mm distance between each other) were 4 x enlarged by overhead projection. All well delineable outer and inner cerebral spinal fluid spaces were outlined on paper and their area was determined by planimetry. The following structures were determined:

1. VBR (ventricle to brain ratio = maximal area of the lateral ventricles in percent of the adjacent whole brain area),

2. relative total area of all frontal and all parieto-occipital sulci (expressed as percent of the whole brain area at the VBR-level, to have a "sulcus to brain ratio") on the first four CT levels,
3. relative total area of the interhemispheric fissure (in percent of the whole brain area at the VBR-level) on the same four CT levels,
4. relative area (in percent of the whole brain area at the VBR-level) of the temporal subarachnoidal space, mainly formed by the lateral sulcus, on four defined levels (T1: level of the first section through the thalamus; T2: level of the pineal gland; T3: level of the cisterna quadrigemina; T4: level of the basal cisterns),
5. maximal width of the 3rd ventricle,
6. maximal area of the temporal horn, situated in the temporal lobe adjacent to the hippocampal formation,
7. ratios of right/left frontal and left/right occipital lobe width. The widths of the frontal and occipital lobes were measured as follows (see Fig. 1a and b). Proceeding from the vertex, the first slice showing the pineal gland was chosen. A vertical line intersecting the most caudal point of the falx, the septum pellucidum, and the pineal was drawn. A line was constructed perpendicular to this, at the level of the posterior end of the falx for the measurement of the left and right frontal lobe widths. A perpendicular line was constructed at the posterior extent of the cerebellar cistern for the measurement of the left and right occipital lobe widths. The right frontal lobe is usually wider than the left, and the left occipital lobe is usually wider than the right.

A detailed description of these methodological issues can be found in Bogerts et al. (1987), Falkai et al. (1993).

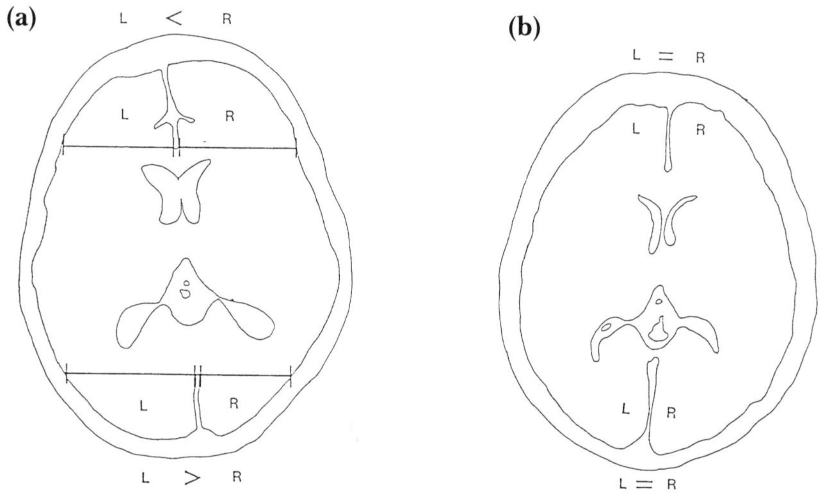


**Fig. 1.** CT-scans of a control (a) with normal and a schizophrenic patient (b) with inverse asymmetry at the level of the pineal gland indicating the distances for frontal and occipital lobe measurements

For the statistical analysis of the data an ANOVA (diagnosis by sex) was performed using program package BMDP 7D.

## Results

There was no significant difference between responders and non-repsonders concerning the VBR (see Fig. 2), third ventricular width (see Fig. 3), relative total area of frontal, parieto-occipital sulci, the relative area of the three upper temporal subarachnoidal spaces (T1 – T3) and temporal horn area. For summary of the values see Tables 2 and 3. There was a trend towards a larger area of the interhemispheric fissure in non-responders (males +36 %, females +66 %; p =.11) and the relative area of the lateral sulcus on level T4 (see Fig. 4) was significantly larger in non-responding schizophrenics on the left side (males: +138 %, females: +7; p =.04) and showed a trend towards an enlargement on the right side (males: +68 %, females: 107 %; p =.08).

Of interest was the observation of *sex differences concerning cortical sulci and temporal horn measurements*. While female non-responders revealed a trend towards enlarged frontal and parieto-occipital sulci, male responders did not point into this direction or even demonstrated the reverse. While temporal horn measurements showed no significant difference between the groups, seperate analysis by sex showed female non-responders had significantly bigger values compared to sex-matched responders (+71%, p<.02, see Fig. 5).

The ratios for frontal but not occipital lobe asymmetry were significantly (p =.018) increased indicating absence of normal cerebral asymmetry in non-responders (see Fig. 6 and 7).

## Discussion

Most morphometric CT scan measures do not seem to distinguish schizophrenic patients responding well to classical neuroleptics from those who do not. Two shortcomings of this study should be mentioned: 1. The *definition of response* to neuroleptics was not based on a standard scale like the BPRS, but by simple clinical judgement – which may have introduced some bias. 2. Using *computed tomography* may be not sensitive enough to detect distinct morphological differences. Magnetic resonance imaging (MRI) is possibly more suitable to detect subtle differences.

Regions, where non-responders significantly or trendwise differed from responders in this study, were the temporobasal level (T4) of the lateral sulcus and the parasagittal cerebrospinal fluid space, which border on important limbic (e. g. hippocampus and amygdala) as well as paralimbic regions (e. g. cingulate gyrus). For further details see Bogerts et al. (1987). Interestingly these regions are identical with those, which are thought to play a pivotal role in the pathophysiology of schizophre-

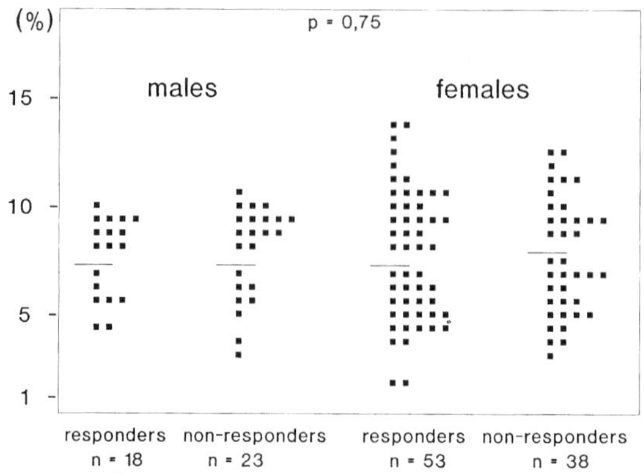


**Fig. 2.** VBR in schizophrenic responders and non-responders

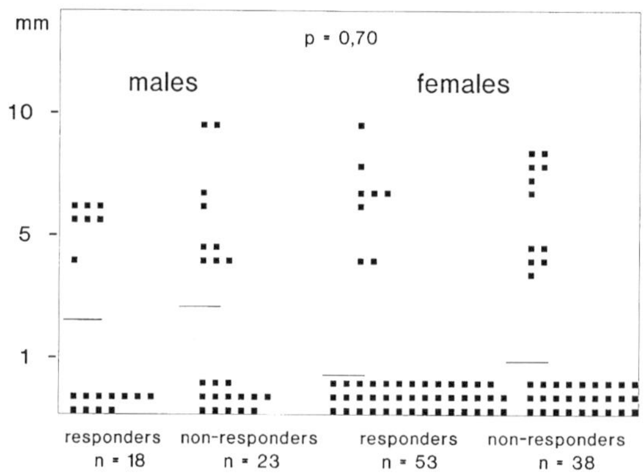


**Fig. 3.** Maximal width of the 3rd ventricle in schizophrenic responders and non-respond-ers

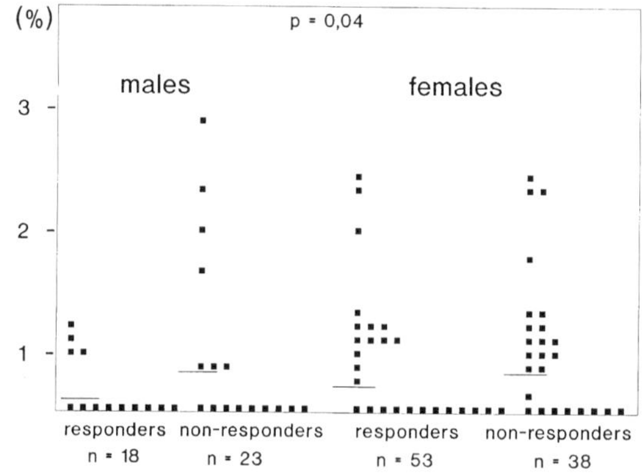


**Fig. 4.** Lateral sulcus in % of whole brain area [tempora-basal level (D)]

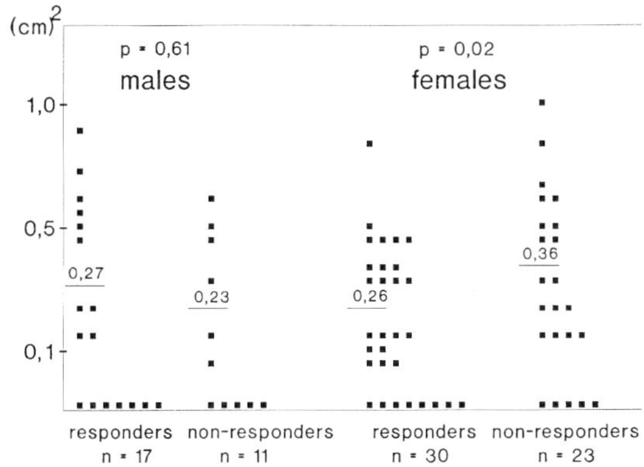


**Fig. 5.** Right temporal horn area in schizophrenic responders and non-responders

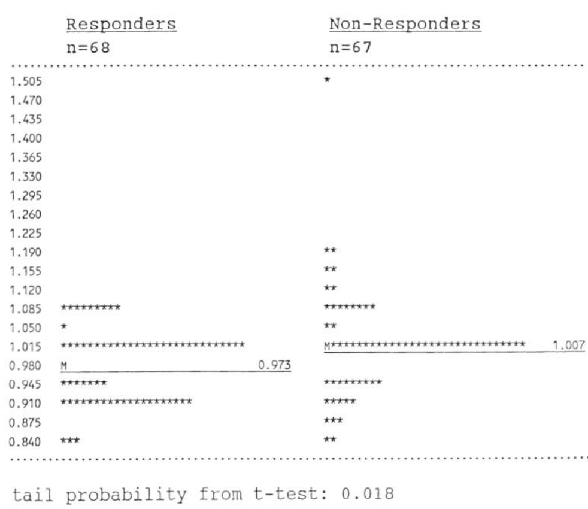


**Fig. 6.** Frontal lobe

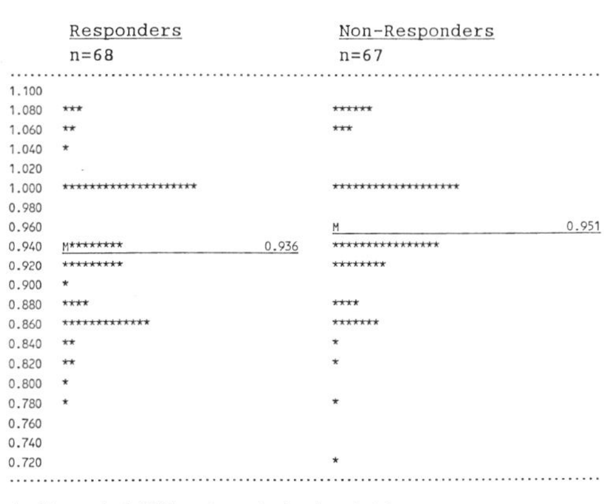


**Fig. 7.** Occipital lobe

**Table 2.** Central and cortical cerebrospinal fluid spaces

| | | Responders | | | | | | Non-responders | | | | | | diff. (%) (Resp. = 100 %) | | |
|---|---|---|---|---|---|---|---|---|---|---|---|---|---|---|---|---|
| | | male | | | female | | | male | | | female | | | | | |
| | | n | mean | (sd) | n | mean | (sd) | n | mean | (sd) | n | mean | (sd) | m. | f. | p-value |
| VBR | | 18 | 7.4 | (2.3) | 53 | 7.8 | (3.4) | 23 | 7.6 | (2.7) | 38 | 8.0 | (3.2) | +3 | +2 | 0.75 |
| III. ventricle | | 18 | 2.2 | (2.4) | 53 | 1.2 | (2.1) | 23 | 2.3 | (3.0) | 38 | 1.5 | (2.4) | +5 | +25 | 0.70 |
| Frontal | l. | 18 | 0.65 | (0.1) | 53 | 0.63 | (1.2) | 23 | 0.73 | (1.3) | 38 | 1.07 | (1.7) | +12 | +70 | 0.34 |
| | r. | 18 | 0.55 | (0.9) | 53 | 0.53 | (0.9) | 23 | 0.52 | (0.8) | 38 | 1.02 | (1.6) | –5 | +92 | 0.30 |
| Parieto-occipital | l. | 18 | 0.49 | (1.0) | 53 | 0.42 | (0.8) | 23 | 0.41 | (0.6) | 38 | 0.71 | (1.3) | –6 | +69 | 0.58 |
| | r. | 18 | 1.14 | (0.2) | 53 | 0.65 | (0.1) | 23 | 0.52 | (1.1) | 38 | 0.88 | (0.1) | –55 | +35 | 0.89 |
| Parasagittal | | 18 | 0.25 | (0.3) | 53 | 0.27 | (0.4) | 23 | 0.34 | (0.4) | 38 | 0.45 | (0.5) | +36 | +66 | 0.11 |

*sd* standard deviation, *m* male, *f* female, *Resp.* Responders

**Table 3.** Peritemporal cerebrospinal fluid spaces and temporal horn area

| | | Responders | | | | | | Non-responders | | | | | | diff. (%) (Resp. = 100 %) | | |
|---|---|---|---|---|---|---|---|---|---|---|---|---|---|---|---|---|
| | | male | | | female | | | male | | | female | | | | | |
| | | n | mean | (sd) | n | mean | (sd) | n | mean | (sd) | n | mean | (sd) | m. | f. | p-value |
| Section | l. | 18 | 0.18 | (0.3) | 53 | 0.58 | (0.8) | 23 | 0.27 | (0.4) | 38 | 0.47 | (0.7) | +50 | −19 | 0.95 |
| T1 | r. | 18 | 0.30 | (0.6) | 53 | 0.50 | (0.6) | 23 | 0.23 | (0.4) | 38 | 0.35 | (0.4) | −29 | −30 | 0.30 |
| Section | l. | 18 | 0.84 | (0.5) | 53 | 0.96 | (0.8) | 23 | 0.77 | (0.7) | 38 | 0.89 | (0.7) | −9 | −7 | 0.64 |
| T2 | r. | 18 | 0.66 | (0.5) | 53 | 0.75 | (0.6) | 23 | 0.39 | (0.4) | 38 | 0.68 | (0.6) | −40 | −9 | 0.15 |
| Section | l. | 18 | 0.81 | (0.6) | 53 | 1.11 | (0.7) | 23 | 0.99 | (0.7) | 38 | 1.06 | (0.7) | +22 | −5 | 0.67 |
| T3 | r. | 18 | 0.67 | (0.5) | 53 | 0.97 | (0.7) | 23 | 0.66 | (0.6) | 38 | 0.89 | (0.7) | −2 | −8 | 0.74 |
| Section | l. | 18 | 0.18 | (0.4) | 53 | 0.30 | (0.5) | 23 | 0.43 | (0.7) | 38 | 0.51 | (0.6) | +138 | +7 | 0.04 |
| T4 | r. | 18 | 0.19 | (0.4) | 53 | 0.28 | (0.5) | 23 | 0.32 | (0.5) | 38 | 0.58 | (0.8) | +68 | +107 | 0.08 |
| Temporal | l. | 17 | 0.28 | (0.2) | 30 | 0.19 | (0.2) | 11 | 0.21 | (0.1) | 23 | 0.27 | (0.2) | −25 | +42 | 0.47 |
| horn ($cm^2$) | r. | 17 | 0.27 | (0.3) | 30 | 0.21 | (0.2) | 11 | 0.22 | (0.2) | 23 | 0.36 | (0.2) | −9 | +71 | 0.36 |

*sd* standard deviation, *m* male, *f* female, *Resp.* Responders

nia (e. g. Bogerts et al. 1987). In addition to this focal pathology, frontal lobe asymmetry was reduced in non-responders. However, the numerical difference is very small and therefore needs replication on another sample.

Despite the trendwise correlation between temporo-basal as well as parasagittal cerebrospinal fluid space enlargement and non-response after four weeks of haloperidol treatment, the large overlap between responders und non-responders does not allow a prediction of the response for individual cases.

In summary, cerebral spinal fluid space area measurements in the CT scans of schizophrenics do not seem to be valuable predictors of neuroleptic response in general. As basotemporal and frontal areas are possibly helpful markers, MRI should be used to examine important temporal structures like the hippocampus or the amygdala.

## References


Bogerts B, Wurthmann C, Piroth HD (1987) Hirnsubstanzdefizit mit paralimbischem und limbischem Schwerpunkt im CT Schizophrener. Nervenarzt 58: 97–106

Boronow J, Pickar D, Ninan PT, Roy A, Hommer D, Linnoila M, Paul SM (1985) Atrophy limited to the third ventricle in chronic schizophrenic patients: report of a controlled series. Arch Gen Psychiatry 42: 266–270

Buckmann TD, Kling A, Sutphin MS, Steinberg A, Eiduson S (1990) Platelet gluthatione peroxidase and monoamine oxidase activity in schizophrenics with CT scan abnormalities: relation to psychosocial variables. Psychiatry Res 31: 1–14

Cazzullo CL (1963) Biological and clinical studies on schizophrenia related to pharmacological treatment. Rec Adv Biol Psychiatr 5: 114–143

DeQuardo JR, Klon R, Tandon R, Aravapalli SR (1989) Ventricular enlargement in schizophrenia: relationships to clinical parameters and DST. Biol Psychiatry 25: 97a

Falkai P, Bogerts B, Schneider Th, Greve B, Klieser E (1993) Gestörte zerebrale Lateralität im CT Schizophrener – Eine morphometrische Studie. In: Baumann P (Hrsg) Biologische Psychiatrie der Gegenwart. Springer, Wien New York, S 517–520

Friedman L, Lys Ch, Schulz SC (1992) The relationship of structural brain imaging parameters to antipsychotic treatment response: a review. J Psychiatr Neurosci 17 (2): 42–54

Gattaz WF, Rost W, Kohlmeyer K, Bauer K, Hübner C, Gasser T (1988) CT scans and neuroleptic response in schizophrenia: a multidimensional approach. Psychiatry Res 26 (3): 293–303

Jeste DV, Kleinman JE, Potkin SG, Luchins DJ, Weinberger DR (1982) Ex uno multi: subtyping the schizophrenic syndrome. Biol Psychiatry 17: 199–222

Johnstone EC, Crow TJ, Frith CD, Husband J, Kreel L (1976) Cerebral ventricular size and cognitive chronic schizophrenia. Lancet ii: 924–926

Kaiya H, Uematsu M, Ofuji, Mishida A, Morikiyo M, Adachi S (1989) Computerized tomography in schizophrenia: familial versus nonfamilial forms of illness. Br J Psychiatry 155: 444–450

Kaplan MJ, Lazoff M, Kelly K, Lukin R, Garver DL (1990) Enlargement of the cerebral third ventricle in psychotic patients with delayed response of neuroleptics. Biol Psychiatry 27: 205–214

Kling AS, Kurtz N, Tachiki K, Orzeck A (1983) CT scans in subgroups of chronic schizophrenics. J Psychiatry Res 17 (4): 375–384

LeMay M, Kido DK (1978) Asymmetries of the cerebral hemispheres on computed tomograms. J Comput Assist Tomogr 2: 471–476

Losonczy MF, Song IS, Mohs RC, Small NA, Davidson M, Johns CA, Davis KL (1986) Correlates of lateral ventricular size in chronic schizophrenia. I. Behavioral and treatment response measures. Am J Psychiatry 143 (8): 976–981

Luchins DJ, Weinberger DR, Wyatt RJ (1979) Schizophrenia: evidence of a subgroup with reversed cerebral asymmetry. Arch Gen Psychiatry 36: 1309–1311

Luchins DJ, Weinberger DR, Wyatt RJ (1982) Schizophrenia and cerebral asymmetry detected by computed tomography. Am J Psychiatry 139: 753–757

Luchins DJ, Lewine RRJ, Melzer MY (1983) Lateral ventricular size in the psychoses: relation to psychopathology and therapeutic and adverse response to medications. Psychopharmacol Bull 19: 518–522

Luchins DJ, Meltzer HJ (1983) A blind controlled study of occipital cerebral asymmetry in schizophrenia. Psychiatry Res 10: 87–95

Luchins DJ, Meltzer HJ (1986) A comparison of CT findings in acute and chronic ward schizophrenics. Psychiatry Res 17: 7–14

MacDonald HL, Best JJK (1989) The Scottish first episode schizophrenia study. IV. Computerized tomographic brain scans in patients and controls. Br J Psychiatry 154: 492–498

Naber D, Albus M, Burke H, Spahn F, Munch U, Reinertshofer T, Wissmann J, Ackenheil M (1985) Neuroleptic withdrawl in chronic schizophrenia: CT and endocrine variables relating to psychopathology. Psychiatry Res 16: 207–219

Nasrallah HA, Kleinman JL, Weinberger DR, Gillin JC, Wyatt RJ (1980) Cerebral ventricular enlargement and dopamine synthesis inhibition in chronic schizophrenia. Arch Gen Psychiatry 37: 1427

Nasrallah HA, Kuperman S, Hamra BJ, McCalley-Whitters M (1983a) Clinical differences between schizophrenic patients with and without large cerebral ventricles. J Clin Psychiatry 44 (11): 407–409

Nasrallah HA, Kuperman S, Jacoby CG, McCalley-Whitters M, Hamra B (1983b) Clinical correlates of sulcal widening in chronic schizophrenia. Psychiatry Res 10: 237–242

Nimgaonkar VL, Wessely S, Tune LE, Murray RM (1988) Response to drugs in schizophrenia: the influence of family history, obstetric complications and ventricular enlargement. Psychol Med 18: 583–592

Nian PT, Yadlam K, Jacobs M, Lieberman JA, Sweeney J, Severe J (1989) CT Morphology and short term outcome in schizophrenia. Schizophr Res 2: 137

Pandurangi AK, Devan MJ, Boucher M, Levy BF, Ramachandran T, Bartell K, Bick PA, Phelps BH, Major L (1986) A comprehensive study of schizophrenic patients. II. Biological, neuropsychological and clinical correlates of CT abnormality. Acta Psychiatr Scand 73: 161–171

Pandurangi AK, Goldberg SC, Brink DD, Hill MH, Gulati AN, Hamer RM (1989) Amphetamine challange test, response to treatment, and lateral ventricle size in schizophrenia. Biol Psychiatry 25: 207–214

Schulz SC, Sinicrope P, Kishore PR, Freidel RO (1983) Treatment response and ventricular brain enlargement in young schizophrenic patients. Psychopharmacol Bull 19: 510–512

Shelton RC, Karson CN, Doran AR, Pickar D, Bigelow LB, Weinberger DR (1988) Cerebral structural pathology in schizophrenia: Evidence for a selective prefrontal cortical defect. Am J Psychiatry 145: 154–163

Silverman JM, Mohs RC, Davidson M, Losoncy MF, Keefe RS, Breitner JC, Sorokin JE, Davis KL (1987) Familial schizophrenia and treatment response. Am J Psychiatry 144 (10): 1271–1276

Smith RC, Maser J (1983) Morphological and neuropsychological abnormalities as predictors of clinical response to psychotropic drugs. Psychopharmacol Bull 19: 505–509

Smith RC, Baumgartner R, Ravichandron GK, Mauldin M, Burd A, Vroulis G, Gordon J, Calderon M (1985) Lateral ventricular enlargement and clinical response in schizophrenia. Psychiatry Res 14: 241–253

Smith RC, Baumgartner R, Ravichandran GK, Largen J, Calderon M, Burd A, Mauldin M (1987) Cortical atrophy and white matter density in the brains of schizophrenics. Acta Psychiatr Scand 75: 11–19

Tsai LY, Nasrallah HA, Jacoby CG (1983) Hemispheric asymmetries on computed tomographic scans in schizophrenia and mania: a controlled study and critical review. Arch Gen Psychiatry 40: 1286–1289

Weinberger DR, Bigelow LB, Kleinman JE (1980) Cerebral ventricular enlargement in chronic schizophrenia: its association with poor response to treatment. Arch Gen Psychiatry 37: 11–13

Weinberger DR, DeLisi LE, Perman GP, Targum S, Wyatt RJ (1982) Computed tomography in schizophreniform disorder and other acute psychiatric disorders. Arch Gen Psychiatry 39: 778–783

Zatz LM, Jernigan TL, Ahumada AJ (1982) Changes in computed cranial tomography with aging: intracranial fluid volume. Am J Neuroradiol 3: 1–11

**Authors' address:** Dr. P. Falkai, Department of Psychiatry, University of Düsseldorf, Bergische Landstrasse 2, D-40629 Düsseldorf, Federal Republic of Germany

# Prediction of neuroleptic response: genetic strategies

**J. L. Kennedy**

Section of Neurogenetics, Clarke Institute of Psychiatry,
University of Toronto, Toronto, Ontario, Canada

## Introduction

There is a revolution occurring in medicine. This revolution is the application of the information available from the mapping and sequencing of the human genome. This information provides the blueprint for the structure of the brain and other organs in any given individual. Genes code for proteins and other information molecules that create the hardware of the organism. For the brain there has been a massive increase in the information available regarding the genetic determinants of brain structure. A recent rapid increase in the detection of genes expressed in the brain has been described by Daly et al. (1991) such that more than 3,500 genes expressed in the brain have been tagged (Adams et al. 1993). This marking process of the brain genes does not define their function, however, it does create a "library" of molecular tools to choose from when dissecting any given brain mechanism. Unfortunately, the function of most of these genes is not yet understood. This library of brain genes will be much more useful when they have been sequenced and more fully characterized. Such a task is large, but not overwhelming, and will be accomplished in the next few years. These 3,500 genes represent approximately 10 % of the number expressed in the brain. Advancing technologies can be used to identify most of the remaining 90 %. In parallel with this molecular neuroscience effort, similar "gene accounting" projects are ongoing for other organs. Thus the stage is being set for a new wave of information that can be utilized in the understanding of the structures of the brain, and the inter-individual variability of those structures. Of course, genes regulate function as well, by coding for enzymes and regulatory molecules.

The strategy to be outlined below shows that the use of genetic factors to predict neuroleptic response will not necessarily be simple. However, neither will this process be overwhelmingly complex. The tools are in place for such work, derived from a broad range of research into genetic factors in basic mechanisms and in disease. It is now possible to genetically dissect the mechanisms involved in an individual's response to a drug using molecular genetic tools. Furthermore, in relative terms DNA analysis is not expensive nor is it time consuming. For example, new genetic typing methods allow the identification of one genetic variant among more than 30 different mutations that might lead to cystic fibrosis. This is done by fixing specific DNA probes in large numbers in a arranged pattern on a membrane. The DNA from the person to be typed is then labelled and poured over the membrane and the variant that that person possesses out of the 30 or more possibilities, will cause a hybridization to one of the molecular probes on the membrane and reveal its identity. Thus it may be possible in the future to pull off the shelf a panel of DNA tests to screen, in one experiment, a large number of variants that had been shown to play a role in response to a particular class of medications.

## Empirical findings

The field of genetic studies of pharmacologic response (pharmacogenetics) has largely been oriented toward the prediction of fast versus slow metabolizers at the debrisoquine metabolizing locus (for a review see Price Evans 1993). A very clear relationship has been identified between fast versus slow metabolizers and genetic variation in this gene. Prior to DNA diagnostic techniques, fast versus slow metabolizers could be ascertained through a challenge test with debrisoquine, sparteine or dextromethorphan. Recently a restriction fragment length polymorphism (RFLP) has been identified that distinguishes fast versus slow metabolizers using a small amount of DNA from a given individual (Gonzalez and Myers 1991). This member of the cytochrome P-450 family of enzymes is the primary breakdown mechanism for most neuroleptic medications. Thus studies have been performed looking at blood levels of neuroleptic medications and the fast versus slow metabolizer genotype (e. g. Lin and Finder 1983). Thus far, however, the debrisoquine metabolizing variant has not been shown to predict clinical response to a significant degree. It might have some correlation with side effects. Further work with the genetic variants at this locus may refine its role in clinical response.

The variation in genes is different across different human populations. This is the basic source of information for population geneticists in their work to identify persons at increased risk for various diseases based on the genetic variant they possess at a particular locus. For example, the sickle cell variant of the haemoglobin gene is much more common in Mediterranean populations. In this particular case of the haemoglobinopathies, the population variation occurs because of selection pressure, favouring the sickling allele in populations that are exposed to malaria. In the heterozygote condition, that is with one sickle and one normal copy of the gene, the individual is protected against the malaria parasite. The homozygous condition of having both sickle cell alleles, leads to a severe form of sickle cell disease, but this homozygous condition, according to Hardy-Weinberg equilibrium, is much less common than the heterozygote condition. Other mechanisms besides selection can change the distribution of gene variants across different groups of humans. This intergroup variation can be caused by population drift or by admixture or by inbreeding for example. Population genetics is a well developed science that has been active for more than one hundred years, however, these methods have only begun to be applied to the variation across different individuals in their response to the same medication.

For the purposes of the present discussion, the focus will be on strategies for prediction of response to the atypical antipsychotic medication clozapine. Clozapine is unique in that it does not have a side effect profile like the more traditional neuroleptics and it can be successful when these other neuroleptics have failed. In some cases the treatment response is dramatic and beyond that observed with other neuroleptics. The D4 gene (DRD4) codes for the dopamine receptor that has the highest affinity for clozapine compared to any of the other dopamine receptors. The cloning of the D4 receptor gene (Van Tol et al. 1991) and the subsequent identification of a remarkable variety of variants in the coding region of this gene by our consortium (Van Tol et al. 1992) has lead to a considerable degree of interest in the relationship between the D4 receptor gene and clinical response to clozapine. Perhaps of most interest is the fact that the different genetic variants of DRD4 have different pharmacologic behaviour with respect to clozapine. The longer version of the gene that codes for seven repeats in the intracellular loop has been shown *in vitro* in transfected cell lines to have a lower affinity for clozapine than the shorter two or four repeat versions. This difference is observed in the absence of sodium in the assay conditions.

There are three other polymorphisms in the dopamine D4 receptor gene that have recently been discovered (Fig. 1). The first is a PCR-based RFLP variant in the 5' untranslated region that is recognized by the restriction enzyme SmaI (Petronis et al. 1994). The poymorphism information content of this site is 0.10, and it's upstream location may mean that it is closely associated with regulatory sites for the D4 gene. Secondly, in the first exon, corresponding to the extracellular portion of the re-

**Fig. 1.** DRD4 Polymorphisms

ceptor protein, there is a 12 base pair insertion/deletion polymorphism that occurs in about 8 % of the normal population. This deletion can be detected using PCR amplification and sequencing gel electrophoresis. The third polymorphism is the mononucleotide G repeat found in the first intron (Petronis et al. in press). This G repeat polymorphism has three common alleles and is the most highly informative of the three markers, although not as informative as the 48-base pair repeat variant in the third exon.

Following our suggestion (Van Tol et al. 1992) two groups have performed preliminary studies of variation in the dopamine D4 receptor gene and clozapine response. Shaikh et al. (1993) examined 64 schizophrenia patients; 43 of these were responders to clozapine and 21 were non-responders. Response was defined as a significant improvement in the global assessment scale (GAS). Those authors found no relationship between clozapine response and the number of 48-base repeats in the coding region of the D4 receptor gene. A trend was noticed in the data towards the longer versions of the gene being more common in the good responder group. The interpretation of this study is limited by several factors. The sample size is relatively small, and the numbers of non-responders is quite small. Secondly, the global assessment scale was administered retrospectively, and thus the baseline symptom profile remains only as accurately assessed as is possible from the medical records on those patients. Furthermore, the interval between stopping the previous antipsychotic treatment and the starting of clozapine was variable and not well documented. Third, the blood levels in the patients were not carefully monitored such that compliance becomes a confounding factor. Fourth, the genetic assay used only polymorphic information from the exon III variation and did not assess any other regions of the gene. A second preliminary study by Rao et al. (1993) also failed to find a relationship between the exon III polymorphism in the D4 gene and clozapine response. This study was limited by the same caveats as mentioned above for the Shaikh et al. study. The sample size was 43 patients in total and there was limited documentation of response.

In our study (Kennedy et al. in preparation) more extensive clinical assessments were performed, a larger number of non-responders to match the responder group was used, and more genetic information was extracted from the DRD4 locus by using four polymorphic sites instead of only one as in the other studies. Furthermore, statistical analysis of the data was carried out using a discriminant function analysis, which is the level of statistical assessment recommended by other authors in this volume in regard to prediction of response. All the patients in this particular study were collected from the research clinic of Dr. H. Y. Meltzer at Case Western Reserve University in Cleveland. Before starting clozapine, the patients were fully documented and ascertained to be either responders or non-responders to traditional neuroleptics. All patients went through a washout period wherein they received no medication prior to starting the clozapine. Baseline measures of several clinical assessment scales including the Brief Psychiatric Rating Scale (BPRS), Global Assessment Scale (GAS), and Quality of Life Scale (QLS) were performed, and then repeated at regular intervals (either every six weeks or three month depending on the measure) throughout the course of treatment. Treatment was continued for a minimum of one year before assessment of responder versus non-responder status to clozapine was defined. The operational definition of response in this study was the traditional measure used by Kane et al. (1988) in recent studies of clozapine response. That definition is a reduction in symptoms as measured by a 20 % decline in the BPRS. Blood levels were measured frequently during treatments to define compliance and provide further correlative data to the clinical measures. Using the repeated measures of the BPRS and the four polymorphic sites in the DRD4 gene, our discriminant function analysis was able to correctly classify patients as responder versus non-responder at a rate of 73.8 %. The sample size for this study remains small, and a great deal of further work is necessary. Replication in a second sample is very important to demonstrate the predictive ability of the DRD4 gene.

Thus the empirical findings in genetic prediction of response to antipsychotic treatment remain preliminary. The use of more extensive polymorphic information at the DNA level and more careful follow-up of patients using a structured baseline assessment before starting clozapine as well structured assessments throughout therapy may prove to be an important set of research design considerations.

The focus of neuroleptic response in schizophrenia remains on the dopamine D4 receptor in light of the recent finding by Seeman et al. (1993) that the D4 receptor protein is elevated six fold in the post-mortem brain tissue (striatum) of schizophrenia subjects compared to controls. This finding of a six fold increase was based on the subtractive difference between a ligand that binds D2, D3 and D4 receptors (emonapride) and raclopride that binds only D2 and D3 receptors. This study showed further that the interaction between D1 and D2 receptors may also be affected in schizophrenics. This latter finding was identified through the use of guanidine in association with raclopride binding to the post-mortem tissue in schizophrenics, Alzheimer's patients, Huntington's patients and controls. Both the Huntington's and Alzheimer's patients had been treated with apparently similar amounts of neuroleptic as had the schizophrenia patients. There was a marked decrease in the raclopride activity and almost no overlap with the control samples. These results, although limited by uncertainty in the lifetime dose of neuroleptic, the subtraction of ligand binding data, and the small sample size, are still quite interesting and provide further support for the dopamine hypothesis of schizophrenia. They point towards research designs that evaluate the D4 receptor, and the mechanism of interaction between D1 and D2 receptors in schizophrenia and neuroleptic response.

## Concepts and methods

As stated in the introduction, the explosion in numbers of cloned brain genes provides the molecular genetic investigator with a large basket of tools to probe any given mechanism in the brain. For neuroleptic response, this molecular genetic probing includes not only the brain, but peripheral mechanisms involved in drug metabolism as well. The following is a list of the components of drug uptake activity and metabolism that might be addressed in a molecular genetic dissection of drug response.

- Absorption
- Bioavailability and carrier molecules
- Blood brain barrier
- Cell membrane receptors
- Intracellular effectors
- Hepatic metabolism and excretion

Extensive research in the pharmacology and biology of these mechanisms has told us a great deal about them as components of neuroleptic action. Now the principles of population genetics can be used to identify the parts of these biologic mechanisms that vary in a significant way from one individual to the next, thereby leading to correlative analyses with variation in clinical response. Our ability to dissect the system in this fashion is dependent on our capacity to measure the genetic polymorphism information in the relevant genes for these components, and on our ability to determine the contribution to the variance in response from each isolated component.

Only the molecular genetic factors in item "Cell membrane receptors" above have been considered here. A full review of potential genetic components of the other parts of the response system identified above would require more space than is available here. The intracellular effector mechanisms are perhaps the most complex of the components listed above. They are a poorly understood system with the intracellular actions and responses to extracellular events difficult to measure. However, molecular biology techniques using transfected cells are breaking ground in this area. The cells can be transformed with specific variants of a given receptor gene, and that gene is then expressed and the protein produced positions itself in the membrane of the cell. Once this cell system is established, ligands can be added to the cell culture and binding behaviour can be studied. Work is in progress in several laboratories to refine the measurement of intracellular effector changes using the cloned receptor as the synthetic gateway. By expressing both D1 and D2 receptor genes in the same cell, Seeman et al. (1993) were able to demonstrate the interaction between the D1 and D2 receptors.

## Future research recommendations

The recommendations for future research can be summarized in the following list:

- Begin the molecular genetic dissection with the dopamine receptor genes and then progress to other parts of the neuroleptic response system.
- Establish a reliable agreed-upon method for quantifying the phenotype of neuroleptic response. This may be a combination of measures including the Positive and Negative Syndrome Scale, Global Assessment Scale, and the Quality of Life Scale.
- Establish multivariate methods for data analyses including discriminant function analysis. Any positive result should be interpreted with great caution until replication is achieved.
- Utilize advances in the molecular biology of the various components of the drug response system as outlined in the concepts and methods section. The rapid rate of accumulation of information in the molecular genetics of the systems will require an alert and energetic following of the molecular biology field.
- Incorporate the best findings of Positron Emission Tomography studies and Magnetic Resonance Spectroscopy to identify brain based variables that are correlated with response. The combination of functional imaging, molecular genetics, and astute clinical observation should provide an effective synthesis.
- Begin with simplified models, and add variables to the analysis as sample size permits.

## Conclusions

The field of genetic studies of response to antipsychotic medication is only at its beginning. There are early promising results, but more comprehensive answers may only follow upon sophisticated analyses of genetic, biologic and clinical data. The molecular genetic investigation of neuroleptic response in schizophrenia patients may well lead to a subphenotype of the disease itself, thus contributing to the elucidation of the genetic factors involved in the etiology of the disease. It must not be forgotten that this research effort across several fields of endeavor requires relatively larger amounts of funding. This kind of research is particularly amenable to combined industry and academic liaison funding.

In summary, the genetics of neuroleptic response is a complex field. However, the secrets of the interplay between genes, clinical response, and medication action will most certainly yield answers and illumination as the new era of molecular medicine evolves.

## References

Adams MD, Kerlavaage AR, Fields C, Venter JC (1993) 3,400 new expressed sequence tags identify diversity of transcripts in human brain. Nature Genetics 4:256–267

Daly AK, Armstrong M, Monkam SC et al. (1991) Genetic and metabolic criteria for the assignment of debrisoquine 4-hydroxylation (cytochrome P4502D6) phenotypes. Pharmacogenetics 1:33–41

Gonzalez FJ, Myers UA (1991) Molecular genetics of the debrisoquine-sparteine polymorphism. Clin Pharmacol Ther 50:233–8

Kane J, Honigfeld G, Singer J, Meltzer HY (1988) Clozapine for the treatment-resistant schizophrenic: a double-blind comparison with chlorpromazine. Arch Gen Psychiatry 45:789–796

Kennedy JL, Meltzer HY, Cola P, Macciardi FM, Petronis A, Athanassiades A (1994) Variations in the dopamine D4 receptor gene predict response to clozapine (submitted)

Lin K, Finder E (1983) Neuroleptic dosage for Asians. Am J Psychiatry 140:490

Petronis A, Ohara K, Kennedy JL, Van Tol HHM (1994) A mononucleotide repeat in the first intron of the dopamine D4 receptor gene. Hum Genet (in press)

Petronis A, Van Tol HHM, Kennedy JL (1994) A SmaI PCR-RFLP in the dopamine D4 receptor gene. Hum Heredity 44:58–60

Price Evans DA (ed) (1993) Genetic factors in drug therapy. Cambridge University Press, Cambridge

Rao PA, Pickar D, Gejman PV, Ram A, Gershon ES, Gelernter J (1993) Allele variation in the D4 dopamine receptor (DRD4) does not predict response in clozapine in schizophrenic subjects. Am J Hum Genet 53 (3):492

Seeman P, Niznik HB, Guan H-C, Booth G, Ulpian C (1989) Link between D1 and D2 dopamine receptors is reduced in schizophrenia and Huntington diseased brain. Proc Natl Acad Sci USA 86:10156–10160

Seeman P, Guan H-C, Van Tol HHM (1993) Dopamine D4 receptors elevated in schizophrenia. Nature 365:441–445

Shaikh S, Collier D, Kerwin RW, Pilowsky LS, Gill M, Xu W-M, Thornton A(1993) Dopamine D4 receptor subtypes and response to clozapine. Lancet 341:116

Van Tol HHM, Bunzow JR, Guan H-C, Sunahara RK, Seeman P, Niznik HB, Civelli O (1991) Cloning of the gene for a human dopamine D4 receptor with high affinity for the antipsychotic clozapine. Nature 350 (6319):610–614

Van Tol HHM, Wu CM, Guan H-C, Ohara K, Bunzow JR, Civelli O, Kennedy JL, Seeman P, Niznik HB, Jovanovic V (1992) Multiple dopamine D4 receptor variants in the human population. Nature 358:149–152

**Author's address:** Dr. J. L. Kennedy, University of Toronto, R-31, 250 College Street, Toronto, Ontario M5T 1R8, Canada

# Design, methodological and statistical issues in prediction research of neuroleptic response

**W. Köpcke**

Institut für Medizinische Informatik und Biomathematik, Münster, Federal Republic of Germany

Of special importance in the design and analysis of medical trials, and in gaining insight into possible disease mechanisms, is the identification of important prognostic factors.

## Inclusion and exclusion criteria

Using these factors, investigators can define prognostically distinct groups of patients that allow for rational design decisions regarding the strictness of inclusion and exclusion criteria.

A list of general factors to consider as criteria for patient inclusion and exclusion can be found in Table 1 (Spilker 1991).

The decision about inclusion and exclusion have an important bearing on the size and design of a study, as well as on the generalizability of the completed study results on other patients populations. Highly restrictive selection criteria have the advantage to provide more precise comparison of the treatments, and the results of the trials are less likely effected by population variability. On the other hand highly restrictive selection criteria increase the cost and time required for patient recruitment, and limit the generalizability of the study findings. Minimally restricive selection criteria have the advantage to make patient recruitment easier and provide base for wider generalization of findings. The disadvantages of minimally restrictive selection criteria may obscure treatment effects because of variability in composition of study population, and the results of the trial may be confusing, especially if an observed effect appears to be associated with a subgroup of patients in the study and the subgroup is too small to yield a reliable treatment comparison.

**Table 1.** Factors to consider as criteria for patient inclusion and exclusion

A. Characteristics of patients
1. Sex
2. Age
3. Weight
4. Education
5. Race and/or ethnic background
6. Social and economic status
7. Pregnancy and lactation
8. Use of tobacco; ingestion of caffeine and/or alcohol
9. Abuse of alcohol or drug
10. Diet and nutritional status
11. Physiological limitations and genetic history
12. Surgical or anatomical limitations
13. Hypersensitivity to a clinical trial medicine or test
14. Other medicine and nonmedicine allergies
15. Emotional limitations

B. Characterstics of the disease and its treatment
1. Disease being evaluated
2. Concomitant medicines
3. Previous medicine and nonmedicine treatment
4. Washout period of nontrial medicines or nonmedicine treatments
5. History of other diseases
6. Present clinical status
7. Previous hospitalizations

C. Environmental and other factors
1. Patient recruitment and cooperation
2. Participation in another clinical trial
3. Participation in another part of this clinical trial or in any other clinical trial using this study medicine
4. Institutional or environmental status
5. Occupation
6. Geographical location
7. Litigation and disability

D. Results of screening examinations

## Stratification

Prognostic factors also have use in stratification of patients during the randomization process to achieve balanced treatment groups. Investigators often produce a long list of factors on which they desire treatment balance. Overstratification in the extreme, however, becomes equivalent to pure unstratified randomization. Thus one choose only important and independent prognostic factors as candidates for stratification. The most important stratification considerations are listed in Table 2 (Spilker 1991).

**Table 2.** Stratification consideration for randomization

- Only variables that are observed and recorded before randomization may be used for stratification in the treatment assignment process.
- Increased statistical efficiency resulting from stratificaiton is minimal for trials involving $\geq$ 50 patients per treatment group.
- It is impractical to control for more than a few sources of variation via stratification at the time of randomization (i.e., generally no more than two or three).
- Use of a large number of allocation strata may allow for fairly large chance departures from the desired allocation ratio if there are only a small number of patients per stratum.
- Any gain in statistical efficiency resulting from stratification using a given variable will be a function of the relationship of that variable to the outcome measure. The gain will be small to nil if the relationship is weak or nonexistent. It will be greatest for variables that are highly predictive of outcome.
- Stratification on any patient characteristic complicates the randomization process; it may prolong the time needed to clear a patient for enrollment if stratification depends on readings or determinations made outside the clinic.
- Variables used for stratification should be easy to observe and reasonably free of measurement error.
- Variables that are subject to major sources of error due to differing interpretations should not be used for stratification. They are of limited use for variance control and the errors made may open the study to criticism when the results are published.
- It is unreasonable to expect that all important sources of baseline variation can be controlled via stratification during randomization. Analysis procedures involving post-stratification and multiple regression will be required to adjust treatment comparisons for baseline differences not controlled via stratification.
- Use of any stratification scheme that involves calculations or complicated interpretations should be avoided, especially in self-administered randomization schemes where the calculations or interpretations are not checked before treatment assignments are issued.
- Clinic should be used for stratification in multicenter trials. This form of stratification will control for differences in the study population due to environmental, social, demographic, and other factors related to clinic.

## Risk measures

From an analysis viewpoint, identification of prognostic factors is important because the analysis of a medical trial should account for variables that affect patient outcome. The importance of a prognostic factor is often expressed as a 'risk'. The odds and the odds ratio are two common measures of risk (Schlesselman 1982). The calculation is illustrated in the following hypothetical example.

| Therapy | Cases $a_i$ | Controls $b_i$ | Odds $a_i/b_i$ | Odds ratio $\hat{\Psi}$ |
|---|---|---|---|---|
| 1 | 10 | 90 | 0.11 | 1.00 |
| 2 | 30 | 70 | 0.43 | 3.91 |
| 3 | 50 | 50 | 0.50 | 4.55 |

$$\text{Odds Ratio } \hat{\Psi} = (a_i/b_i)/(a_1/b_1) \quad (1)$$

The cases are persons with a certain event (e.g. relapse): controls are persons without such an event. The odds are a measure for the chance of getting an event in a specific therapy category (e.g. 0.5 in therapy category 3).

The odds ratio is a measure for the change of risk in a specific therapy group compared to the risk in a reference category (e.g. the risk in therapy group 2 is roughly four times higher compared to therapy 1).

A test, whether odds ratios are different, is similar to the simple $\chi^2$-test. Often a trend in the odds is suggested. A general statistical **test of trend** (either a progressive increase or decrease in the odds of an event) has been derived by **Mantel**. The test statistic, which has to be computed, is $\chi^2$ distributed with one-degree-of-freedom (1DF) (Mantel 1962).

## Logistic regression

Regression methods have become an integral component of any data analysis concerned with describing the relationship between a response variable and one or more explanatory variables. The most common example of modeling is the usual linear regression model where the outcome variable is assumed to be continuous.

What distinguishes a logistic regression model from the linear regression model is that the outcome variable in logistic regression is binary (e.g. relapse yes/no).

In the early 1960s, the **logistic model** was proposed for the multivariate analysis of the individual and joint effects of a set of variables on the probability of an event (Hosmer and Lemeshow 1989). The logistic model specifies that the probability of an event depends on a set of variables $x_1, x_2 \ldots, x_p$ in the following way:

$$px = p(e = 1 \mid x) = \frac{\exp(\Sigma\, \beta_i x_i)}{1 + \exp(\Sigma\, \beta_i x_i)} \quad (2)$$

The variable $e$ denotes either the presence ($e = 1$) or absence ($e = 0$) of an event, and x denotes a set of $p$ variables, $x = (x_1, x_2, \ldots, x_p)$. The variables $x_i$ represent any potential risk factor. The $\beta_i$ are parameters that represent the effect of the $x_i$ on the probability of an event.

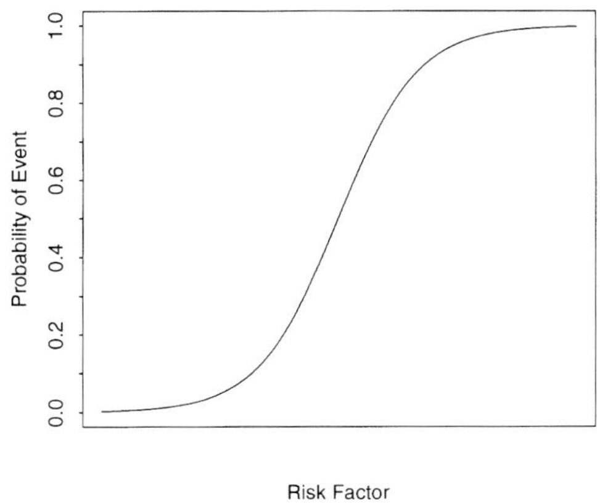


**Fig. 1.** Logistic function

A function having the shape of

$$\Pi(x) = \frac{\exp(\alpha + \beta x)}{1 + \exp(\alpha + \beta x)} \tag{3}$$

is called the **logistic function**.

The graph of the function (Fig. 1) shows the advantages of such an approach.

1 like probabilities the values of the function $\Pi(x)$ are bounded between 0 and 1.
2 the increase of risk in many biological situations is similar to the shape of the logistic function.

There is a link to the odds mentioned above. The odds for an event $e = 1$ are

$$\frac{p(e = 1 \mid x)}{p(e = 0 \mid x)} = \exp(\Sigma\, \beta_i x_i) \tag{4}$$

This formula provides a basic interpretation for the $\beta_i$. The odds increase multiplicatively by $e^{\beta_i}$ for every unit increase in $x_i$.

## Cox regression (proportional hazard model)

In many medical studies not only the occurrence of an event (e.g. relapse) is of interest but also the time from a starting point (e.g. diagnosis, begin of therapy) until the event gives valuable information. In such a case $S(t)$ denotes the so-called survival function, which is the probability that the event time $T$ occurs after the time $t$:

$$S(t) = p(T > t) = 1 - F(t) \tag{5}$$

$F(t)$ is the probability distribution function. The density function $f(t)$ is the first derivative of the distribution function $f(t) = F'(t)$. The basic function in the context of evaluating prognostic factors for event time data is the hazard function $\lambda(t)$.

$$\lambda(t) = \frac{f(t)}{S(t)} = \lim_{\Delta t \to 0} \frac{p(t \leq T < t + \Delta t \mid t \leq T)}{\Delta t} \tag{6}$$

$\lambda(t)$ is the probability, that, if an event has not occured till $t$, the event occures in the next moment $\Delta t$. In the Proportional Hazard Model by Cox (1972) it is assumed that the hazard function $\lambda(t,x)$ for a given vector of potential risk factors $x = x_1, \ldots, x_n$ is

$$\lambda(t,x) = \lambda_0(t) * \exp(\Sigma\, \beta_i x_i) \tag{7}$$

The expression $\exp(\Sigma\, \beta_i x_i)$ shows the similarity with the logistic regression. Formula (7) means that $\lambda(t,x)$ is proportional ($\exp(\Sigma\, \beta_i x_i)$) to a baseline hazard $\lambda_0(t)$ at every time point $t$ and the proportional factor is independent of time.

## Classification and regression trees (CART)

This method was proposed by Sonquist (1970) for the first time. But the founding mathematical solution of this method was done in the monography of Breiman et al. (1984). The principle of all CART-methods is very simple: construct subgroups in such a manner that they are internally homogenous as possible and at the same time externally to other subgroups maximal different with respect to a dependent variable (e.g. relapse).

In a typical situation we have a binary dependent variable (e.g. relapse (yes/no)) and several metric or binary prognostic factors. The data are splitted with respect to that variable, which generates subgroups with maximal different relapse rates. A measure for the heterogeneity of the split is the simple Pearson $\chi^2$-test: the bigger the $\chi^2$-value the more inhomogeneous are the relapse rates in the subgroups. Thus the CART procedure works as following: we split the data according to all variables with all possible cutpoints, calculate the $\chi^2$-test statistic, select the variable and the cutpoint with the highest $\chi^2$-value and split the data in two subgroups. The same procedure goes on with the remaining variables independent in each subgroup. The procedure stops if either the subgroups are too small or the maximal $\chi^2$-test statistic too unimportant.

## ANI-study

For the illustration of the methods we used the data of the ANI-trial, a German multicenter study on neuroleptic long-term treatment strategies (Pietzcker et al. 1993).

### Goals, study design, hypotheses, and treatment evaluation

The overall goal of the study was to contribute to the optimization of neuroleptic long-term treatment in schizophrenia. A major aim was to determine whether a decrease in the use of neuroleptics in comparison to standard treatment can produce the same or even better treatment success and can reduce the rate of side effects. A related aim was the examination of prodromal symptoms and their significance as predictors of impending relapse. The study group also investigated the extent to which patients' expectations and their satisfaction with the treatment influenced their compliance and hence affected the success of therapy. Finally, with respect to treatment planning the question whether different therapeutic strategies are suited for different patients was also addressed.

To attain these goals three treatment strategies were compared under routine outpatient conditions:

#### *Prophylactic maintenance treatment (MT)*

This strategy represented the standard treatment, i.e. continuous maintenance administration of neuroleptics in which the dosage of neuroleptics was individually adjusted in accordance with the patient's clinical demands at a given time. However, a minimal neuroleptic dosage was maintained at all times, corresponding to at least 100 mg chlorpromazine equivalents (CPZE) per day.

#### *Prophylactic early intervention (EI)*

This strategy represented the targeted use of neuroleptics. It consisted of complete, step-by-step discontinuation of neuroleptic treatment after clinical stabilization. Neuroleptic treatment was, however, reintroduced as soon as prodromal symptoms – suspected predictors of impending relapse – occured. Once restabilization was attained, the neuroleptics were again discontinued until prodromal symptoms re-occured.

### *Neuroleptic crisis intervention (CI)*

This control-strategy also represented a temporally limited use of neuroleptics, consisting in gradual, but complete withdrawal of neuroleptics after clinical stabilization. Neuroleptic treatment, however, was reinstalled only in case of relapse (defined according to specified criteria), and was discontinued again after restabilization.

Table 3 shows the inclusion and exclusion criteria of the ANI-study. We only used one stratification factor for randomization: the different participating clinics. For further details see the publications on the ANI-study (Gaebel et al. under publication).

**Table 3.** ANI-study – inclusion and exclusion criteria

*Inclusion criteria*
- Schizophrenia
- Age 18 – 55 years
- Recent acute episode
- Discharge from inpatient to outpatient treatment

*Exclusion criteria*
- Organic brain disease
- Drug and alcohol abuse
- Intelligence deficit
- Pregnancy
- Suicide attempts
- Tutelage/treatment guardianship

**Table 4.** Logistic regression GAS ≤ 60 at $t_2$

| Variable | Regression coefficient $\beta$ | SE ($\beta$) | $e^{\beta}$ | $\beta$/SE | p |
|---|---|---|---|---|---|
| Strauss/Carpenter-$t_0$ | –1.7367 | 0.4055 | 0.176 | –4.28 | 0.0001 |
| Clinic 1,2,4 | 1.7573 | 0.4123 | 5.797 | 4.26 | 0.0001 |
| Social scale-$t_0$ | –1.1724 | 0.3884 | 0.310 | –3.02 | 0.0025 |
| Duration of disease | 1.2398 | 0.5271 | 3.455 | 2.35 | 0.0187 |
| Intercept | 0.5481 | 0.4627 | - | 1.18 | 0.2362 |

**Table 5.** Cox regression on time to the first relapse

| Variable | Regression coefficient $\beta$ | SE ($\beta$) | $e^{\beta}$ | $\beta$/SE | p |
|---|---|---|---|---|---|
| Intermittent therapy | 1.3055 | 0.2123 | 3.69 | 6.14 | 0.0001 |
| PDS-P | 0.0709 | 0.1709 | 1.07 | 0.41 | 0.6780 |
| PDS-D | –0.1003 | 0.1730 | 0.90 | –0.58 | 0.5623 |
| CGI | –0.1523 | 0.1622 | 0.86 | –0.94 | 0.3479 |

To illustrate the three procedures for evaluating prognostic factors, we used the following baseline variables from the ANI-study as potential prognostic factors (Gaebel et al. 1994).

Clinic, Age, Sex, Therapy, BPRS-$t_o$, GAS-$t_o$, Social Scale-$t_o$, Philips-Scale-$t_o$, Strauss/Carpenter-Scale-$t_o$, EPS-$t_o$, PDS-D-$t_o$, PDS-P-$t_o$, PDS-KV-$t_o$, Duration of Disease, SRS-1-$t_o$,..., SRS-5-$t_o$, Diagnosis. As dependent variable we show the results for the variable GAS $\leq$ 60 (Table 4) (logistic regression and CART), and time to first relapse (Cox regression) (Table 5).

With the values of table 4 one can calculate $\Sigma\beta_i x_i$

$$\Sigma\beta_i x_i = 0.5841 - 1.7367 * \text{Strauss/Carpenter} + 1.7573\begin{pmatrix} * \text{ 1 if clinic 1,2,4} \\ * \text{ 0 else} \end{pmatrix}$$

$$-1.1724 * \text{Social Scale} + 1.2398 * \text{Duration of Disease}$$

The probability to have a GAS $\leq$ 60 after two years is then

$$p(\text{GAS} \leq 60) = \frac{\exp\ (\Sigma\ \beta_i x_i)}{1 + \exp\ (\Sigma\ \beta_i x_i)}$$

A positive (negative) value of the regression coefficient $\beta_i$ means that the prognostic factor increases (decreases) the risk. E.g. higher values of Strauss/Carpenter Scale and Social Scale at time $t_o$ decrease the risk having a GAS-Score $\leq$ 60 after two years (at $t_2$). The importance of a risk factor can be measured by the expression $\beta$ / Standard Error of $\beta$ (SE), which is approximately standard normal distributed ($\beta$/SE = 1.96 means p = 0.05).

The CART-procedure for the same dependent variable (GAS $\leq$ 60 at $t_2$) is shown in Fig. 2.

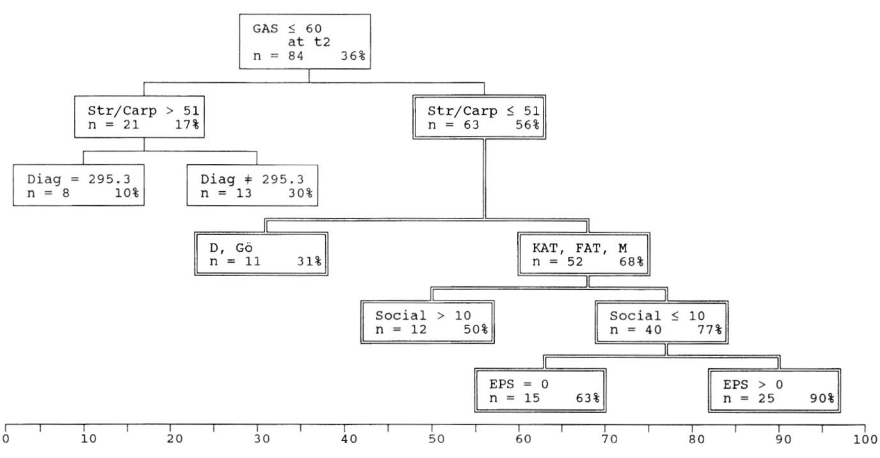


**Fig. 2.** CART-analysis for GAS $\leq$ 60 at $t_2$. Study centers: *D* Düsseldorf, *Gö* Göttingen, *KAT, FAT* Berlin, *M* München. *Social* Social scale score. *EPS* Extrapyrenidal Symptom scale score

36 % of all patients have a GAS ≤ 60. Only 17 % of the patients with a Strauss/Carpenter Scale > 51 at $t_0$ have a GAS ≤ 60 at $t_2$, while 56 % of the patients with a Strauss/Carpenter Scale ≤ 51 at $t_0$ have a GAS ≤ 60 at $t_2$. The highest percentage (90 %) of GAS ≤ 60 at $t_2$ is in the patient group: Strauss/Carpenter-$t_0$ ≤ 51 and Clinic 1,2,4 and Social Scale-$t_0$ ≤ 0 and EPS-$t_0$ > 0. Some of the prognostic factors (Strauss/Carpenter, Social Scale, Clinic 1,2,4) are consistent with the results in the logistic regression.

As in the logistic regression a positive (negative) regression coefficient $\beta_i$ increases (decreases) the risk. Thus intermittent therapy increases the risk to have an early first relapse. One can see from the expressions $\beta$/SE and $p$ that the only significant prognostic factor in this model is the variable 'Intermittent Therapy'.

## Summary

Inclusion and exclusion criteria definition and stratification are instruments for using prognostic factors in the design of clinical studies. In the evaluation phase logistic regression, Cox regression and CART-analysis are highly valuable multivariate methods for detecting prognostic factors.

## References

Breiman L, Friedman JH, Olshen RA, Stone CJ (1984) Classification and regression trees (CART). Wadsworth, Monterey

Cox DR (1972) Regression models and life tables. J Roy Stat Soc 34: 187–220

Gaebel W, Köpcke W, Linden M, Müller P, Müller-Spahn F, Pietzcker A, Tegeler J (1994) Prediction of neuroleptic response in the ANI-schizophrenia study (under publication)

Hosmer DW, Lemeshow S (1989) Applied logistic regression. John Wiley, New York

Mantel N (1963) Chi-Square tests with one degree of freedom: extensions of the Mantel-Haenszel procedure. J Am Stat Assoc 58: 690–700

Pietzcker A, Gaebel W, Köpcke W, Linden M, Müller P, Müller-Spahn F, Tegeler J (1993) Intermittent versus maintenance neuroleptic long-term treatment in schizophrenia – 2-year results of a german multicenter study. J Psychiatry Res 27: 321–339

Schlesselman JJ (1982) Case-control-studies-design, conduct, analysis. Oxford University Press, New York

Sonquist JA (1970) Multivariate model building. Institute for Social Research, University of Michigan, Ann Arbor

Spilker B (1991) Guide to clinical trials. Raven Press, New York

**Author's address:** Prof. Dr. W. Köpcke, Universität Münster, Institut für Medizinische Informatik und Biomathematik, Domagkstrasse 9, D-48129 Münster, Federal Republic of Germany

## Panel Discussions

Every presentation on both days was followed by a brief discussion with participation from the audience. In additon, all speakers presenting during the first day participated in a panel discussion. At the end of the second day, all speakers from both days participated in a general discussion. Following is an abridged version of such discussions. Unfortunately, the audio recording system did not pick up the names of those participants from the audience who took part in the discussions.

*Gaebel:* We try to differentiate between general predictors and neuroleptic specific predictors in clinical trials by including placebo-treated groups. How should we do that in the individual case?

*Möller:* I believe before coming to the question of individual prognosis, we must first have a reliable and valid prognosis with respect to group differentiation. Probably Professor Köpcke can elaborate further on this issue.

*Köpcke:* If you look outside the window you see that you are now in the autumn. All of us know that in autumn the leaves fall down from the tree but often you cannot predict for a specific leaf when it will fall down. You can only give the probability, but if this probability is true for a specific patient, we do not know. We have a group problem and we can predict on the whole relatively good under some circumstances but in the individual case, it is still problematic, we can give probabilities but we may also be wrong.

*Falkai:* How can you differentiate drug effect and time effect? If you try three different drugs after each other, and at the end the patient improves, then always the question is, what effect is that?

*Gaebel:* Obviously the last drug always wins. This is a very difficult question to answer but it shows clearly that when we are going to compare different drugs in different patients, we should be aware that patients are at a comparable stage of their illness.

*Falkai:* When you put a patient on fluphenazine, for example, 20 mg a day for four weeks and he/she is not responding, would you switch immediately to clozapine?

*Kane:* That would be the implication, however, that needs to be tested. We need to demonstrate that clozapine is superior in that population at that point and time and that has not been done yet. In our original study we have looked at patients who have been tried on three different drugs and have been ill for 15 years at least. However, I would argue that there is no point in raising the dose or switching the drugs as it does not seem to have that much impact. Whether clozapine is the answer or electroconvulsive therapy, that needs to be studied.

*Seeman:* Could it be in that example that the dose is too high for some of those patients? Might you consider lowering it especially if you are getting side effects?

*Kane:* This is a good point and is certainly possible, however, I am less optimistic that lowering the dose is going to do it. The study by Volavka who manipulated patients in and out of potential therapeutic window was unable to show an effect. One can argue that maybe his patients were relatively non-responders and we should not generalize from that study. I still think that somewhere between 15–20 mg of haloperidol probably is the best dose in terms of producing response in most patients and that 10 mg of haloperidol was not effective as we have seen in the risperidone-haloperidol multinational study.

*Gaebel:* Returning back to Dr. Falkai's question, what do we consider as an appropriate time for expecting response, is it two weeks, four weeks?

*Kane:* I believe this requires more research. I believe we are a bit timid to put our research into practice. From the work that has been reviewed here already, the response at one week may be very important in terms of future response but yet we have not acted upon that information. With clozapine, given the expense and the risk of agranulocytosis, I would like to see a study before making such recommendation of switching patients immediately to clozapine.

*Buchsbaum:* We have not talked about different classes of conventional neuroleptics. For instance, in PET studies, opposite effects have been found by haloperidol and thiothixene. So it could be that shifting to another drug class even among conventional drugs would increase the number of responders.

*Kane:* I am not sure we should necessarily conclude that all drugs are the same based on the fact that we have not done those studies.

*Audience:* I have a question for both Drs. Lieberman and Kane. From Dr. Lieberman's data about response rate over a relatively long period of time, the curve looked almost linear for the first 30 weeks and did not flatten out until after six months. Does this suggest that our drug trials are much too short? For Dr. Kane's data, if the trial had gone on further data may have looked different and may have told a different story?

*Lieberman:* It gets back to the distinction in terms of what we are trying to predict. Are we trying to predict the degree of response within a certain time frame? Or are we trying to predict how much somebody is capable of responding if you follow them indefinitely? Most clinicians, I think, are probably more interested in the former rather than in the latter. If you could devise a treatment plan that would speed up response, that is what everyone is interested in at present for economic and other reasons. But it is correct, what we end up emphasizing at present is predicting rapidity of response rather than ultimate response.

*Kane:* I would agree. What we were showing in the first episode sample was the proportion of the sample that was meeting a conservative definition of remission, not the percent response over time nor the degree of improvement that was occurring as reflected by the rating scales over time. Had that been depicted the curve would have been much steeper in the sense that there would have been a much greater rate of response earlier. But looking at remission rate that way if you are waiting for patients to improve to some criterion level, there is an advantage to wait and observe them over a longer period of time. The issue is germane to what an optimal treatment trial is with a given treatment particularly with clozapine which is a somewhat limited resource. Here, if you look at the time course to response, there also appears to be a protracted recovery curve. Where then do you draw the line as to what an optimal time period is: six weeks, 12 weeks, 24 weeks, one year? In part that depends on how long the physician is prepared to wait to allow the patient to have the chance to respond.

*Lieberman:* Going back to the discussion before about when to switch someone to clozapine, looking at that data it would suggest to me that you should wait six months. Since there were so many responses between 12 and 30 weeks, to conclude that someone is a non-responder would take 26 or 30 to 60 weeks before one could reach that conclusion and therefore switch them to clozapine.

*Kane:* Obviously, the data that Dr. Lieberman presented is related to the first episode and the question is whether you might not want to intervene with clozapine in the episode until you have gone six months. In other patients who have had already three to five episodes it is not clear whether you are going to do that much better by waiting for six months.

*Awad:* Related to such question you have to consider not only the time but also the type of population that you are dealing with. A small percentage of improvement in an acute sample may not be that significant but if you are treating a chronic population a small improvement may be important in the larger picture.

*Gaebel:* My question is for Dr. Lieberman. There are interesting findings from episode to episode; the time to response seems to increase or put differently, the response rate seems to decrease. So is there any explanation of the underlying mechanism? Is it a kind of kindling effect? Or a kind of illness toxicity? Does that mean that the first episode responder will be the ultimate non-responder after a certain number of episodes?

*Lieberman:* In terms of what mechanism for any progressive decrease in response I can only speculate theoretically in terms of mechanism along the line of certain animal models. However, I do think in terms of what we can learn of treatment resistance is that not all patients who are ultimately treatment resistant are really so from the beginning of their illness. Now, if this is a consequence of experiencing many subsequent episodes of illness then perhaps that is preventable.

*Fleischhacker:* Clinicians have been under pressure to do placebo controlled trials in schizophrenia as it is required by regulatory agencies. In light of the data presented the treatment response becomes worse the longer you have a patient untreated, can we still afford to do placebo controlled trials in these patients?

*Lieberman:* That raises an important but controversial point. Looking strictly at data suggesting potential damage to individual patients who experience resistant psychoses or repeated episodes, this raises questions about the ethics and consequences of doing placebo or drug discontinuation trials. But on the other hand, as Dr. Kane stated in his chapter for the NIMH guide lines for clinical trials, that if placebo controlled trials are the quickest way involving the smallest number of patients to get a definitive answer, then maybe that can offset to potential liability for the sake of the collective good of humanity.

*Kane:* I would agree. One question is: do we have any data that suggests that four weeks is long enough to produce the effect that Dr. Lieberman is taking about? His data came from patients that had been untreated for six to 12 months. The other concern is that the need for placebo controlled trials is probably greater now than it was. At present, we tend to be getting more and more refractory patients into clinical trials because it is harder to get drug responsive patients to enroll. The question then whether we are seeing any drug effect at all becomes absolutely critical. Without a placebo and without an active effect of control, we do not know where we are. In the long-term discontinuation studies, it is harder and harder to justify. From all the studies so far, the intermittent strategy is not very effective so it is hard to justify long-term placebo studies at this point.

*Möller:* I would like to ask whether it is really proven that early treatment leads to a better outcome. In my opinion, this is only based on statistics but not proven in a controlled group design. My question then is whether these results are confounded with acuteness of illness as a disease variable?

*Lieberman:* This is an important point. The speed at which patients come to treatment can be influenced by a number of factors, one of which is the mode of onset of symptoms, the more florid onset symptoms may come to treatment quicker. However, I would like to emphasize that though when we did our analysis of data to examine how duration of psychotic symptoms was a robust predictor, taking into account variables like premorbid adjustment, mode of onset, etc., the duration of active psychosis still remains significant.

*Buchsbaum:* One could interpret Dr. Lieberman's data as the more you are treated with neuroleptics, the worse you are going to do. Had the second episode patients been untreated in the first episode, they might have responded faster.

*Lieberman:* In trying to explain the reason for increased time to recovery, on one hand we suggest that it may be an illness progression effect. On the other hand it may be a cumulative treatment exposure effect in which tolerance to antipsychotic effects of medications are developing. This is the type of confound that Professor Möller and Professor Kane were alluding to. We can only attempt to control for it statistically. My intuition is that I do not think that it is purely explainable on the grounds of a treatment effect and this gets back to some of the issues raised a long time ago by Loren Mosher suggesting that if you avoid exposure (to neuroleptics) this may be beneficial. I would dismiss that as being unfounded at this point.

*Kane:* I would like to comment on Professor Möller's earlier comment as well as those of Professor Buchsbaum. In Philip May's original study, patients were randomly assigned to placebo, ECT, or neuroleptics. Those patients who got placebo ultimately did not do as well in the long-term. This is the only random assigned study that has ever been done and probably will ever be done. To respond to Professor Buchsbaum's point about placebo, by looking at all the placebo controlled maintenance trials that were done, if the suggestion made was true we might see that those patients that relapsed on placebo had a better treatment response than those patients who relapsed on medication. This certainly was not the case just from looking at the old NIMH data as well as our's.

*Möller:* In our Munich follow-up study we had some critical results indicating that those patients with the longest duration of treatment with neuroleptics had the highest score of psychopathology after five years. Obviously, we were concerned about this so we tried to control for other confound-ing variables. Putting together a multiple regression analysis of several predictors of poor outcome in schizophrenia, the effect of neuroleptic treatment could not be detected any more.

*Falkai:* I think as Professor Lieberman pointed out, time is a very important variable. The question then is: can we actually leave patients over six, eight, 12 weeks on the same medication? Is it not necessary that we switch after four weeks in order to stop illness progression?

*Lieberman:* If you know that there is a treatment you could switch a patient to and will achieve a more rapid response then I think that might be warranted. The reality is that we do not know. As suggested earlier by Professor Kane quoting the study which increased dose and changed to a different neuroleptic did not seem to produce any differential improvement suggesting that the most important factor is the passage of time when the patient is on a presumed adequate dose of medication.

*Gaebel:* To summarize my impression from the morning session we have heard quite a lot about potential predictors. My impression is still that many of these predictors are not used in clinical practice. We think about predictors only when we are in a situation of non-response or high side effects but certainly not before we start treatment. Put differently then, do we really need predictors when we start treating a patient? Alternatively, we treat patients with neuroleptics and it is only when we are in some trouble we try to use certain variables as for example looking for a CT scan.

*Kane:* This is the old story. However, as the treatments get better, the need for predictors becomes more important. Right now for any patient with schizophrenia probably anywhere in the world they are going to be treated with neuroleptics regardless of what we see in terms of predictors. But in some day we have a different treatment, or better treatments, or we are able to better delineate subtypes, the predictors will become very important. The availability of an alternative treatment as happened with clozapine stimulates discussion and research about how we decide when to switch to clozapine.

*Awad:* I have to admit that I lost a grant because one of my reviewers felt strongly that there is no need for prediction on the basis that every schizophrenic patient will be treated with neuroleptics any way. I obviously disagree with such approach. First of all I think we have problems with the term "prediction" since "predicting" means really something concrete. I believe we are talking here about prohability of response. Prediction also is important in terms of understanding the variability of outcome.

*Möller:* I would like to make two comments on the presentation by Professor Awad. You were sceptical on the issue of combining predictors in the field of neuroleptic outcome. From my experience this is not true. The second point, on the other side, you were somewhat optimistic with respect to biological predictors as for example CT and ventricular size. In my estimate, the literature in this field is still full of controversies.

*Awad:* Combining predictors certainly improves predictive power. However, when you review the extensive literature, combining several predictors still leaves a good deal of variance unexplained. It is true that the literature on structural brain changes is quite controversial but on balance I believe there is a trend more toward a poor outcome associated with CT scan or MRI abnormalities. To make this point related to the earlier point, there is good evidence that if you combine such structural brain changes with soft neurological signs as well as certain neurocognitive deficits in the same patient, the outcome is certainly more unfavourable.

*Gaebel:* I would certainly agree, we have the same observations. Let me ask a question; what will the future be? We are sceptical about biological measures but the question is what are the scales as for example the Strauss-Carpenter or others are measuring? Should it not be our goal to get to the underlying mechanisms? The more we understand about the pathophysiology of the illness, obviously the better we might be able to tap the right variable.

*Audience:* I have a question for Professor Kane. In your clozapine study you stated that only hostility and paranoid symptoms were related to good outcome. I am a bit astonished that negative symptoms did not figure up in a similar way.

*Kane:* Negative symptoms did not come out at as predictor in the multicentre study but it is also important to emphasize that those patients were selected on the basis of positive symptoms.

*Seeman:* We have been speaking so far about prediction to neuroleptics as if the process that causes psychosis is all the same in every single person. I wonder if that is not a very false assumption and if we could improve our studies if we thought of it more the way oncologists think about cancers in that there are many different kinds of cancers and they use different chemotherapies at different sequences.

*Awad:* I agree, we have also uncritically accepted that all the conventional neuroleptics are similar. It may actually not be so. It may be that the differential response to one medication is really overlooked as it gets buried in the group means as we usually express our results. No one has taken a critical look into that issue. It is possible that a certain drug is more useful for a subpopulation or a certain cluster of symptoms. This brings up the issue of homogeneity as a means for clarifying some of these issues.

*Audience:* Professor Seeman, could you say some more about handedness?

*Seeman:* One of the theories of why women have an advantage over men in schizophrenia is that the defect in brain function may be more on the left side. Women are less lateralized. In women the separation of the two sides of the brain is not as marked as it is in men. For instance after a stroke women can recover for the most part quicker than men because women can use the other side of the brain. This is true of course for left handers as well, for some left handers anyway, they are more bilaterally represented in the brain.

*Gaebel:* It is well established that in women the onset of illness is about four to five years later than in men. Could it be a hormonal effect? Or could it be a maturational effect?

*Naber:* There is another difference, men tend to have more negative symptoms and that may have implications. Have we reached a point now that we have to separate our data as we do in prolactin studies according to sex?

*Lieberman:* Do you think it would be useful to examine the efficacy of adjunctive estrogen treatment with neuroleptics?

*Seeman:* I really do. Using the same kind of reasoning that estrogens are protective or self preserving, estrogen treatment is studied now in Alzheimer's disease.

*Kane:* Are you aware of any clinical studies about adjunctive estrogen use in the literature?

*Seeman:* There was one clinical study from Quebec involving men with tardive dyskinesia given estrogens. My recollection is that the results were not definitive.

*Audience:* Given the protective effects of estrogen, have any examinations been carried out during menopause and its effects on symptoms?

*Seeman:* They tend to worsen.

*Fleischhacker:* This is a question to Professor Marder about implementation of research findings into clinical practice. Do you actually monitor regularly plasma levels at your site?

*Marder:* We do not routinely measure plasma levels and we do not advocate it. What we do is when a patient has been on a neuroleptic and after couple of weeks is not responding and if they are on haloperidol we order haloperidol levels. Most patients for example with haloperidol if they are given a dose between 10 and 20 mg they are likely to be within the therapeutic range so I do not consider it useful to do it on a routine basis. Fluphenazine is hard to recommend because there are so few laboratories that have analytical methods with adequate sensitivity to measure this neuroleptic. We do it because we have a radio immunoassay which is adequately sensitive. I do know many clinicians as I go frequently around to hospitals, they order thiothixene levels as well as other neuroleptics. I find those levels very hard to interpret so I am not sure I would advocate such routine use.

*Gaebel:* As far as I know, there is data that responders and non-responders are not different with respect to receptor occupancy in PET scanning. If that is the case, could it be something beyond the receptor that explains difference in response?

*Marder:* It appears that if one has an adequate haloperidol concentration one will end up occupying the maximum number of receptors. Once those receptors are occupied, it becomes an issue of the responsiveness of the particular individual.

*Buchsbaum:* I would like to make a comment on the PET studies. The studies of Farde and also of the Brookhaven group have tended to suggest that even at low neuroleptic levels receptors are largely occupied. This suggests that differences between responders and non-responders are not due to receptor occupancy. Dr. Wolkin had 10 subjects who were tested for their dopamine receptor concentration before treatment. In that study, though only on a few patients, there was a hint that the more receptors are available, the more likely the person is a neuroleptic responder. To my knowledge, no one has followed this up.

*Kane:* It was my impression from the Brookhaven data that the levels of haloperidol were low but they were still at the plasma concentrations that the patients had when they had 70 %–80 % occupancy. Generally the concentrations were above 2–4 ng which most people would say is around a threshold. This would support that the threshold haloperidol plasma concentrations is probably about the threshold of blocking 70 %–80 % of the $D_2$ receptors.

*Buchsbaum:* Yes, I think that we agree on the interpretation namely that if you give a threshold dose of haloperidol the receptors are likely to be blocked. My inference then was that the difference between responders and non-responders was not reflected in receptor occupancy since everyone had their receptors at least 75 % occupied even at such low dose.

*Möller:* Perhaps receptor blockade measured by PET techniques is principally not a good predictor. It is difficult to find any predictor relationship if you don't have variance in the possible predictor variables since a small dose is occupying the majority of receptors. The other point coming back to plasma levels, Professor Marder, you have not mentioned anything about predicting treatment response based on early plasma level measurements.

*Marder:* Yes, I should have commented on it as there was an important work done by the late Van Putten in which he looked at plasma levels 24 and 48 hours after receiving a test dose. The results showed such observation as statistically significant indicator of response. I have never quite understood it. At that time we found that the patients' subjective response was a much stronger predictor so we somehow lost interest in plasma levels within 24 or 48 hours.

*Kennedy:* In the pharmacodynamic studies most of it to my knowledge has been done on $D_2$ receptors. I want to remind everyone that molecular biology has been pushing the elucidation of these families of receptors to $D_3$ and $D_4$ which may be far more predictive of clinical response. It could well be that $D_2$ is high in the striatum and may be important for side effects, the anatomical distribution of $D_3$ and $D_4$ receptors is much more commensurate with clinical action of the drugs.

*Awad:* Professor Fleischhacker, I believe our study that you quoted in your presentation did not have the objective to test the impact of extrapyramidal side effects on outcome. We were interested if there was a difference in extrapyramidal symptoms between those who responded by being dysphoric or non-dysphoric. Our analysis at 24 or 48 hours after initiating treatment revealed no differences in extrapyramidal symptoms between the dysphoric and non-dysphoric groups. However, the interesting observation is that by day 21 there was a significant difference between the two groups with the non-dysphoric group experiencing more extrapyramidal symptoms.

*Audience:* Dr. Fleischhacker, when you talk about treatment of akathisia having no impact on the final outcome, are there any data about decreasing the dosage when akathisia is present?

*Fleischhacker:* Probably that would be the first option I would choose. Of course, there is a whole bunch of problems around EPS that we have to deal with in terms of predictive value of EPS. Do we change drugs, do we increase or decrease dose? I do not think there is so far any evidence in any direction that would improve treatment outcome.

*Möller:* Dr. Naber, in your study, you described your recently developed scale as predictive of compliance. Did you also look to see if other scales as for example the POMS are also predictive?

*Naber:* We did, but it was not predictive.

*Gaebel:* Dr. Naber, how can we really be sure that subjective response on neuroleptics is a drug specific effect? Has anyone looked for subjective response on placebo?

*Awad:* The issue of placebo certainly is quite important, however, when we developed our scale for measuring subjective response to neuroleptics (Drug Attitude Inventory) we had to do retests after a few months. We were markedly surprised with the consistency of responses over time. So in some way I tend to think it is not just placebo though I believe such studies have to be done. The problem is so far we are not yet clear about what factors contribute to the genesis of such subjective feelings on neuroleptics, it could be biological, it could be side effects, it could be previous experiences or possibly have something to do with values and attitudes towards health and illness. There was an excellent study some years ago by Kelly who demonstrated that at least 20 % of the variance in compliance in an outpatient population had to do with values and attitudes.

*Naber:* We tried to explore some of these issues. We have data about patients' concept of illness and there was no relationship. I believe it is not only motor side effects as some of the patients did not have any motor side effects but still they did not take medications for a long time.

*Awad:* This also reminds me about the work of Peter Weiden in New York. He found that stigma contributes quite significantly to noncompliance. There must be a number of issues at play in such situations.

*Naber:* We did some comparisons; acute versus chronic and so on and there were only a few significant differences. For example with regard to dosage we found no significant relationship.

*Seeman:* I wonder, Dr. Naber, if you have found any differences between men and women?

*Naber:* There were none.

*Möller:* Did you compare the findings from your scale with a more global judgement of the patient? The reason I am raising is that in some of the remoxipride studies it became apparent that patients were able to differentiate the effects of whether they are on remoxipride or a classical neuroleptic according to their subjective well-being. The other point, you brought up the concept of subjective well-being in relation to the concept of pharmacogenic depression. The two concepts probably are different.

*Naber:* This illustrates the problem with terminology. With regard to other scales, as I mentioned earlier, we gave a portion of our sample the POMS. In our scale we selected our items by checking the literature for what subjective effects are most commonly mentioned. That is why I am not so surprised that with our scale we were able to detect some differences.

*Gaebel:* Although this was not your topic, did you look for a relationship with response, particularly early response?

*Naber:* We have not. We thought we wanted to be on the safe side and decided to test our patients using our scale at the end of their treatment. I believe it may be worth trying our scale in an acute population though I may have some doubts about feasibility. At time of discharge, almost 90 % of patients were able to respond to the scale.

*Audience:* Did you measure patients' response in follow-up?

*Naber:* We only asked the doctor responsible for the outpatient treatment if the patient has improved but only in a very global way.

*Bilder:* It seems to me from the psychometric construction of the scale and the results that you had, the negative scale was sensitive and predicted compliance while the positive scale really didn't. Yet your factor analysis showed that there was really only one factor. If so, both scales should be measuring the same construct. Yet if only the negative items are predictive then this suggests that there could be a response bias, in fact to include neutral items which might indicate that there are some nonspecific factors about patients' tendency to be negativistic and might be a good predictor of future dysphoria. Such relationship has been observed in patients with depression. If you just ask patients to recall happy and sad memories you get greater recall of sad memories that are correlated with dysphoria. Even other kinds of cognitive indices of response bias that are negative and that predict dysphoria seem to be another predictor of compliance as well.

*Naber:* It is not that we have two different scales, it is just that we have a mixture of positive and negative statements. For this analysis we separate them into the positive and negative components.

*Kane:* I would like to raise a question for Drs. Lieberman and Fleischhacker in terms of the disparity between the first episode patients and the more chronic patients in the relationship between extrapyramidal side effects and outcome. I would like also to comment on the McEvoy study. One of the interesting points about their first episode subgroup study is that he had crossed their neuroleptic thresholds at half the dose of the more chronic patients. One wonders then, whether there is some change in the vulnerability test or extrapyramidal side effects from the first exposure to subsequent episodes.

*Fleischhacker:* I think this will be the first guess. Pharmacological responsivity changes as the patient gets older. Or maybe again as Dr. Lieberman has mentioned, schizophrenia is a toxic process. Maybe the toxicity of the illness itself changes the viability of certain symptoms to respond to antipsychotics and maybe this is different in different dopaminergic systems of the brain. I think that all that we are doing at this point is just guessing where it might come from. I was also similarly surprised by that lower neuroleptic threshold but again shorter time to remission that Dr. Lieberman has also shown in his first episode trial that can be a strong indicator in that direction.

*Lieberman:* I agree, it is a puzzling finding and the only thing we can do is to sort out the differences between that study and the other studies in the literature which have shown a negative association between EPS and treatment response. The biggest difference is that it is a first episode treatment-naive population, so to the extent that chronic exposure alters specific anatomical structures that mediate extrapyramidal responses, then perhaps there is some progressive effect that occurs in terms of tolerance or sensitization that may produce an interaction between side effects and therapeutic effects. The other point is that in the first episode sample, no prophylactic anticholinergic medications were used whereas in some of the other studies including our study where chronic multi-episode patients were studied prophylactic anticholinergic medications were used. As a result, the EPS there was associated with poor treatment response as it is the kind of EPS that was occurring despite an adequate dosage of anticholinergic medication. Still I think there remain curious differences between the first episode sample in that study and the other studies which need further clarification. One other curiosity in our clozapine database is that higher levels of extrapyramidal side effects also predicted good response to clozapine which is another slant on the whole matter.

*Kennedy:* I am just wondering, no one mentioned today racial or ethnic differences in response to neuroleptics. I have not read anything about this other than in asians it relates to plasma levels. Can anyone comment on differences between blacks, caucasians or asians in terms of there response to neuroleptics?

*Seeman:* Asians have the same difficulty with neuroleptics that they have with alcohol. I do not know whether it is a related enzyme, but certainly they do require lower dosages of medication. They develop EPS much more readily.

*Gaebel:* There has been at least one study in the Japanese population where differences have been looked at. The results indicated that the higher the inactive metabolite, the poorer the outcome judged by a test dose of chlorpromazine. Such study has not been replicated as far as I know.

*Fleischhacker:* The work of Altamura in Italy demonstrated that the higher the reduced haloperidol, the less likely the patients are good responders.

*Kane:* What data sets might the panellists point to that might allow us to explore the relationship between subjective response and biological factors?

*Lieberman:* I believe in the past doing studies of subjective response was limited by the toxicity of the neuroleptic which was a limitation because the dose response curve for toxicity was so close to the dose response curve for clinical response. I believe with clozapine and other new antipsychotics, these two dose response curves are further apart. That will allow us to study the subjective effects of the drug associated with its biological effects without EPS interfering as much. Most of us have attributed the large proportion of the subjective response to EPS, however, with Dr. Naber's clozapine data there may be intrinsic subjective responses to clozapine that are driven by something other than the fact it is just not a toxic antipsychotic.

*Awad:* There is another issue related to that. One has to test whether this phenomena is unique in schizophrenia or also can be observed with other psychoactive medication beside neuroleptics. There exists only one study from the

Berlin group about the same phenomena, i. e. subjective response to antidepressants predicted outcome. To extend the point further, in order to understand the nature of such subjective responses, maybe we have to pick a non-psychiatric illness such as hypertension which is similarly long-term, requires long-term treatment with hypotensives that also cross the blood brain barrier and affect many receptors. It is known that the compliance rate with beta blockers in hypertension similar to schizophrenia is not that high. In essence, testing the same concept in a non-psychiatric population is what we are doing at present. I am curious as to whether there have been any observations, systematic or otherwise between subjective response to antipsychotic drugs and the presence of negative symptoms.

*Naber:* Unfortunately I am not aware of such data.

*Gaebel:* From what we have heard so far, most of the predictors we have talked about are treatment related predictors. Apart from sex, all other predictors were related to treatment, so my question is: should we stick more to treatment related variables on different levels: be it subjective responses, plasma levels, receptor blockade, and using gender as a moderator variable? Or should we still stick to what Professor Möller recommended, i. e. to have at least a variable that does what it should do: predicting?

*Marder:* It would be premature to drop the idea that there are baseline clinical and biological factors that can serve as predictors. The range of drugs that are effective seem to have changed. The antipsychotic medication that we are going to use in the mid and late 90s will include a number of drugs with different mechanism, i. e. low affinity $D_2$ blockers, $5HT2/D_2$ drugs, clozapine type drugs. I believe then many of these predictors need to be re-investigated to see whether or not they predict the type of drug that a patient responds to. There have been a number in particular that have not been explored adequately with the new drugs, i. e. baseline levels of dopamine activity as measured by HVA, PET investigations of dopamine receptor occupancy using different ligands. I believe that there should still be some optimism driving the field as these new drugs come in.

*Gaebel:* Would it be then a recommendation to include routinely some predictors in future drug trials?

*Lieberman:* In response to that, many studies of predictors are done sort of after the fact, they are not really designed to measure particulars. For example if one were to study how a particular biological variable affects response to one drug versus another, there should be random assignment after the patient is categorized. I would argue against the idea that all of us should study the same particular and just enter them into any clinical trial that we do. These issues could be answered probably with carefully developed designs.

*Seeman:* My prediction would be that in not so many years from now we are going to be targeting drugs for specific DNA mutation and that is the way the field is going to go. Maybe then what we should be doing now is collecting blood samples and growing them in cell cultures and then we can look backward to see if indeed we were correct that some of our responders/non-responders could be distinguished easily because they have totally different DNA.

*Kane:* I would echo Professor Marder's statement. I would not be as pessimistic in regard to predictor variables. The treatment dependent predictors have been the most informative because there you are looking at a dynamic test. We are probing the system in some way as opposed to looking at a basic resting state variable and therefore the magnitude of the response of the variable is enhanced and gives you a greater predictor power. That certainly may enhance the capacity to demonstrate relationships. There is evidence simply by the consistency of findings across studies to suggest that other variables do have predictor validity such as structural brain pathology as well as a number of historical variables, e. g. premorbid adjustment, duration of illness, mode of onset. There are other biological variables, too, such as resting HVA or growth hormone levels. The problem is as alluded to earlier, no single variable by itself accounts for a great amount of the outcome variance and that is a limitation of their sensitivity or our sensitivity or our ability to measure them. Thus we need to use multiple variables jointly to enhance the predictive power.

*Awad:* Maybe our expectations are too high at this time. Thinking in terms of response, we tend to think that it is an "all or none" phenomenon. Indeed, most of the time it is a continuum. It is very useful to use a combination of predictors, at least a reasonable number together because certainly that adds more to their predictive power. However, I want to raise another issue which has not been raised so far in our discussion. Are neuroleptics useful for every patient? It has been alluded to that some patients do indeed deteriorate in some aspects of their functioning on neuroleptics. It may be also that some outcome particularly in functional status can be impacted upon more effectively by different interventions beside or other than neuroleptics.

We are not yet clear about the adjunctive role of other therapies added to neuroleptic as for example psychosocial intervention. There are many such challenges that require clarifications. It may be that we just have to persist in our strategies a bit longer.

*Audience:* I feel always a little bit uncomfortable when we list all possible variables that are used as predictors, particularly that they come from very different sources. I remember working with students as healthy volunteers in an experiment to find that they responded to a drug in a different way even probably not related to the biological effect of the drug but mostly to their personality characteristics. We probably have to look for predictor variables not in the variables relating to personality, drug, or disease but variables relating to the interaction between dose and these variables.

*Kane:* In a classic experiment by Schachter in Columbia several years ago, normal volunteers were given epinepherine, the three groups were told very different things about what was going to happen. The responses to the same drugs were vastly different based upon the expectations of every individual. This is something we usually don't talk about and not necessarily tell our patients that they might feel lousy and then gauge the response accordingly.

*Naber:* This issue can be dealt with by studying placebo response, it should be easy then to find the relationship between placebo response and personality. However, the literature is rather controversial.

*Bilder:* There was an editorial in *Biological Psychiatry* some time ago calling for variables of the second order, i. e. something that is normally behind the variables usually taken into account as plasticity and responsivity. These variables might be those that we are looking for to identify those who respond and those who do not. In the very end it goes back to DNA but is still a long way. We have the possibility to find probes before that because it would be rather difficult to make a DNA evaluation in each patient who comes to the outpatient clinic, whereas it might be very easy to say he is a "classic guy, he is going to respond."

*Gaebel:* I agree with your ambitious goal. As I stated earlier, all variables that relate to treatment response in a certain way are hints to certain processes that we do not yet understand. The question is how to get to the second layer?

*Bilder:* It seems as if a lot of effort has been spent on trying to identify the number of predictors that might be used. Yet there seems to be a tendency to lapse into thinking about outcome again as a unitary variable although it has been pointed out through all our discussions that it is a polyfactorial construct as well. I wonder if we can speculate about what are the main underlying latent variables; the latent construct that we need to identify in outcome and would help us to focus prediction uniquely. I am thinking instead of using multiple regression models, that we use economical correlation models so as to identify the sets of variables. We have already heard that the best predictor of future outcome in certain domains as for example is past occupational performance. This may sound a bit boring but unless we account for the other variance first and get rid of it and then look at what is left, it does not seem that we would be able to make much progress. I am wondering then if we could address the question: What are the useful domains we should focus on?

*Audience:* I wonder how specific motor function is as predictor in schizophrenia. L-Dopa can affect motor performance in Parkinson's patients. I suppose this would suggest that such aspect is not specific to schizophrenia. The other question relates to the complexity of the tests you are using and whether you are able to relate such function to anatomical region?

*Bilder:* In terms of the complexity of the tests I think the complexity comes from me not explaining clearly that our goal has really been to try to study the simplest functions and those we believe stand a chance of assessing something that is relatively specific in functional anatomy. For example the most widely used neuropsychological test in schizophrenia is the card sorting test. It is virtually impossible to interpret why a patient does poorly on such a test. Here we have a complete range of perceptual, motor and conceptual aspects of the different functions involved. I think the tests we are using control a whole host of such variables and in fact is about as simple as you can get to assess things like switching of responses or two-choice guessing tests. The other point was about the specificity of defects of these types in schizophrenia. I would argue that motor defects and their predictor validity and treatment outcome are not necessarily specific to schizophrenia. The example about Parkinson's disease is interesting because this is another disease that involves the frontal striatal system. In that sense defects in motor performance may be predictive of the severity of pathology that is relevant to outcome. In our studies, tests of correlation coefficients showed that the motor measures are significantly better predictors than other kinds of measure. However, we need further studies to answer the question of specificity.

*Gaebel:* Dr. Bilder, you seem to take us through some of the deeper layer. I would like to ask you which kinds of tasks would you recommend as potential predictors? Are those tests better trait related deficits because they tap functions that cannot be addressed by neuroleptic drugs and therefore are related to potential systems which reflect non response?

*Bilder:* Using neuropsychologic methods to predict outcome, we can assess so much of these traits. Neuropsychology is really designed to tap traits. The Wisconsin Card-Sorting Tests used after patients have had some treatment can predict longer-term vocational and occupational functioning quite well. The difficulty that comes: what do we do at the time of acute psychosis? Can we add anything to predictive validity at that point, particularly can we use these kinds of measures to determine whether a patient should get a particular kind of neuroleptic treatment? One of the pragmatic uses of neuropsychological methods potentially is in monitoring of treatment: behaviourally titrated treatment. It would be nice for example if we could watch neuroleptic dosing to see how it alters patient's capacity for redundancy and get them to a point where their response repertoires are more flexible. Rather than looking at patients for tremor, why can we not look at them for evidence of motor slowing? Additionally, the memory defect that accompanies anticholinergic treatments, can we try to determine whether or not we are causing more iatrogenic harm to outcome while we may be alleviating some of the side effects of neuroleptics? If we have objective measures of these deficits we are in a better position to measure the costs and benefits of different treatment options. This certainly is a future clinical use of these kinds of psychological measures. The other purpose is to try to understand pathophysiology better using the kind of measures that look at response organization, the hierarchic organization of such controls.

*Audience:* This brings us back to the issue of specificity, are these specific (psychological) tasks specific for a system like the motor system?

*Bilder:* None of these tasks have a great deal of specificity. Certainly finger tapping tends to be more specific than for example the pegboard. The tapping test is actually a specific motor task, however, you cannot interpret them as having any specificity unless you are looking at them in the context of other preserved functions. It is only by saying that they are differentially predictive compared to other measures of attentional control that are sensitive to perceptual process, one could infer that there is anything specific about damage in the motor system which may be important and predictive. Although these measures tend to show long-term stability and predictive validity, I do not mean to imply that they do not change with treatment. In fact, these motor measurements show significant decrement following the introduction of treatment. We have good evidence about the initial motor slowing effects on these tasks after the introduction of neuroleptics during the first eight weeks of treatment. However, when we look at patients at six and 18 months later, it looks as though they are back to baseline. This is consistent with the literature which shows it is difficult to detect any effect of neuroleptic treatment on cognition in patients with schizophrenia other than acute motor slowing effects.

*Möller:* Did you look for background variables like the P300? The other point, do you think that the cognitive functions are predictive of treatment response or are they only predictors of the natural course of illness?

*Bilder:* In some of the earlier studies by Weaver and Brooks, as well as Cancro's original study RT had relatively moderate to strong effects. These probably are maximally accounting for 30 %–40 % of variance in global outcome measures. I think this is what most studies had in terms of effect size. Some of the more recent studies have shown smaller but significant results. Such studies focused more on measures of attentionally controlled memory functioning as predictors.

*Marder:* This is a question to Dr. Müller-Spahn. From your presentation, it seems that levels of plasma homovanillic acid is one of the most promising predictors. If you were going to design a large multicentre study what questions would you be looking for? Would it be the prediction of response, would it be whether or not it is the change in levels?

*Müller-Spahn:* This is a rather difficult question. We are a little bit sceptical about the biological measures since we do not have exact information about the underlying pathophysiological process. However, for neuroleptic treatment I think plasma HVA levels, baseline levels, and change over time, particularly the latter would be one of the major premises for a new study.

*Lieberman:* In respect to the plasma HVA as a potential marker of course, could you comment on the role of the washout period and the effect of washout on the results from various studies?

*Müller-Spahn:* The washout in our study was about four weeks. In the literature it ranges from one to three weeks. I think the washout period must be longer.

*Lieberman:* I agree. In order to enhance the predictive power on the value of the plasma HVA level we need to have a sustained washout period which is a limitation in its clinical applicability.

*Müller-Spahn:* I believe it is the change over time that is the most important, not necessarily the absolute baseline levels.

*Lieberman:* That is true except that the change over time depends on where the patients start from in terms of their baseline. One line of reasoning is that if chronic neuroleptic treatment produces the reduction of plasma HVA by a depolarization blockade or some other process that reduces neural dopamine activity and then medication is withdrawn, there is some period of time before the neural pathways are reactivated. Where in that process the study begins or the treatment is reinstituted, it can affect the observed pattern.

*Audience:* When you state that results from challenge tests are inconsistent, are you referring mainly to acute neuroleptic treatment response?

*Müller-Spahn:* Yes. We investigated acute schizophrenic patients with three of the neuroleptic drugs for at least four weeks in the acute period and then we investigated the same patients without neuroleptic treatment after six or seven months in the so called symptom free state. We found that those patients who had elevated growth hormone response to apomorphine and those patients who responded very well had no stimulation effects after six months. I think that the apomorphine challenge test might be a state dependent variable and might give some information about dopaminergic activity processes, but from my experience it is not a good predictor for short-term clinical effects.

*Audience:* That is our experience as well. The most consistent results from a challenge test being related to clinical outcome has been in the maintenance treatment data where there seems to be an association between behaviour response to dopamine agonist and likelihood of relapse if medication is withdrawn or the dose is reduced. When I first read the paper by Bondy on lymphocyte-spiperone binding I was almost euphoric as I thought we had already a peripheral marker for dopamine receptor measures. However, to my knowledge over the years apart from the data from the Munich group this work has not been consistently replicated.

*Müller-Spahn:* This work has been done in our laboratories in Munich. What consistently has been found was that schizophrenic patients, especially of the paranoid type have significantly elevated spiperone binding. This was not a predictor of clinical outcome, only a so-called traitmarker or something like that for acute schizophrenia. I agree, this has not been replicated and so it is difficult to know its significance.

*Gaebel:* It looks as if the indicators of the dopaminergic system activities seem to be the most interesting. Is the pathophysiological mechanism of the illness itself directly related to the dopamine system? Or is it more a kind of buffer function which is mediated by this system? The Davila paper cited showed a relationship between plasma HVA pretreatment levels and negative symptoms: the higher the negative symptoms the lower the HVA levels.

*Müller-Spahn:* Yes. The relationship between the negative symptoms and the HVA levels is not surprising since there is a lot of data demonstrating that the negative symptomatology might be related to a lower activity in the forebrain. A drug like clozapine might increase the forebrain dopaminergic activity and accordingly patients show some improvement. The balance between low and high dopaminergic activity is the most convincing interpretation of the dichotomy; positive and negative symptomatology.

*Möller:* You demonstrated significant differences in the means of HVA concerning responders and non-responders, could that be a clinically relevant predictor? This is a rather difficult question as the data from the literature are still conflictual, 50 % of the studies demonstrated a significant correlation between elevated baseline HVA and the clinical short-term outcome, but the other 50 % failed to do so. I believe it is a relative predictor.

*Audience:* This is a question to Dr. Buchsbaum; have you found a correlation between activation of the ventral part of the striatum and changes in symptomatology during clozapine or haloperidol treatment? Supposedly, the ventral area is somehow correlated, its blockade would probably be correlated to anhedonia, depression or some negative symptoms.

*Buchsbaum:* We examined the correlations in a much larger group of patients between symptoms as measured by the BPRS scales and metabolism in all parts of the brain. This study has just been published in the American Journal of Psychiatry and involved 70 unmedicated schizophrenic patients. The only area consistently correlated with symptoms was the medial frontal cortex. The primary correlations were with negative symptoms, low metabolism in the medial frontal cortex was much more dramatically associated with negative symptoms. These conclusions were similar to that of Andreasen who published in the Archives and reported that the medial frontal cortex was the area most decreased and most correlated with her negative symptoms score. We did not find the basal ganglia to be correlated with any of the schizophrenic symptoms. The medial frontal lobe is the area of the frontal cortex richest in $D_2$ receptors and also the richest in the enzyme tyrosine hydroxylase. Other investigators have found that medial areas of cortex in the monkey were very rich in dopamine. It is possible that this is part of the story that we are trying to unravel. Our difficulty is that haloperidol did not affect the medial frontal cortex, only clozapine did. The medial frontal cortex is also very rich in serotonin receptors and a number of investigators including Dr. Meltzer believe that clozapine acts through the serotonergic system advancing a serotonin hypothesis for schizophrenia. So we are still puzzling over these seeming contradictions, but at the moment we have not been able to tie the symptoms in schizophrenia to basal ganglia.

*Lieberman:* Dr. Buchsbaum, this is a fascinating line of investigation. I have a couple of questions and a comment. First, the findings of increased glucose metabolism in non-responders at baseline and decreased metabolism in responders is a little bit puzzling being that the non responders look more like "normal" pretreatment.

*Buchsbaum:* What I have been hypothesizing is that the responders have increased dopaminergic innervation of the striatum, increased dopaminergic firing from the ventral areas. This produces an inhibitory effect on the striatum which decreased metabolism there. So they have hypodopaminergia when blocked with neuroleptics, then the basal ganglia metabolism is allowed to rise to normal levels. Individuals with high or normal metabolism in the basal ganglia have average or low amounts of dopamine and therefore when they are given a dopamine receptor blocker they do not get any better, they may feel worse.

*Lieberman:* Is it possible given your design that patients who are non-responders may have had residual drug activity at the time of their placebo scan? This persisting drug activity may be what is accounting for the increased metabolic activity.

*Buchsbaum:* This would be a correct hypothesis if the five week washout was not enough so non-responders would show normal metabolism in the basal ganglia as a leftover effect from their previous neuroleptic medications. However, one might have expected during the washout period to see receptor supersensitivity and the reverse effect. It would be difficult to postulate that one failed to washout and for some reason the same group who failed to adequately washout were patients who were especially likely to be non-responders. However, it cannot be ruled out without a longer washout period. I would cite the data we obtained on the first day in which a lot of the drug response really occurred within the first week. So if a lot of the drug response occurs within the first week, maybe a five week washout is enough for most of the drug response to be lost.

*Lieberman:* One could postulate that your most severely ill or most refractory patients got larger amounts of medications prior to coming into the study and this is more slowly washed out over the course of the washout period. Did the patients deteriorate during the five week washout?

*Buchsbaum:* We saw some deterioration, we only lost two or three patients from the study during the five week washout period. One of the patients dropped out as he felt tired on neuroleptics which interfered with his work and two others dropped out for other reasons unrelated to drugs. To respond fully to your point, we should really look at the preceding neuroleptic levels in the non-responders and responders.

*Lieberman:* You mentioned that when you looked at the caudate putamen that there was an association with treatment response, was it size?

*Buchsbaum:* That was size morphometrically in our 1989 study. In that study, drug treatment did not change the size of the basal ganglia but we did find individuals with wider putamen who were more likely to respond to medication as measured by MRI before and after drug treatment one month apart.

*Kane:* How does the time course of this change in basal ganglia metabolism correspond to clinical change and change in HVA? This may help us understand how promising it is as a viable predictor.

*Buchsbaum:* Unfortunately we do not know because we have only tested people at five weeks. One of my thoughts about a future grant is to look at 24 or 48 hour response to neuroleptics in addition to five and 50 weeks so as to get some idea of the time course.

*Lieberman:* This is a question to Dr. Falkai about the relationship of morphology to the response to clozapine. There was a report from Dr. Meltzer's group in a CT study suggesting that increased hemispheric width was associated with clozapine response. In a subset of patients receiving clozapine in our study, who also had MRIs, there did seem to be an association between likelihood of response to clozapine and abnormal morphology. From all the structures we examined, lateral ventricular volume and most particularly the frontal horn seem to be the best predictors of treatment response.

*Falkai:* There are two MRI studies that showed an increase of sulcal prominence in the frontal lobe which interestingly corresponds to PET data. Sulcal prominence and non-responsiveness are correlated in the clozapine study.

*Lieberman:* With the finding about the lateral sulcus in the basal temporal region associated with response, do you think that it is a specific effect in that region or is it due to crude or insensitivity of CT that you are finding a generalized enlargement of subarachnoid space?

*Falkai:* I do not believe it is nonspecific as we have analyzed 200 CT scans of schizophrenic patients compared to normal controls. We found a significant enlargement of these lateral sulcal areas up through almost all levels especially on the left-hand side. We analyzed the 200 CT scans and replicated Dr. Crow's finding. We found a drastic increase of the temporal horn area on the left-hand side in the schizophrenic group, this supports the idea of abnormal temporal lobe morphology in schizophrenia.

*Buchsbaum:* The measure of sulcal atrophy and ventricular enlargement are normally related all over the brain. One would be interested in seeing a multivariate approach to generalized brain shrinkage as a correlative response rather than trying each variable on its own.

*Falkai:* We calculated ratios but just for frontal and occipital separately. We looked at brain size and tried to correct for that but we did not correlate the variables, this seems to be a good suggestion for future work.

*Gaebel:* Dr. Falkai, you mentioned that we should find new ways of subtyping patients to get better results, do you have any suggestions? Have you tried other kinds of response criteria?

*Falkai:* We thought about looking for length of neuroleptic treatment, hospital stay and other measures but in retrospect we found it very difficult to find any other measures.

*Audience:* This is a question to Dr. Kennedy. I would like to tie up the modern genetic research with the old work that has been done on twins as for example in the Shield's study. Do you think that these old risk factors would be expressed in DNA sequences?

*Kennedy:* This is a good point. There are so-called familial cases of schizophrenia where there is another relative in the family affected and the majority of cases are non-familial, so-called sporadic. We have not factored that in. It may be an interesting variable to put in our studies of clozapine response, whether the patient has another relative affected. Therefore, in a familial at risk group it may be that prediction in that group would be higher if we could partial out the sporadic cases. I have other perspective on that, the recent discovery of the genetic base for Huntington's disease and myotonic dystrophy. In those cases the sporadic disease group was explained by their DNA sequence. The DNA changed from parent to child enough to go over the threshold. The child expressed the disease, but all the ancestors have not crossed the threshold. In those cases, the DNA expands and becomes more unstable and at some point crosses the threshold. It may be in schizophrenia we are looking at a similar situation where in those sporadic cases the DNA crosses over a threshold but it certainly could be also an environmental cause.

*Audience:* In a recent paper by Dr. Philip Seeman in Nature it was shown that spiperone also binds to $D_4$ receptors which might be enhanced in number in schizophrenic patients. The question is, do you think the response to traditional neuroleptics is a question of dirtiness in the sense that they do not only fit to $D_2$ but also to $D_4$? One then should give a huge amount of these traditional neuroleptics but obviously we are hampered by their side effects which relate to their $D_2$ action.

*Kennedy:* This is an interesting point but it is hard for me to predict what might be the true case. The PET data as opposed to the genetic data is the best way to disentangle the $D_4$ versus the $D_2$ story. The fact that the genetic variance in $D_4$ seemed to predict clozapine response does support the idea that $D_2$ is less important than $D_4$. My work in genetics is consistent with that and we are seeing some converging evidence that $D_4$ is a more pivotal receptor than $D_2$. The older neuroleptics bind to $D_2$ and $D_4$ but we were not able to discriminate the degree of $D_4$ binding in the past.

*Gaebel:* Dr. Köpcke, when you compare different treatment strategies it might be necessary sometimes to have a base rate of a certain event included. Let's say if you compare two dosages it might be important to include the base rate of a placebo-treated group, would that be possible in your model?

*Köpcke:* Yes, it must be possible especially in the logistic regression.

*Marder:* I would like to propose a question to both the panellists and the audience as well. We have already discussed a number of elegant predictors that we can measure with reasonable precision as for example plasma HVA. One of the dilemmas is that we are trying to take these elegant predictors and pairing them against outcomes that are relatively crude to measure. What kinds of innovations in the field should be made in so far as measuring outcome, diagnosis, patient selection, etc., that will help move the field forward?

*Awad:* One of the basic issues there which is quite important is the question of choosing outcome criteria. You have to choose outcomes that are sensitive to the intervention. Maybe we should not rely on one measure like symptom change or improvement on one scale but we should use multidimensional outcome that taps a number of areas.

*Kane:* I agree completely with Dr. Awad's comments. We also need to identify populations that are sensitive to the treatment. You can dichotomize patients into responders and non-responders or you can try to identify people who are capable of responding and then assess the degree of response that you can bring about with a particular treatment. We have a hodge-podge of different treatment approaches, whether it be different dosages of neuroleptics, different durations, different stages of the illness. It is going to take a lot of careful consistent work with attention to all aspects of methodology in order to be able to advance the field. The problem we all have is that each of us tends to be expert in one area and focuses on that so it is rare to get groups of people together who can bring to bear different types of expertise in designing studies which is obviously one of the exciting aspects of this meeting. It sets a framework to do that and hopefully we can take advantage of that.

*Gaebel:* I would like also to add that we should include measures that until now we were reluctant to include as for example, neurocognitive measures as proposed by Dr. Bilder, not so much to use them as outcome measures but as measures to monitor the treatment and its potential side effects.

*Marder:* I would like to suggest a strategy to see if people will agree with me. There has been too much emphasis on patients who are relatively poor responders. I have consulted frequently to state hospitals in California seeing some of the most psychotic individuals one could see. I have had patients who said that they are non-responders to antipsychotics until the antipsychotics were discontinued and then we saw people who were terribly sick become even worse. I think that when one gets to the part of the continuum where you have poor responders or non-responders, it is very hard to do prediction research with that group. Maybe it would be better to look at the predictors in patients who are relatively highly responsive and measure things like rapidity of response. What I think happens with many of these non-responders, we treat them with a drug, they may get slightly better but we really do not have the technology to measure it. The sensitivity of our measures is much better on the patients who are good drug responders.

*Kane:* That would be a useful approach to focus on responsive patients as a way of maximizing the potential for changes in a population. Coming back to the question: what kinds of measure of outcome ought we to include? Traditionally treatment outcome research has focused on psychopathology exclusively or predominantely. Although for short-term acute antipsychotic treatment response that may seem appropriate, for assessing the wider spectrum of efficacy of the newer compounds and longer-term outcome based research, it is increasingly important to incorporate other dimensions of response related to social functioning, vocation, neurocognitive performance as well.

*Buchsbaum:* I want to say something about the selection of appropriate measures. Many of the neurocognitive measures that have been selected are based on studies comparing schizophrenics and normals who obviously are not on medications. We might want to re-examine which attentional and cognitive measures are sensitive to neuroleptic action that can then be used in drug studies. Another point is that our difficulty with non-response may be related to some other neurochemical abnormalities. No one on this panel has pushed the GABA theory of schizophrenia or glutamate theory of schizophrenia or the glutamate-dopamine theory nor a viral theory of schizophrenia. Presumably, non-responders to haloperidol would make up those categories so we need to have a more positive characterization of non-responders according to other biological models. This would help our studies not just being responder – non-responder to haloperidol. It may be more helpful to also include whatever other drugs have been used in responders to clarify the biology of response.

*Seeman:* The most frequent clinical question is: if you have somebody on antipsychotics for months or years and they are doing well and you want to know if it is safe to take them off, how do we predict that with the knowledge we have at present?

*Kane:* I have two thoughts on that. First I do not think it is safe to take them off. We tried to find all the studies in the English language literature that identify patients in good remission for a long period of time and then taking them off medication. We were able to find six such studies done in New Guinea, Hong Kong, U.S. and Scandinavia. Patients were in remission for up to five years and when they were taken off medications and followed for the next year to year and a half, 75 % relapsed. My conclusion is that it is probably not safe. In terms of predictors, the work that Dr. Lieberman has done with methylphenidate is interesting and suggests who may go the longest interval without relapsing. However, patients still do relapse and it seems difficult to identify those who are free of that risk. The problem is that there are so few of them that it is increasingly difficult to identify them.

*Fleischhacker:* Let me come back to the point of differentiating responders from non-responders initially in order to get good correlations for outcome. We do not know that till we treat patients responders will respond and the non-responders would not have responded. In other words, the sample cannot be separated in the beginning when you start the study.

*Kennedy:* Perhaps the genetics can sort that out. If you give me for example blood samples I can type them for the $D_4$ receptor and tell you which ones I think will be responders and which will not. In terms of this idea of response – non-response, it does not worry a genetics person too much. The power to predict will probably come from those who do respond, starting with the person who responds the best and working downward doing genetic correlations. Probably the non-response group can also be separated into subtypes. It may require those other variables as for example morphology studies or PET studies to augment as co-variants the genetic variables. It may be possible then when we pool these variants together we can subdivide the non-response group based on these biological tests.

*Falkai:* One of the issues for me that is still unclear is that response and non-response remains to be a clinical question. It is important then to have criteria that all of us will use in defining response in order to be able to compare results across studies.

*Bilder:* I have a comparable concern about the plurality of outcome dimensions. Essentially, we are talking about outcome at such a high behavioural level, where do the patients do well or do not do well in a complex psychosocial environment. This is the dimension we are trying to predict from a set of fundamental biological variables including things like plasma HVA. There is no reason we should believe that a person's psychosocial adaptation be related principally to plasma HVA. The fact that we find correlations or that we can explain 30 %–40 % of the variance in this kind of measure is astounding given the lack of reliability on both ends of the equation. On one hand we are clinically obliged to try to make patients as well as they can be in their psychosocial matrix; at the same time in doing predictor research, it seems imperative when we are using biological predictor variables to come up with a set of functional brain dimensions that we are affecting with neuroleptic treatment. There is the kind of work that Dr. Buchsbaum is doing: isolating abnormal patterns of brain activity, that is what we are treating; some kind of dimensional abnormality in certain key functional brain systems. If we can identify those that is what we are treating. We are not treating the patient's psychosocial problems. We are treating those biological abnormalities. The next step then is to determine what the relationship of those is to other social latent variables.

*Buchsbaum:* It could even be that we have failed to use the technology of neurocognitive studies to devise the reliable psychosocial measures that could be used and clearly related back to the biology. We know that in animal pharmacology there are paradigms for studying social behaviour that have a close relationship with lesions in the brain or drug treatment and are used reliably. We do not have that kind of laboratory facility for people where we get a good social measure or whatever the operation situation would be which would be a clear index related to the underlying biology.

*Kane:* I would take a different view point. What we are really looking at most immediately in terms of response in relations to plasma HVA, brain morphology, plasma norepinepherine, or any other variable is psychopathologic response to treatment. That is a limited variable and certainly does not account for the wide range of morbidity that the disease imposes on the individual. Clearly, we need to extend beyond that to a range of social functions in this complex environment but methodologically that is the more problematic. The instruments used to assess that probably have lower validity and lower sensitivity as well as lower reliability. In addition, once you get into measuring performance, vocationally/socially, cognitively, you have to measure that in relation to premorbid. Although we have a premorbid psychopathological rating, i. e. they were ill when they came into the study and that is our baseline, we do not have a good baseline for the other functional measures. All of us know that patients do not start from the same point functionally and we do not always know what the point they started from is and whether that was influenced by their illness in some prodromal fashion or whether it was in the normal range of human variation on those performance measures. Methodologically, it is more complicated to do as it is incumbent on the field to try to develop ways of characterizing those measures of outcome.

*Gaebel:* Coming back to the question of how to define response. It is true we are not treating psychopathology but we are acting on certain biological systems but we do not know yet how we do it. On the other hand the definition of non-response is still made clinically and is not made in advance; it is a post hoc definition. The question really is: are we talking about non-response in general to any drug or to a certain drug? How do we define it? Are four weeks of treatment enough? Must two drugs be used? Only when we have clear ideas how to identify the non-responder may we be able to sort out this kind of patient and do research on them and hopefully come up with the characteristics which can be used as predictors in the future.

*Marder:* I am wondering if we can approach this issue differently. Instead of defining it as response or non-response, we look at variables such as suggested by Dr. Lieberman, i. e. the time it takes a patient to reach a certain responsiveness. This has some advantages. It includes the patient who eventually responds but it takes them 5–6 weeks or even 6 months. That also may give the biostatistician something more to work with.

*Gaebel:* Would we then rephrase non-response and call it slow response?

*Kane:* Or maybe the time to reach a certain response?

*Lieberman:* I believe we may be looking at different dimensions of outcome. There may be patients who are slow responders but ultimately good responders. It is not clear whether we should go after the psychobiological differences among the responders in that sense or look at more profound differences. Probably that at this point we should be doing all of that but using definitions or criteria that we can agree on. Unfortunately, we are not at this point yet. I am still struggling to answer the question of how to define non-response. I do not think we have worked that out well enough because we have not validated it. I was interested in Dr. Buchsbaum's presentation where he talked about haloperidol non-responders. It would have been interesting if he had the clozapine data on those patients to see what would happen then and what we would like to be able to do is more alternative treatments in serial fashion.

*Buchsbaum:* One of the things that is really missing in the field is cross-over studies. There are only very few neuroleptic cross-over studies so we do not know whether responders to for example thiothixene are really non-responders also to haloperidol. We stayed away from cross-over strategies because of the belief that neuroleptics would hang on over a long period of time and that cross-over studies are uninterpretable. We already heard data about drug effects occurring within 24–48 hours after initiating treatment.

*Marder:* I certainly agree with that but with one caveat. We still have to control for time and that whenever we cross over we need a control group.

*Lieberman:* The point raised by Dr. Marder about looking at the dimension of time to respond is useful. As an example, in studies of brain morphology and treatment outcome, dichotomous definitions of response were used. In reality by non-response we do not mean "no response." We mean partial response. In the study that I presented, the first episode study, if we were to define response categorically as non-response or response and then look at presence or absence of brain morphology in the specific region there might be a trend towards an effect but it would be far from statistically significant even with a sample size of 70 which is an adequate number. It is only when you use a survival analysis and look at time to remission that the relationship becomes fully apparent. It is interesting both clinically and therapeutically as well as biologically because what it says is that patients who exhibit such morphologic abnormality they are somewhat less responsive rather than non-responsive. The less response has to do with their time to and to some degree their level of ultimate recovery. It is a graded phenomenon and I believe it is a useful way to look at it to enhance the sensitivity of our approaches to predictor variables.

*Bilder:* I would like to follow-up on the issue of time as a key dimension. Time is not only a key dimension in defining response, but it is the key clinical dimension as well. When you are treating patients, it is really how rapidly you can achieve a beneficial result and that is the key decision for the physician to deal with. It would seem to be a Bayesian problem of what is the possible pay-off at a certain point of treatment of making a decision: to stay with one drug or switch to another one. If you have a finite probability of patients doing significantly better on drug D then it would seem possible to define the optimal time points to switch and the optimal pay-off matrix in terms of the potential outcomes. I do not know whether there is enough data existing to enable these calculations even to be approximated, but if not I would think that would be the kind of data we would like to obtain.

*Kane:* The problem is in discussing all that is that we tend to lose sight of how enormously difficult it is to do the clinical studies that are necessary to answer many of these questions. It took us four years to do the study I presented in a 237 bed hospital devoted to research. If you think about the implications of deciding what the Bayesian results would be, think about clozapine. You start with drug A. At what point do you switch to clozapine, is it two weeks, three weeks, five weeks or six months? To be able to answer that question would require an enormous amount of data. We are still debating whether you should give clozapine for 12 weeks or six months or one year and that question has been posed for the last four years and we still do not have a clear answer. I do not mean to throw cold water, but we have to do things that are a little bit crisper to get some answers.

*Naber:* As all of us recognize the difficulties in doing large studies, is it time to consider other design alternatives? For example in oncology they use more alternative designs than the classic designs as for example well-time or time to relapse.

*Bilder:* I am wondering whether the single case study designs have been adopted in psychopathology research?

*Kane:* Unfortunately, we have the confound of time. Here we are talking about time to remission, the confound of time in treatment and treatment changes which make intensive designs very difficult and what to some extent has misled the field and clinicians for all these years.

*Lieberman:* I wonder what you think of Dr. Awad's suggestion. Instead of using an intensive treatment design, you could use a much larger sample in a quasi-experimental approach and then find some outcome that could be measured in a treatment setting.

*Kane:* To my mind it is very hard to get away from the basic design and methodology problem. This kind of work is very difficult if you are trying to control a variety of factors optimizing treatment so that you can optimize potential to respond. So all of these things require a lot of control and attention. I think that is why we are no further advanced in being able to predict response.

*Lieberman:* Let me see if I understand Dr. Awad's suggestion. If Dr. Kennedy, for example, wants to see how one of his models works, could you take a proportion of patients receiving clozapine, use the measure and test their responsiveness over a year to study their relapse rate or improvement rate rather than put them into complex designs that take years? This is something that could be done with a larger sample but a cruder design.

*Awad:* Although I agree with Dr. Kane that the factor of time may play an important role, I do not know statistically what problems that creates since you will have end points at various intervals. Is it possible statistically to have meaningful conclusions?

*Köpcke:* You can make very complex designs with simple case studies but the problem always seems to be generalizability to other patients. For a single patient of course it may be possible to get the correct dosage, the correct drug but the overall problem to try to predict response is not solved by this. I think that Bayesian analysis is sometimes attractive but in reality not easy. I am perhaps more pragmatic. What you should do is to try a solid definition of what is a responder and what is a non-responder, try to define a basic variable set which is documented in every study and then each study centre has its own specific additional variables. Maybe, the first approach is to put together all the different data you have all collected. That would help us in the near future but not in the very distant years.

*Kane:* I would be curious what you would think, Dr. Köpcke, if we take some of our predictor variables and dichotomise our patients into extreme groups. It may be possible to identify for example 10 patients at each extreme where there is no overlap and then we do a prospective trial with whatever treatment approach rather than try to work with all this noise.

*Köpcke:* It is a good strategy because the intermediate noise, the people with moderate metabolism in the basal ganglia or a little bit of brain shrinkage disappears. You only have individuals that are clearly abnormal. For example, if you have the 200 people scanned you could take the 10 top and the 10 bottom on the CT scan for ventricular size and give them methyphenidate challenges. That may be a real shortcut. Biological studies are intensive. They are hard to do in large populations so that screening followed by intensive biological probe might be very effective.

*Lieberman:* Let me get back to the question that Dr. Awad's proposal raises: is it feasible to do predictor research in a less methodologically controlled or sophisticated design as, for example, an open study with the appropriate outcome measures which are operationally defined and the predictor variables appropriately assessed using the proper characterization and method of assessment? The key would be standardization and assurance of treatment. One of the problems that may occur in some of the less structured studies that have looked at correlates of outcome or predictors of outcome is that it has been naturalistic treatment and that patients may not have been treated well or others have been treated too well or toxically and the key is: could comparable and adequate treatment be administered and could it be done in an open fashion without controlled or parallel treatment design?

*Fleischhacker:* Let me just pick that point up because it is very important from a pragmatic approach. If we consider what brings us all together in research this could be a big efficacy study that we do for the pharmaceutical industry. That would be probably one of the possibilities where we could extend predictor research.

*Naber:* In medicine, quasi-experimental or naturalistic studies have been used frequently and have yielded good results provided as has been said, that there are adequate controls about the conduct and observation of treatment.

*Kennedy:* Thinking about these two approaches put forward, taking the 10 top variable and the 10 bottom versus the large sample: from a genetic point of view, we could take that small group, i. e. the people with the greatest brain morphology changes and explore a wider number of genetic loci specifically genes that control brain development. In the large sample studies genetics could be done relatively cheaply and efficiently taking a small amount of blood from a larger number of patients and looking at the best-guess genetic hypothesis and folding data from one or two genes into this large data set and trying to go at it from both angles: the large data set with a not so intensive study and the small data set with the very intensive biological study.

*Lieberman:* That would make sense but would also suggest a process where the one kind of design where you use extremes might be very good for generating hypothesis, whereas a larger quasi-experimental design might for example be useful in confirming whether or not in a larger sample size the hypothesis generated from the smaller more intensive study can be verified. That would make sense with your kind of variable but not so much with PET scanning on the other hand.

*Gaebel:* To what extent are we still able to conduct any drug studies besides those which are sponsored by drug companies? All the new EC guidelines of good clinical practice make such independent studies nearly impossible unless you get a sponsor. Obviously, there is no interest in the old neuroleptics though it might be interesting to look at these old drugs first before going to the new ones. It is presently a problem at least in Europe.

*Möller:* This good clinical practice guidelines in the European community is only valid for new drugs that are not yet on the market. As far as I can see then, it is not a problem for drugs that are already on the market.

*Gaebel:* Every drug that is already on the market would be considered in such design as a phase-III study.

*Audience:* Probably phase-IV.

*Gaebel:* Not any more. As you randomize, it becomes phase-III and has to be handled according to these guidelines. This is difficult without having external funds to do it.

*Audience:* This could be the reason for non-randomized studies to detect prognostic factors and then it becomes phase-IV.

*Awad:* I always tell my students before you even start thinking about design you have to invite a biostatistician. How do we go about adopting standard approaches?

*Audience:* Perhaps that can be done by holding a consensus conference to define the standards.

*Audience:* I would like to comment on this issue as I think that would not be a good idea to come together and have a consensus on what is a responder or a non-responder and what predictors should be taken. At present we have not yet found the appropriate predictors nor have we agreed on the definitions. For instance, we heard from Dr. Gaebel and Dr. Awad that it is important to look at the early behaviour of the patients after initiation of drug treatment. That might be a good predictor of future outcome. I am afraid if we standardize our approaches and stick to fixed definitions we may not be able to detect potential predictors because we would not look for them.

*Kane:* I believe this would be a good moment to close the conference, so I will ask for the concluding remarks.

*Awad:* We had a wonderful few days. The speakers were superb, they did exactly what we hoped they would do: bring a strong focus to many of the issues related to prediction research. We are indebted to all the speakers not only for taking the time but also for their major contribution to the conference. This conference has brought together the best experts in the field. It is my hope as that of my co-organizer, Dr. Gaebel, that this conference may usher the beginning of an interest group in predictive research in schizophrenia. I would like also to pick more on the idea proposed by Dr. Köpcke that maybe we can all work together to get a consensus on some of the basic issues and which then can be applied to a multicentre international study. This would be a challenge for all of us and in some way put to the test what we are preaching to other.

Our many thanks to Dr. Gaebel and the staff of the institute who have done a superb job in organizing the meeting and for their kind hospitality. The measure of success in any conference is when some of the participants inquire about the time for a follow-up conference. I hope that not before long, say in two to three years, we meet once more and rate our progress. On behalf of Dr. Gaebel and myself, once more I would like to thank all the speakers as well as the audience whose participation has made this conference a success.

# Prediction research in neuroleptic therapy – future directions

**W. Gaebel** and **A. G. Awad**

Prognosis (Gk. *prognosis*) means to know in advance. To predict (Lat. *praedicere*) means to state, tell about or make known in advance. Prediction is the more technical term compared to prognosis. Prognosis is a prediction especially of the probable course of a disease. This makes clear that in prediction research we deal with probabilities. One aim of this kind of research is to increase the probability of correct prediction. The clinical aim is to improve the course of illness by tailoring the treatment to the individual patient.

One of the major problems in prediction research is that despite a good deal of empirical findings, these findings have not been translated into clinical practice. Many of the identified predictors proved too weak and frequently not replicable. Another explanation is that drug treatment itself may be so effective in most of the situations that a patient would be treated irrespective of the prognostic status. Based on the presentations and discussions of the panel of experts as outlined in the previous chapters, following is a synthesis of the recommendations and future directions for optimization of strategies in prediction research of outcome to neuroleptic therapy.

## Recommendations for future research strategies

### *Patient/illness characteristics and sampling procedure*

An inherent dilemma in the recruitment of patients is to select a sufficiently homogeneous sample which also guarantees representativeness. An acceptable compromise would be to define clinical or biological subgroups by using agreed upon operationalized criteria. Treatment outcome could then be assessed within each of these subgroups relative to other potential predictors.

## Diagnosis

Schizophrenia is a heterogeneous disorder with regard to aetiology, pathobiology and treatment outcome. The currently used diagnostic systems for schizophrenia do not claim to classify nosologically distinct clinical groups of illness. Nevertheless, the patient sample should fulfill the criteria of commonly accepted diagnostic systems. One important defining criterion in most diagnostic systems is duration of symptoms (e. g. DSM-IV and ICD-10 $\geq$ 4 weeks). Given the importance of the time dimension in prediction and outcome research it should be clear that the classificatory process already contributes to the selection of different prognostic subtypes. On the other hand the logical algorithm for diagnosis according to these systems leads itself to the recruitment of patients with heterogeneous symptom clusters. By taking into account further defining variables, only then the task of achieving a sufficiently homogeneous sample can be accomplished.

## Patient and illness characteristics

There are a number of criteria related to the prognosis and course of the disorder according to which the sample could be defined:

- Gender
- Age at first onset
- Stage of illness
- Time since recent onset
- Number of previous episodes
- Symptom type (e. g. positive/negative)
- Symptom severity
- Social adjustment

This list could easily be expanded, e. g. by psycho-biological variables such as cognitive dysfunction, eye movement disturbances, brain structural abnormalities, etc.. A more treatment-related classifying criterion could be:

- Previous neuroleptic treatment response.

To include potential responders to certain neuroleptics (i. e. patients with previous episodes) according to predefined response criteria would allow to explain the outcome variance within responders (maximum to minimum response) by certain predictors.

## Patient recruitment and sample size

Because of generally used inclusion/exclusion criteria the recruited sample frequently is only about 10 % of the original screened number of patients. This raises serious doubts about the generalizability of the study results. To assure generalizability, basic characteristics of the screened and the recruited sample should be compared. Although the above mentioned patient and illness characteristics are predictors by themselves, they could also be used as defining the sample in order to improve homogeneity. Obviously, there has to be an optimal match between homogeneity and feasibility.

## *Design characteristics*

### Treatment strategies

Prediction should be tailored to specific drugs and dosages in order to be able to answer the question whether a patient will respond to drug A or B. Although in statistical group means, all neuroleptics have been demonstrated as equally effective, this may not be the case for the individual patient. According to the stage of illness, predictor studies can be either for acute or long-term treatment. Additionally, long-term treatment studies can include maintenance or intermittent treatment approaches. All these types of studies can be further differentiated according to the type of drug used, drug application (e. g. oral versus depot), drug dosage (e. g. standard versus low dose) as well as adjunctive treatments (e. g. psychosocial interventions). Another important type of study would be a combination of short- and long-term strategies. To test whether the same drug is useful for both short- and long-term indications stability and reliability of predictors over time have to be examined. It is important besides designing specific prediction studies to include some prediction strategies in future clinical trials of new neuroleptics.

### Time to switch to another drug

An open question is when to switch from one drug to another in case of non-response. Studies utilizing the test dose model have demonstrated that early symptom change (at 24–48 hours after initiation of therapy) is a consistently good predictor of response. In clinical practice and according to present treatment guidelines, however, no one would change medication before 4–6 weeks. Empirically there is evidence that response can still occur after this time. The question that arises is whether response and non-response are different in degree and/or time course of remission. A related question is whether a non-responder to a drug would benefit from being switched to another drug belonging to another pharmacological class as usually recommended in psychiatric standard texts. In situations of non-response to both drugs predictors of non-response could be considered non-specific. However, in case of response to drug B compared to drug A, predictors of non-response are then likely to be considered as specific to drug A. As a research recommendation it is important to emphasize the need for more cross-over studies. This design could easily incorporate the strategy of test dose model as well as other strategies such as using different dosages within groups.

## Treatment characteristics

Fixed dose strategies or an open titration by clinicians is another important question. Such open titration has led to erroneous interpretations as was demonstrated in studies of neuroleptic plasma levels. Since nonresponders ended up receiving higher dosages, this created the apparent impression that high drug levels were associated with poor response. It is hoped that PET studies in the future can contribute to the choice of appropriate dosages based on receptor occupancy. As such data are not yet available, one has to ensure adequate dosages. Within this context, continuous monitoring of patient compliance should be applied given the high noncompliance rates particularly in outpatient studies. To ensure that prediction is specific to the drug, the treatment setting as well as the context in which the treatment is given should be standardized as much as possible.

## Control groups

A placebo or standard neuroleptic control group ought to be included in prediction studies. An alternative design, e. g. quasi-experimental studies have been advocated to test identified predictors since such studies are more feasible and generally approximate what happens in clinical practice. Naturalistic studies, however, have certain short-comings with respect to interpretation of results since they cannot differentiate between response "to drug" (specific drug effect) and response "on drug" (overall outcome). Single case studies, particularly when using a placebo-controlled double-blind A–B–A design, may also be useful in exploring individual predictors.

## Organizational issues

Given the restrictions discussed above, it is very unlikely that one single centre will be able to recruit an adequate sample. Therefore, multicentre studies have been advocated which also allow to address the question of generalizability of results. However, in such studies the number of patients recruited in a single centre should be high enough to allow separate analyses with regard to additional specialized assessments applied by the particular centre. For instance, one centre may provide specialized psychophysiological assessments or brain imaging while another centre may provide detailed biochemical assessments. Given a common definition of sample characteristics, treatment strategies, time frame of assessments, and response/outcome, this would allow not only to test for general predictors applied in all centres but also for cross-referencing from special predictor-outcome relationships in a single centre. This approach can be helpful in generating new hypotheses which then can be put for further tests.

The introduction of "Good Clinical Practice" (GCP) guidelines in the European Community has been a major step in the improvement of quality of clinical trials. On the other hand, the possibilities to pursue clinical studies with already approved drugs have become rather difficult. Randomized studies with these drugs also have to fulfill the GCP standards and as usual in these situations it requires extensive monitoring which unfortunately pharmaceutical companies are reluctant to sponsor since interest in these "old" neuroleptics is becoming limited. Conducting independent studies is becoming difficult as a result of the expense and declining external funding. Therefore it may be important to persuade pharmaceutical companies to include predictive strategies in their design of clinical trials of new neuroleptics.

### *Research specific variables – selection and measurement*

#### Predictors

Potential predictor variables are traditionally selected from a number of domains including:

- Patient characteristics
- Illness characteristics
- Treatment characteristics
- Environment characteristics

Some of these variables also serve to define the sample characteristics (see above). A more hypothesis-driven classification of predictors partly overlapping with the traditional one refers to the bio-psychosocial model in psychiatry. Examples of these variables have been discussed throughout the previous chapters. It seems that prediction research will only progress through the future developments in basic research. What is needed as a concept for prediction is a coherent theory of the determinants of illness course which has to be embedded in a concept of aetiology and pathogenesis. The vulnerability-stress model currently offers the best heuristic conceptual framework and can be applied for prediction and outcome. In general, a functional approach should be given priority. Illness dynamics, predisposition and determinants as well as responsivity to treatment should be conceptualized in terms of underlying psycho-neuro-biological disorder. The test-dose approach or a pharmacological challenge procedure can tap some of the aspects of the functional status. Methodologically, a multi-level assessment approach is needed using standardized measuring instruments.

## Response

For defining response, target areas and time are the key dimensions to be taken into account. Such target areas should be sensitive to treatment change and should be of the kind of "state" and not "trait" variable. A psychological or biological episode marker would be an ideal measure at least for acute treatment studies. For its measurement standardized instruments should be used for which a certain percentage of decrease within a certain period of time could be defined. To control for the initial deviation from normal values in certain measures a minimum degree of deviation or "severity score" should be defined for inclusion. It has to be kept in mind that response is a concept which is not categorical but dimensional. By using operational definitions, response and non-response can be defined. It may be even helpful in terms of maximum contrast to refer to the extremes in groups, e. g. the lower and upper third on a variable. Although response primarily refers to a clinical concept tied to gross psychopathology, measures referring to motor behavior and neurocognitive functions should be included as response variables. It could be that these measures are more sensitive to treatment change and thus give an earlier clue to clinical response. For long-term studies, other measures come into play such as relapse rate, time to relapse, well-time, and other measures such as rehospitalization, time out of hospital, social adjustment, etc.. This once more refers to the concept of the multidimensionality of outcome.

## Outcome

Outcome refers more to the ultimate baseline of illness course than to a time related gradient of recovery. Some of the above comments related to response are also applicable to the concept and measurement of outcome. Long-term outcome in particular has to be conceptualized and assessed as multidimensional in nature requiring the same approaches using standardized instruments. Although symptomatology and relapse are still important characteristics of illness course, they should be complemented by measures from other domains such as psychosocial functioning or quality of life.

## *Statistics*

It is important to employ the most appropriate statistical model for data analysis. It is essential to involve the biostatistician from the initial phase of study design through data gathering and final analysis. Important for future post hoc comparisons across studies is to do meta-analysis. This requires to make available the raw data of predictors and response/outcome measures. The ROC-method (Receiver Operating Characteristics) allows qualitatively and quantitatively to analyze such data with respect to sensitivity and specificity of certain predictor-outcome relationships.

## Key selected references

Awad AG (1993) Methodological and design issues in clinical trials of new neuroleptics: an overview. Br J Psychiatry 163 [Suppl 22]: 51–57

Carpenter WT, Heinrichs DW, Hanlon TE (1981) Methodologic standards for treatment outcome research in schizophrenia. Am J Psychiatry 138: 465–471

Clements K, Turpin G (1992) Vulnerability models and schizophrenia: the assessment and prediction of relapse. In: Birchwood M, Tarrier N (eds) Innovations in the psychological management of schizophrenia. Wiley, Chichester New York Brisbane Toronto Singapore, pp 21–47

Engel GL (1980) The clinical application of the biopsycho-social model. Am J Psychiatry 137: 535–544

Gaebel W, Renfordt E (eds) (1989) Objective methods for behavioral analysis in psychiatry and psychopharmacology – examples and concepts. Pharmacopsychiatry 22 [Suppl]: 1–50

Helmchen H, Gaebel W (1987) Strategies of clinical research on neurobiological determinants of psychosis. Psychiatr Dev 5: 51–62

Hsiao JK, Bartko JJ, Potter WZ (1989) Diagnosing diagnoses. Receiver operating characteristic methods and psychiatry. Arch Gen Psychiatry 46: 664–667

Kissling W (ed) (1991) Guidelines for neuroleptic relapse prevention in schizophrenia. Springer, Berlin Heidelberg New York Tokyo

May PRA, Van Putten T, Yale C, Potepan P, Jenden DJ, Fairchild MD, Goldstein MJ, Dixon WJ (1976) Predicting individual responses to drug treatment in schizophrenia: a test dose model. J Nerv Ment Dis 162: 177–183

May PRA, Goldberg SC (1978) Prediction of schizophrenic patients' response to pharmacotherapy. In: Lipton MA, Dimascio A, Killam KF (eds) Psychopharmacology: a generation of progress. Raven Press, New York, pp 1139–1153

Nuechterlein KH (1987) Vulnerability models for schizophrenia: state of the art. In: Häfner H, Gattaz WF, Janzarik W (eds) Search for the causes of schizophrenia. Springer, Berlin Heidelberg New York Tokyo, pp 297–316

Van Praag HM, Kahn RS, Asnis GM, Wetzler S, Brown SL, Bleich A, Korn ML (1987) Denosologization of biological psychiatry or the specifity of 5-HT disturbances in psychiatric disorders. J Affect Disord 13: 1–8

Woggon B, Baumann U (1983) Multimethodological approach in psychiatric predictor research. Pharmacopsychiatry 16: 175–178

# Subject Index

## *Springer-Verlag and the Environment*

We at Springer-Verlag firmly believe that an international science publisher has a special obligation to the environment, and our corporate policies consistently reflect this conviction.

We also expect our business partners – printers, paper mills, packaging manufacturers, etc. – to commit themselves to using environmentally friendly materials and production processes.

The paper in this book is made from no-chlorine pulp and is acid free, in conformance with international standards for paper permanency.